THE HOLISTIC CARE AND DEVELOPI
OF CHILDREN FROM BIRTH TO THRE

The Holistic Care and Development of Children from Birth to Three provides students and practitioners with the knowledge and understanding they need to meet the complex needs of babies and toddlers. With a focus on the fundamentally holistic nature of young children's development, and emphasising the role of play and the emotional and physical environment throughout, the book shows its reader how to maximise each and every opportunity for learning when caring for the under-threes.

The text addresses both theory and practice, foregrounding the vital link between the two as the reader learns how to integrate theoretical approaches into their own setting and ways of working. From personal, physical, social and emotional development, to cooperation with parents, SEN and enabling environments, a wealth of topics are discussed in the depth and detail required to ensure that children can be given the best possible start in their critical first three years.

Throughout the book, the following features help the reader to reflect on, and develop their own practice:

- 'Case Studies' put key topics in context
- 'Reflective Questions' help the reader test and consolidate their knowledge of key topics
- 'Review your Practice' boxes invite the reader to reflect on their own practice
- 'Further Reading and Research' suggestions inspire independent study in key areas.

The book is also supported by a companion website featuring links to videos and articles, as well as an interactive flashcard glossary.

Kathy Brodie is an Early Years training specialist and author. She has worked in the childcare industry for over 15 years, during which time she has worked as a practitioner, Special Educational Needs Coordinator (SENCO) and Early Years Professional (EYP) in a variety of settings.

THE HOLISTIC CARE AND DEVELOPMENT OF CHILDREN FROM BIRTH TO THREE

An Essential Guide for Students and Practitioners

Kathy Brodie

Routledge
Taylor & Francis Group

LONDON AND NEW YORK

First published 2018
by Routledge
2 Park Square, Milton Park, Abingdon, Oxon OX14 4RN

and by Routledge
711 Third Avenue, New York, NY 10017

Routledge is an imprint of the Taylor & Francis Group, an informa business

British Library Cataloguing-in-Publication Data
A catalogue record for this book is available from the British Library

Library of Congress Cataloging-in-Publication Data
A catalog record for this book has been requested

ISBN: 978-1-138-21103-2 (hbk)
ISBN: 978-1-138-21105-6 (pbk)
ISBN: 978-1-315-45377-4 (ebk)

Typeset in Interstate
by Florence Production Ltd., Stoodleigh, Devon, UK

Visit the companion website: www.routledge.com/cw/brodie

For Ian, Chris and Robs

Contents

A VISUAL TOUR OF
THE HOLISTIC CARE AND DEVELOPMENT OF CHILDREN FROM BIRTH TO THREE

Pedagogical feature

Birth to Three offers an array of features specifically designed to enhance your learning experience.

Reflective Questions

'Reflective Questions' test the reader's knowledge and understanding of key topics and challenge the reader to consider how theoretical approaches might be best reflected in practice.

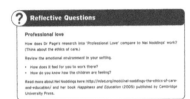

Review your Practice

'Review your Practice' boxes promote self-awareness, encouraging the reader to reflect on the implications of their actions and approaches.

Case Studies

'Case Studies' put the topics under discussion into context and help to illustrate key points.

Quick Summaries

These boxes contain key information on central topics, reminding the reader of the context in which further theoretical approaches are to be understood.

Further Reading and Research

Each chapter concludes with a list of recommended further reading, including relevant books, articles and websites. This feature serves as a guide to independent study and provides a useful point of departure for students and practitioners wishing to extend their knowledge in a particular area.

Companion Website

Visit the companion website for a whole host of student and lecturer resources that support and enhance the book, including:

- An interactive flashcard glossary
- Links to relevant video clips
- Links to useful websites.

www.routledge.com/cw/brodie

Acknowledgements

There have been many people who have supported and helped me during the writing of this book, and I extend my sincere thanks to them all. In particular, Sharon Skade for her insights into physical development (I hope I have been brave enough for you); Des Forrest for her love of babies and sharing that with me; to Ann, David, Joan and Arch for their continued support and discussions about babyhood; to all the reviewers who have helped to shape the book into a coherent style; to Annamarie Kino, who started me on this adventure; and to Elsbeth Wright, who has helped me to the finish line.

1 Introduction to holistic development

The first years of life are a critical opportunity for building healthy, resilient and academically competent children, young people and adults.

Burton, 2015

All areas of learning and development are intricately intertwined, young children develop and learn holistically and their emotional and social development seems to form the bedrock of other areas.

David *et al.*, 2003: 76

Introduction

Children's development from birth to three is an explosion of learning, growth and progression in every aspect. This is a vital time and getting it right at the very beginning lays the good foundations for subsequent development. This is being recognised more and more, especially with initiatives such as 1,001 (conception to age two years) Critical Days (Leadsom *et al.*, 2013) and encouraging Early Years Teachers to work in baby rooms in preference to pre-schools (Hadfield *et al.*, 2012).

The surge of young children's development between birth and three may or may not match some theories, 'norms' or typical development for any number of reasons. Each child develops and learns uniquely, depending on their unique circumstances. Children in the same family experience life differently, depending on their sibling position in the family, the family circumstances, and living conditions at the time of their birth, their own biology, as well as any number of other situational differences. Even twins are likely to have different perspectives. There may be noted similarities when you start to observe children, but care must be taken not to over-generalise or apply theories unthinkingly. Part of supporting holistic development is not only recognising the links but also viewing development from many perspectives. Reflection and thought is essential to stop practice becoming too focused on one or two areas of development over all others.

Holistic development

'Holistic' goes across content (enjoying and making books comes under every area of the English curriculum, the Early Years Foundation Stage, for example) as well as the areas of learning and development. Working in the baby room or having babies in your setting requires practitioners to have an immense range of skills, for example: 'being there' both physically and emotionally; sustained interactions (talking, eye gaze, cuddles) with babies and adult conversations with parents; high levels of care and intuition to pick up on the small cues that indicate stress or happiness as well as thinking about early education. This complexity and variety of communications in a fast-changing environment means that the practitioners for this age group must be flexible, responsive and closely attuned with the children in their care. Yet practitioners in the baby room may still be the least valued in a setting (Powell and Goouch, 2012).

The importance of holistic development in the birth to three age range

Holistic means dealing with something as a whole, even if you can subdivide the whole into separate areas. Holistic child development is where every area of learning, development and growth is entwined with every other. For example, this can be envisioned as a 'mat' woven with the different threads of learning and development, as in the New Zealand Early Childhood Curriculum – Te Whāriki; or a complex spider's web of criss-crossing strands of development, reinforcing and supporting each other to make a strong and resilient whole. In addition to New Zealand, Germany and Denmark both employ 'a holistic perspective and objective for Early Childhood Education and Care, as do other Nordic countries, emphasising the importance of socio-emotional development' (Wall, Litjens and Taguma, 2015: 41).

In practice, holistic development means that, right from birth, the learning, growth and development of young children are interdependent and concurrent. Babies and children don't arbitrarily subdivide their learning into neat little boxes and choose one day to learn how to talk, the next day how to sit up and the next day to count blocks. This will all be happening all at once, in a matter of minutes in the life of a baby. However, there are some very well-recognised and researched groupings of areas of learning that seem to develop simultaneously. For example, 'language and thought are developmentally linked and each promotes the development of the other' (David et al., 2003: 13). Inevitably, the corollary to holistic learning is that if there are areas of developmental delay, this may influence the other areas of learning and development.

It is therefore proposed that the 'pedagogy of care' is the most appropriate for the birth to three-age group (Ionescu and Tankersley, 2016: 22), because care and learning are inseparable in this holistic approach.

Quality in the birth to three age range

Mathers *et al.* (2014: 5) identify four key dimensions of pedagogy when practitioners are working with the birth to three-age group:

1. Stable relationships and interactions with sensitive and responsive adults
2. A focus on play-based activities and routines which allow children to take the lead in their own learning
3. Support for communication and language
4. Opportunities to move and be physically active.

They go on to state five 'key conditions' for quality:

1. Knowledgeable and capable practitioners, supported by strong leaders
2. A stable staff team with a low turnover
3. Effective staff deployment (e.g. favourable ratios, staff continuity)
4. Secure yet stimulating physical environments
5. Engaged and involved families.

These findings probably reflect the pedagogy and good practice already in settings (for example, all three prime areas of the Early Years Foundation Stage (EYFS) are represented here). However, it is interesting to note that this research is drawn from reviews conducted in the US, Australia, New Zealand as well as the UK, demonstrating that quality and good pedagogy crosses international boundaries. Similarly, David *et al.* (2003: 14) note that practitioners are a key part of holistic care and development: 'For babies and young children, being cared for and special to someone is important for their physical, social and emotional health and well-being'.

Quality interactions

Having 'quality' interactions with children is desirable at all ages. However, it can sometimes seem easier to sit talking to a chatty pre-schooler about their latest discovery or their newest toy than to have a quality interaction with a pre-verbal toddler who is still learning how to control his or her emotions. Nevertheless, any interaction, whether they are verbal or shared joint attention or proto-conversations, should always be considered to be a vital part of a baby or child's holistic development.

Sustained shared thinking

Sustained shared thinking was defined as 'an episode in which two or more individuals "work together" in an intellectual way to solve a problem, clarify a concept, evaluate activities, extend a narrative, etc. Both parties must contribute to the thinking and it must develop and extend' (Sylva *et al.*, 2004). Note that there is no age limit and that this is a two-way exchange, with both adult and child or baby getting something from the exchange.

Older toddlers can often be found having an in-depth conversation of their own devising, where they are trying to work something out together or negotiate a game plan.

Playful interactions

Not only do children need to play, but practitioners need to ensure that their interactions are playful, i.e. interactions rather than interrogations or interruptions or interference. This is especially important for younger children, because they don't yet have the ability to walk away or 'object'.

Educational curricula

Many curricula are moving towards birth, or even antenatal, care and education as the importance of birth to three is recognised. The guidance for the EYFS has been adjusted to reflect the wide range of progress that can be made during the birth to three age range. The Scottish curricula start at pre-birth, and in Wales the early years are defined as 'the period of life from pre-birth to the end of the Foundation Phase'.

Early Years Foundation Stage

The Early Years Foundation Stage (EYFS, 2017) is the statutory (mandatory) framework for all early years providers in England, maintained schools, non-maintained schools, independent schools, all providers on the Early Years Register and all providers registered with an early years childminder agency. The inspecting body for the EYFS is Ofsted (or for independent schools, their own inspectorate). The legal provision on which it is based is twofold – first the learning and development aspects of the framework and second the safeguarding and welfare. These are section 39(1)(a) of the Childcare Act (2006) and section 39(1)(b) of the Childcare Act (2006), respectively (EYFS, 2017: 3).

There are several supporting, guidance documents that accompany the statutory document, the most applicable being *Development Matters* (Early Education, 2012), which has guidance on child development so that practitioners can see at a glance the types of activities and environments that support children in the different areas of learning and development in various, overlapping, age bands. *Development Matters* also details the Characteristics of Effective Learning, which describe the ways in which the child engages with other people and their environment.

Care in the UK

Integrated care and education were the basis of Sure Start centres, with an emphasis on early engagement with families. Although the Sure Start programme has evolved, there is still a strong rhetoric of quality care for the youngest children. This has been further tested by the government's commitment to free (at the point of contact) care for children while parents are at work – in settings that are deemed to be high quality. Consequently, the concepts of 'quality' care have been revisited and redefined.

Education and care

Children develop holistically and so quality experiences in settings should embrace and reflect this. Quality and level of care will impact on physical, cognitive, language and personal, social and emotional (PSE) progress and development. Practitioners with specialist skills are needed to appreciate the rate and complexity of development of children in the birth to three age range, as well as being able to meet the needs of dependent babies and young children. Separating education and care is unrealistic and unreasonable. Babies and young children are learning all the time, through their play and through their life experiences. Simultaneously, they are still dependent on the adults in their life for care, affection and daily needs.

Wider influences on holistic development

Following Bronfenbrenner's theories, babies and young children are influenced most by their close family and their sociocultural context. There will be affects from the wider society, which may be both positive and negative influences; for example, there may be negative effects from the wider society with things like racism even if a child is being raised within a loving family (National Association for the Education of Young Children, 2009). Babies and young children need to have the best possible care in settings where practitioners can have the most influence, to build self-esteem, self-confidence and resilience, in case they do encounter negative influences.

Chapter summaries

The chapters have been chosen to represent every major area of development for babies and young children. Prime areas, identified by the EYFS, are communication and language, physical development and personal, social and emotional development, and therefore each of these chapters, and the chapter on play and creativity, are larger than the others. This partly reflects their importance in children's development, and partly is due to the extremely large number of theories and discussions that these topics elicit. The holistic links for each chapter are the core influence in that area of learning and development, which then has a significant effect on other areas of learning, and development. For example, the key person is a major, recurring theme throughout personal, social and emotional development (PSED). It is also a vital component in partnership with parents, play and setting up suitable physical environments. Therefore, for easy referencing, the key person description is repeated wherever relevant.

Chapter 2

Chapter 2 focuses on PSED and how this underpins all other learning. It is well documented that stress plays a negative role in 'cognitive functioning with regard to learning, memorizing, and retrieving information' (Desautels, 2016: 1) for adults, and that there are similar effects of all types of stress for young children (for example, Wiley and Karr-Morse, 2012; Marmot, 2016). However, most adults have some strategies to be able to cope with stressful situations and emotional upheaval. Babies and young children still have to learn how to recognise emotions and then control them and/or articulate their feelings in some form (whether that is behaviour as communication or verbally). Therefore, supporting babies' and young children's PSED is essential if they are to have positive learning experiences from their interactions with the world around them.

The holistic links in this chapter relate to the other major areas of learning and development, namely physical development and communication and language. The three areas of PSED, physical development and communication (whether pre-verbal, verbal or non-verbal) form a virtuous circle of reinforcement and holistic development. For example, a baby with secure attachment (PSED) who can confidently reach for a toy (physical development) and then smile happily (communication 'I am happy' and PSED, emotional well-being) is demonstrating his or her holistic development. If this is met with a joyful response of 'You got the teddy! Well done!' from an adult, this builds confidence, encourages further communication and rewards the physical effort this has taken. Although these exchanges may only take a second or two, they are essential experiences for a baby's developing brain.

The key holistic themes in this chapter are:

Key person

A key person in a setting is a named person who has special responsibility for their key children, their family and any other agencies involved with the family. This good practice is the practical application of Attachment Theory, which says that a baby's emotional well-being is greatly improved if he or she has at least one adult who they can 'attach' to or bond with.

The key person role includes emotional support, keeping the child in mind, observing (and acting on, where necessary) any changes in mood, health or behaviour, liaising with parents and being a special person for their children.

This includes all areas of development, and often the key person is the first one to notice progress or problems with their key children, in all areas of learning and development.

Theory of mind

Theory of mind is realising that other people may have different views and perspectives to yourself. At about one year old, young children start to appreciate that other people are different, with different ideas.

Up to this point of realisation, babies and young children will always assume that everyone else will have had the same experiences, have the same knowledge and are experiencing the same emotions as they are.

Professional love

This is a concept formulated by Dr Jools Page to explain the love that practitioners feel for the babies and children in their care. It is the affectionate and caring behaviours that happen when you care for babies and children, even though it is part of your professional role. Dr Page's research started with a focus on babies, but the concept is equally applicable to older children.

Secure attachment

Secure attachment is typical for the majority of children and is described as emotionally healthy. It is characterised by a child who is in distress after a brief separation, but can be comforted and settled by the caregiver reasonably quickly.

Page, Clare and Nutbrown (2013: 36) theorise that:

1   High-quality caregiver relationships are central to emotional development and learning in infants and toddlers
2   Relationships take time to develop, so the key person must be given that time and opportunity to become attached to their key baby or key toddler.

Chapter 3

Chapter 3 reviews physical development of babies and children from birth to three years old. It is considerably easier to see and measure children's physical growth, although their skills development is not as easy to determine. From birth, as a tiny baby who is totally dependent on adults for every need, to an independent, mobile and capable young child in three short years is remarkable. The physical growth of babies and young children enables almost every other area of learning, from being able communicate effectively to cognitive function to a sense of learning through oneself (embodiment). Consequently, this is an area of learning and development that permeates every other area and therefore the holistic development links for physical development have been chosen to reflect the links in the PSED chapter, but viewed from the perspective of the role of physical development. For example, being able to purposefully grasp a spoon (physical development) and feed themselves gives babies self-confidence and independence (PSED), demonstrates knowledge of food and will usefully elicit positive interactions with the adults. Physical development is also a necessity for some other areas of learning and development.

The key holistic themes in this chapter are:

The seven senses

The first five senses are well known:

- sense of smell
- sense of sight
- sense of hearing
- sense of touch
- sense of taste.

However, there are two other senses that we also rely on.

Proprioception is knowing where your body is in space, so that you can sit on a chair without looking behind you or pick up a plastic cup without squashing it or dropping it.

Vestibular is having a sense of balance and motion, so you can walk on a moving ship, balance on a log or spin round in a circle without falling over.

Tummy time

Tummy time (putting babies on the carpet on their tummies) is key for neck strength and trunk control (try doing a jigsaw yourself on the floor!). Tummy time builds up core stability in the trunk, which is needed before children can have secure arm and leg movements, as children develop physically from the centre of their bodies outwards. Archer and Siraj (2015) explain how babies using their arms to push up from the floor give the strength and alignment in the spine that will be needed for an upright posture. Interestingly, lots of tummy time stimulates the pelvic area, helping to support toilet training when the time comes. Good core stability is essential for children later on when writing or doing other activities sat at a desk, because they need to be able to support their bodies sufficiently to support their arms, elbows, wrists and finally finger movement. Babies should be on their tummy from ten weeks old until seven months (unless sleeping or being held).

Chapter 4

In Chapter 4 the third element of the virtuous circle, language development, is explored in greater depth. As with PSED and physical development, language and communication is a complex, multifaceted and substantial area of development. It has been suggested that newborn babies have an innate knowledge of language, but there are practical issues with this. They certainly communicate from birth, with looks and coos and cries. From this beginning, a typically developing child will be talking, using a range of vocabulary and using language to explain, explore, question and interact with the world around them in just three years. Sometimes this is in more than one language.

Having good language skills means that children can interact socially with peers and others; explain their feelings verbally; share their thoughts and ideas; solve problems jointly with others; express their personalities; construct a cultural identity and lay the foundations for early literacy. They are transformative skills to have and enhance progress in the other areas of learning and development significantly.

The key holistic themes in this chapter are:

Language chain

This is a way of describing the series of processes that the brain has to go through before speech can be attempted.

- Receptive language: recognising, understanding and interpreting the language that is being used
- expressive language: choosing the words, syntax, grammar and social norms before talking
- speech: coordinating the facial muscles, tongue and voice box to make speech sounds.

There can be disconnects at any of these stages, which will need different approaches to resolve.

Summary of stages of language development

- Birth to six months: Babies will turn towards sounds, watch faces and start to make a range of noises.
- Six to 12 months: Babies will babble and hold proto-conversations.
- Twelve to 18 months: Understand words, simple instructions, gesture and use a few words themselves.
- 18 to 24 months: Children will understand 200 words or more and be using 50 or more words of their own.
- Two to three years: Use around 300 words and create sentences.

These three chapters explore the core areas of babies' and young children's learning and development, which are closely intertwined, interdependent and transformative.

Chapter 5

Chapter 5, which follows these chapters, focuses more on the process of holistic learning and development, specifically through play. Children have a natural disposition to play, but the type of play that they engage in as they grow from babies to children changes to encompass more and more areas of learning. Physical growth and development enable different types of play, and social mastery draws other children into the play arena. Children reveal their thoughts, skills and personalities during play so it is essential that this is recognised as a formative element of holistic development. Key holistic themes for this chapter are:

Language chain

This is a way of describing the series of processes that the brain has to go through before speech can be attempted.

- Receptive language: recognising, understanding and interpreting the language that is being used
- Expressive language: choosing the words, syntax, grammar and social norms before talking
- Speech: Coordinating the facial muscles, tongue and voice box to make speech sounds.

There can be disconnects at any of these stages, which will need different approaches to resolve.

Summary of stages of language development

- Birth to six months: Babies will turn towards sounds, watch faces and start to make a range of noises.
- Six to 12 months: Babies will babble and hold proto-conversations.
- 12 to 18 months: Understand words, simple instructions, gesture and use a few words themselves.
- 18 to 24 months: Children will understand 200 words or more and be using 50 or more words of their own.
- Two to three Years: Use around 300 words and create sentences.

Chapter 6

It may seem strange to think of babies as having mathematical awareness, but more research and neuroscience revelations are showing that even babies are curious about mathematical improbabilities and that young children may be more mathematically aware than we have previously realised. Mathematics in Early Years' settings poses a double dilemma: first that many practitioners are not confident with traditional or 'academic' mathematics themselves (even though they may have excellent practical mathematics), and second that mathematics is often considered to be a pre-school or school subject, so can be neglected in the birth to three age range. However, mathematics has a constant influence on both children's and adult's lives, from spatial awareness to throwing a ball to calculating ratios.

Chapter 6 considers how practitioners can incorporate mathematics into regular activities and be aware of their own skills in this area as well: for example, encouraging babies to problem solve and be aware of numbers all around them, encouraging toddlers to use number names and using accurate, suitable mathematical language with all children. Laying out this foundation will help children to be mathematically aware from the very beginning.

The key holistic theme in this chapter is:

Integration of mathematics

Using mathematical language while doing everyday things around the setting helps young children to both learn a wider range of vocabulary, and also to understand the specific, meaningful mathematical terms heard in the correct context (Hutchin, 2012). For example including 'I wonder how much this jug will hold – what is its capacity?' or the 'symmetry' of a pattern or the 'orientation' of a shape. After all, if they know there is a dinosaur called 'Tyrannosaurus Rex', the 'capacity' of a jug is pretty tame!

Chapter 7

Babies and young children are developing cognitively (intelligence and mental abilities) from birth and have 'phenomenal learning abilities, unique gifts, deep thoughts and emotions' (Lansbury, 2014: 8). The type of experiences that they have in their first three years can support and even reinforce their cognitive abilities.

In Chapter 7, some of the core influences on cognitive development – self-regulation, metacognition, executive function, physical development and cultural perspectives – are discussed.

The key holistic themes in this chapter are:

Why incorporate 'neuroscience' into Early Years practice?

Neuroscientists affirm that 'billions of synaptic connections are made within the first five years of life' (Conkbayir, 2017: 22) and that practitioners are part of this process, through planning environments, developmentally appropriate activities and sensory experiences.

The process of incorporating neuroscience into early years settings with practitioners may have challenges (including a proliferation of 'neuromyths'), but is worthwhile because it vindicates good practice based on science (causation, not correlation) and adds another layer of knowledge to understanding about how young children think, learn and develop.

Learning theories

There are many theories about how babies and children learn, some based on behaviours, some on social context and some on environment. A few of the major theorists are listed here.

Bandura proposed a Social Learning Theory. Bandura showed that children learn by imitating what they see other people doing in their own environment. The actions of others become the model that children will copy.

Vygotsky hypothesised that children's learning is within a social context, that the two cannot be separated and that language (and use of language) is central to cognitive development.

Piaget believed that children 'interiorised' (David *et al.*, 2003) actions, so their cognitive ability was a series of assimilations and accommodations to build up their knowledge and beliefs.

Skinner theorised that children repeated actions that were positively reinforced (e.g. praised or got a reward) and undesirable behaviour could be ameliorated by punishment.

For much more detailed information and links to the EYFS (as well as to other curricula in the UK), see Featherstone (2016).

Chapter 8

Some children will have additional needs or Special Educational Needs (SEN), which may only become apparent as they grow. For some children these will be significant and lifelong, whereas for other they may be transitory – for example, glue ear causing hearing loss for a few weeks of the year. Embracing the philosophy of children's holistic development, Chapter 8 reviews good practice that supports all children, whether there is an SEN or not. There are a number of ideas in this chapter that will help practitioners in any type of setting to support, stretch and challenge babies and children in all areas of learning and development. These have been developed from practical experience and advice from a range of multi-agency professionals, such as speech and language therapists, occupational therapists and specialist teachers.

The key holistic theme in this chapter is:

Top three thoughts on good practice

1   Consider all the senses during sensory play. Do you always include a sense of smell? Do you present prickly or scratchy items?
2   Visual timelines support all children. How do children know what will be happening next? How can they judge how long until home time?
3   Regularly review your environment from the children's perspective. Is it cluttered? How would a child with a hearing or visual impairment experience the environment?

Chapter 9

Holistic growth, learning and development are contextualised, so the importance of the physical environment is discussed in Chapter 9, suitable physical environments. This is considered via the practitioner's effective use of the environment to support independence, talking and listening, cognition, playing outdoors and partnerships.

The key holistic theme in this chapter is:

Is the environment suitable?

There are a number of assessment tools available to help to determine the suitability of the environment. For the physical environment there is the American-based ITERS (Infant/Toddler Environment Rating Scale, ITERS-3) (Harms *et al.*, 2017) and the Early Years Quality Improvement Support Programme (EYQISP) (National Strategies, 2008). In addition there are the Leuven Scales (Laevers, 1994) and the Sustained Shared Thinking and Emotional Well-being scales (SSTEW) (Siraj *et al.*, 2015) for the emotional environment.

How do you know whether the environment is suitable for babies, toddlers and young children for this area of learning and development? Is it an enabling, a creative and a learning environment? Think about how this group of babies or children may have grown and developed since the environment was last reviewed.

Chapter 10

Effective partnerships between practitioner and parents; practitioner and baby or young child; and practitioner and other professionals depend on practitioners being able to understand the nuances of these different roles.

Therefore, Chapter 10 first explores the relationships between parents and practitioners, the key person role and the home learning environment. This, however, does not take place in a vacuum, so the cultural influences on practice and the 'quality' of pedagogy are also discussed.

The key holistic theme in this chapter is:

Share with parents

The activities and environment at home – for example, positive parenting, the home learning environment and parents' level of education – are some of the most important factors in driving children's outcomes (Field, 2010: 38) in the early years.

Therefore, consider how practitioners can share this with parents to continue the learning and development at home.

Chapter 11

Chapter 11 looks to the future of the Early Years sector. It recognises that the babies and children of today will be living in a future that could be very different, especially with the exponential rise in the extent and power of technology, so how can practitioners allow for this? The childcare sector itself may look very different in the future, as work expectations evolve, childcare 'norms' change and research may start to identify trends in children's holistic development that have resulted from this in the past. In addition, the exciting developments in neuroscience and biology may change the way that child development is currently understood altogether.

The key holistic theme in this chapter is:

Sustained shared thinking

Sustained shared thinking is defined as:

> an episode in which two or more individuals 'work together' in an intellectual way to solve a problem, clarify a concept, evaluate activities, extend a narrative etc. Both parties must contribute to the thinking and it must develop and extend.
>
> Sylva *et al.*, 2004: 36

These are the two-way interactions that occur from birth and which support babies' and children's thinking processes and knowledge base.

Conclusions

Holistic learning and development focuses on the intersections between all these different areas of learning, development and growth, and most importantly how these connections can then be used to improve outcomes for babies and young children in settings. Holistic development is also about how practitioners can create quality emotional and physical environments that will support all children, through care, early education and play.

Further Reading and Research

Sound Foundations, a Review of the Research Evidence on Quality of Early Childhood Education and Care for Children Under Three by Mathers *et al.* (2014) has some excellent in-depth investigations of aspects of 'quality' in the Early Years, from practitioners and pedagogy to home-based care and service integration. It is a good reference document for students, with sections on practice and policy too. It can be downloaded from the Sutton Trust here: www.suttontrust.com/researcharchive/sound-foundations/

References

Archer, C. and Siraj, I. (2015) Measuring the quality of movement-play in Early Childhood Education settings: Linking movement-play and neuroscience. *European Early Childhood Education Research Journal* Vol. 23 Iss. 1, pp. 21–42.

Burton, A. (2015) *Supporting the Best Start in Life*. London: PHE.

Conkbayir, M. (2017) *Early Childhood and Neuroscience: Theory, Research and Implications for Practice*. London: Bloomsbury.

David, T., Goouch, K., Powell, S. and Abbott, L. (2003) *Birth to Three Matters: A Review of the Literature Compiled to Inform The Framework to Support Children in their Earliest Years*. London: DfES.

Desautels, L. (2016) *How Emotions Affect Learning, Behaviors, and Relationships*. Available from: www.edutopia.org/blog/emotions-affect-learning-behavior-relationships-lori-desautels. Accessed 27 May 2017.

Early Education (2012) *Development Matters*. London: DfE.

EYFS (2017) *Statutory Framework for the Early Years Foundation Stage. Setting the Standards for Learning, Development and Care for Children from Birth to Five*. London: DfE. Available from: www.gov.uk/government/publications/early-years-foundation-stage-framework–2. Accessed 28 May 2017.

Featherstone, S. (2016) *An Anthology of Educational Thinkers*. London: Featherstone Education.

Field, F. (2010) *The Foundation Years: Preventing Poor Children Becoming Poor Adults. The Report of the Independent Review on Poverty and Life Chances*. London: Cabinet Office.

Hadfield, M., Jopling, M., Needham, M., Waller, T., Coleyshaw, L., Emira, M. and Royle, K. (2012) *Longitudinal Study of Early Years Professional Status: An Exploration of Progress, Leadership and Impact*. Final report. London: DfE.

Harms, T., Cryer, D., Clifford, R. and Yazejian, N. (2017) (3rd edn) *Infant/Toddler Environment Rating Scale (ITERS-3)*. New York: Teachers' College Press.

Hutchin, V. (2012) *The EYFS: A Practical Guide for Students and Professionals*. Abingdon: Hodder Education.

Ionescu, M. and Tankersley, D. (2016) *A Quality Framework for Early Childhood Practice in Services for Children under Three Years of Age*. International Step by Step Association (ISSA).

Laevers, F. (ed.) (1994) *Well-being and Involvement in Care Settings. A Process-oriented Self-evaluation Instrument*. Leuven: Leuven University.

Lansbury, J. (2014) *Elevating Child Care: A Guide to Respectful Parenting*. Createspace Amazon.

Leadsom, A., Field, F., Burstow, P. and Lucas, C. (2013) *The 1001 Critical Days*. Wave Trust and NSPCC.

Marmot, M. (2016) *The Health Gap: The Challenge of an Unequal World*. London: Bloomsbury.

Mathers, S., Eisenstadt, N., Sylva, K., Soukakou, E. and Ereky-Stevens, K. (2014) *Sound Foundations: A Review of the Research Evidence on Quality of Early Childhood Education and Care for Children under Three. Implications for Policy and Practice Research*. London: The Sutton Trust.

National Association for the Education of Young Children (2009) *Developmentally Appropriate Practice.* NAEYC. Available from www.naeyc.org/DAP. Accessed 5 June 2017.

National Strategies (2008) *Social and Emotional Aspects of Development (SEAD).* Nottingham: DCSF.

Page, J., Clare, A. and Nutbrown, C. (2013) (2nd edn) *Working with Babies & Children from Birth to Three.* London: SAGE.

Powell, S. and Goouch, K. (2012) Whose hand rocks the cradle? Parallel discourses in the baby room. *Early Years: An International Research Journal* Vol. 32 Iss. 2, pp. 113–27.

Powell, S. and Goouch, K. (2014) *Two-Year-Old Children in Three Counties: Improving Provision through Research-led Development.* Canterbury: Research Centre for Children, Families and Communities.

Siraj, I., Kingston, D. and Melhuish, E. (2015) *Sustained Shared Thinking and Emotional Well-being (SSTEW) Scale for 2–5 Year Olds Provision.* London: IOE.

Sylva, K., Melhuish, E., Sammons, P., Siraj-Blatchford, I. and Taggart, B. (2004) *The Effective Provision of Pre-School Education [EPPE] Project. Effective Pre-School Education: A Longitudinal Study funded by the DfES 1997–2004.* London: DfES.

Wall, S., Litjens, I. and Taguma, M. (2015) *Pedagogy in Early Childhood Education and Care (ECEC): An International Comparative Study of Approaches and Policies.* London: DfE.

Wiley, M. and Karr-Morse, R. (2012) *Scared Sick: The Role of Childhood Trauma in Adult Disease.* New York: Basic Books.

2 Personal, social and emotional development

> What must also be acknowledged is that understanding about self and others is dependent upon social and emotional interactions in which cognitive processes come into play. It is the holistic nature of this interweaving of all aspects of development and learning, which is now recognised.
>
> David *et al.*, 2003: 66

Introduction

Personal, social and emotional development (PSED) is the bedrock of child development, and is justifiably one of the three prime areas of the Early Years Foundation Stage (EYFS), meaning that it is fundamental to supporting all other areas of learning and development. Although there is a description here of each of these elements, in real life they are so interrelated that to examine them separately seems unreasonable. However, it is important to note that each of the areas does represent a different form of development and that children will develop, from birth, at different rates and in different ways in each of their personal and social and emotional capacities. In this chapter the ways that PSED underpins some of the other areas of learning and development are examined.

First of all, it is useful to have some descriptors of each area of PSED, to help untangle some of the overlap and to acknowledge the unique aspect of each area.

Personal

Children's personality becomes more obvious as children grow from birth to three. This is a combination of their temperament, self-esteem and self-confidence.

Social

Traditionally social development has been associated with older children, but more and more research is finding that even very young babies are social. As children's social skills develop, they also start to push boundaries and test out behaviours, which can be challenging for adults but highly emotional for the children ('terrible twos' is now considered outdated – all behaviour is a form of communication).

Emotional

Emotional development is rooted in attachment, but also encompasses managing children's own feelings and emotions. The essential emotional life skills, such as resilience and self-regulation, are part of a baby's emotional development.

Practitioner's role

The change from baby to toddler physically, cognitively, emotionally - in fact in all areas - is astonishing. Practitioners need to be conscious that the development of the baby they are caring for will be almost imperceptible from day to day, so they need to constantly assess, review and adapt to meet the growing needs of the babies and children in their care to ensure that practice keeps up with growth and development. As children grow older and become more independent, the care element subtly changes. Practitioners need to use a number of highly developed skills for the children in their care to make the successful transition from a totally dependent baby to an independent and resourceful toddler. Similarly, they need to be able to support parents and families in different ways as babies develop into young children.

Personal, social and emotional development relies on the whole setting, from the manager/ owner right through to the least experienced apprentice, to value the vital and longlasting value of the baby room for the foundations of PSED and to also recognise the challenges of a baby room, which can be hard both physically and emotionally. Spotting the nuances of the baby's wellbeing, changing care routines, retaining information about the family, and being the key person are a demanding combination of roles and responsibilities. In addition, the requirements are changing almost daily, for example, going from a non-mobile baby to crawling, to cruising, to walking means constantly re-evaluating the physical environment, as well as assessing the baby's PSED. As a childminder, there will be changes in how children of different ages and abilities in the same setting interact and can be supported with their interactions. This takes skill and good observational techniques to be effective.

Typical PSED developmental patterns

From the very start, babies enjoy the company of others, particularly their main caregivers. They are fascinated by faces and face patterns and will reciprocate with games such as sticking out tongues. Babies will usually respond with their whole body when being spoken to, waving their arms and legs. Gradually babies start to recognise and respond more enthusiastically for their main carer and will show delight at cuddles or being rocked. Babies will start to smile and maintain eye contact. Other emotions, such as frustration or fear, will be displayed through body language and facial expressions, as well as crying. Initially, babies are totally reliant on their caregivers, whether that is a parent or a baby's key person in a setting. The adult's ability to meet the needs of their baby has 'a profound impact' (Cuthbert, Rayns and Stanley, 2011). As more physical control is developed, babies will start to grow relationships, seeking attention for social gain (rather than to meet a physical need), in addition to becoming wary of ' strangers'. Contact with others will include asking others to help. Comforters will still be used regularly and even young babies will start to show clear signs of different 'personality traits' (Dowling, 2014: 9).

As a toddler, he or she will start to interact with other children, with mum as a secure base to come back to. There may be special friendships and play patterns will start to emerge. This is also a time when the toddler's independence becomes more obvious and boundaries are tested, especially with behaviour. Self-confidence and self-esteem will grow at different rates, but should be more obvious by now. A toddler's self-confidence is influenced and moderated by 'self-concept, self-esteem and self-knowledge' (Dowling, 2014: 10). As a three-year-old, he or she may be sufficiently self-assured to talk to other adults and to understand that others may have feelings different to theirs.

It is evident that PSED is reliant on frequent, high-quality interactions between babies and adults, but practitioners also need to be sensitive to the fact that young children may need a 'social break' to get away from over-stimulation. Babies need a darker, calm room whereas older children could use a den, quiet reading area or hidey nook outdoors. Some settings (such as Pen Green in Corby) provide sleep nests, which are large baskets on the floor, so that children can crawl into them independently whenever they are tired or need some time alone.

'Measuring' personal, social and emotional development

It is a relatively simple task to measure a baby's weight or a child's height. However, measuring children's PSED is considerably more difficult, especially as it is still emerging and the baby may be pre-verbal. There are some areas that can only be appraised in certain circumstances. For example, resilience can only be 'tested' after observing the reaction to a stressful situation. Recent research (Halle and Darling-Churchill, 2016) has found that it is possible, but difficult, to measure PSED effectively. Starting with 120 types of assessment, Halle and Darling-Churchill (2016) narrowed these down to 75 effective measures. When these were reviewed, only six were found to be 'strong' measures, i.e. they had a majority of 10 identified and desirable key features, such as reliability, validity, cost, time, training and age range. This wide-ranging review of measurement techniques demonstrates just how difficult it is to find a way to an effective, efficient and reliable measure for children's personal, social and emotional development. Add to this the busy (emotionally and physically) day in an Early Years setting and measuring PSED seems to be an impossible task. Nonetheless, the Early Years Foundation Stage (and many other worldwide curricula) requires practitioners to make professional assessments on young children's PSED. Therefore, practitioners need to be attuned with the children they are caring for and be sensitive to changes, however small these may be. With babies this includes liaising thoroughly with parents and carers and being mindful of the information that they bring.

SSTEW scales

One measure used widely in England is the Sustained Shared Thinking and Emotional Well-being (SSTEW) scale, which focuses on young children's (two to five years old) well-being, self-regulation and quality interactions (Siraj *et al.*, 2015). The relevant developmental areas are social and emotional development, and cognitive development. The scales can be used to evaluate settings, review and reflect on the practice and guide towards better practice. In these scales, the authors suggest that children develop different emotional expressions and emotional understanding as they grow up.

Well-being

Well-being is not a single entity or feeling. It can be defined in several domains:

- Emotional well-being – this includes being happy and confident and not anxious or depressed.
- Psychological well-being – this includes the ability to be autonomous, problem-solve, manage emotions, experience empathy, be resilient and attentive.
- Social well-being – has good relationships with others and does not have behavioural problems – that is, they are not disruptive, violent or a bully.

NICE, 2012

All areas of well-being impact on each other, but it may be useful to try to isolate one area, especially if there are concerns about well-being.

Emotional expressions

Trying to understand a baby's emotional state is hard until you are really attuned and know the baby well. Being able to read their facial expressions, and to put those in context of the baby's emotional understanding, can help practitioners to understand the baby's emotional responses.

Newborn:	Startle, disgust, distress
0–20 months:	Social smile
	Laughter, anger, interest, surprise, sadness, fear, stranger distress
16–36 months:	Shame, pride, envy, guilt, embarrassment.

Emotional understanding

0–20 months:	Social referencing (taking emotional cues from adults to moderate their own response – for example, looking towards a practitioner for reassurance or a smile before reaching out to touch a treasure basket)
30–60 months:	Emotional display rules.

Siraj *et al.*, 2015: 50

Quick Summary

Is the environment suitable?

There are a number of assessment tools available to help to determine the suitability of the environment. For the physical environment there is the American based ITERS-Infant/Toddler Environment Rating Scale (ITERS-3) (Harms *et al.*, 2017) and the Early Years Quality Improvement Support Programme (EYQISP) (National Strategies, 2008). In addition there are the Leuven Scales (Laevers, 1994) and the Sustained Shared Thinking and Emotional Well-being scale (SSTEW)(Siraj *et al.*, 2015) for the emotional environment.

How do you know if the emotional environment is suitable for babies, toddlers and young children for this area of learning and development?

Is it an enabling, a creative and a learning environment?

Think about how this group of babies or children may have grown and developed since the environment was last reviewed.

YouTube video from November 2016 with Professor Ferre Laevers talking to Early Years Scotland about his thoughts on well-being, involvement and the improvements in children's outcomes: "Well being and involvement can be improved in a short time" www.youtube.com/watch?v=5RZDYK8tsvk&t=10s

Reflective Questions

Developmentally appropriate practice

What do we mean by 'developmentally appropriate'? Is this determined by the curriculum (and what evidence or research has the curriculum been based on?) or based on culture and customs? (Think about 'appropriate' to this particular baby or young child, in their own circumstances, environment, irrespective of the curriculum.)

What is your own favourite pedagogy or theorist and why does that particularly resonate with you?

Emotional environments in settings and professional love

The emotional environment can be defined as 'the atmosphere and ethos created by all who are part of the setting' (National Strategies, 2008). Critically, the emotional environment is all about the people in the setting, not the bricks and mortar. The emotional availability of practitioners for their babies is vital for babies to flourish (Hutchin, 2012), not just being there in body, but also being responsive, genuine and expressive. The emotional environment starts for babies pre-birth. Gerhardt (2004) explains how 'corrosive cortisol', which is a stress hormone that can be produced during pregnancy if mum is stressed, can affect a baby's response to stress and social interactions. As a practitioner working with babies and young children, it is sensible to be aware that babies may react very differently to 'stressful' situations, such as change in key person, even if the change is managed in exactly the same way.

Traditionally, practitioners have been cautious to say that they 'love' the babies in their care, in case parents were upset or felt that practitioners were trying to take over. However, Dr Jools

Page has opened a very useful and interesting dialogue about 'Professional Love' with her project Professional Love in Early Years Settings (PLEYS) (Page, 2017: 1), which was established 'to examine how those who work in early years settings can safely express the affectionate and caring behaviours which their role demands of them'. This has produced an attachment toolkit, containing resources to improve on reflective practice and an evaluation form for settings. Professional development such as this will help practitioners to ensure that their emotional environment is suitable for the babies and toddlers they are working with.

The emotional environment is important for everyone, but for very young children, who are laying the foundations of their emotional literacy and emotional health, is it essential that they have appropriate experiences. Depending on the amount of time that children spend in the setting, it may be that practitioners will be providing a large proportion of a child's exposure to their emotional environment. How practitioners approach this opportunity will affect children's PSED as well as their holistic development. For example, what is valued and what is valuable will affect children's perspectives (Page, Clare and Nutbrown, 2013). If being able to write your own name is valued, i.e. it is encouraged, praised, displayed and shared with others, but a painting receives a smile and a comment of 'put it out to dry', then children will very quickly realise that writing is 'valuable' but their paintings are not. Babies need to grow and develop in a suitable, developmentally appropriate environment. Very young children and babies are totally dependent on the conditions that are supplied by their parents, carers, community and world in which they find themselves. Adults should be good role models, talk about their own feelings and be aware that their responses and feelings will have an effect on the PSED of the children in their care.

Reflective Questions

Professional love

How does Dr Page's research into 'Professional Love' compare to Nel Noddings' work? (Think about the ethics of care.)

Review the emotional environment in your setting.

- How does it feel for you to work there?
- How do you know how the children are feeling?

Read more about Nel Noddings here: http://infed.org/mobi/nel-noddings-the-ethics-of-care-and-education/ and her book *Happiness and Education* (2005) published by Cambridge University Press.

What do you do to plan an emotional environment? (Think about the role that leadership AND management play in setting the emotional environment.)

Is it embedded throughout the setting? (Think about the physical indications of this throughout the setting, e.g. key person pictures with descriptions, children's pictures.)

Is the emotional environment developmentally appropriate? (Think about how a baby may need different emotional support than a two-year-old.)

Practitioners' own emotional health

Caring for young children can be physically demanding, but a practitioner's own 'emotional demands are great' (Elfer, Goldschmied and Selleck, 2011: 38) too. As a key person, practitioners need to have regular and well-planned supervision meetings and to be aware of their own care needs too. These may difficult to fit into the busy schedule of a nursery setting and may need some creative thinking for childminders (consider your childminding networks, online support groups or linking with local settings), but are nonetheless essential for practitioners. Research by Page and Elfer (2013: 553) found that there were few specifications about 'nursery attachments in theoretical or practical terms to guide staff critical reflection and judgement about managing these close relationships', which left practitioners working intuitively to the best of their abilities. The research concludes that the importance of attachment-based pedagogy needs to be understood from management onwards.

Reflect on your own emotional health

How do you support each other and how does your setting support *you* emotionally? Read Chapter 7 in Sonia Mainstone-Cotton's book *Promoting Young Children's Emotional Health and Well-being*, which is about 'Adult Well-being' for practical ideas on how to support your own emotional health.

Attachment Theory

John Bowlby (1969) is considered the pioneer for Attachment Theory. He investigated family separations and how this affected children's progress, development and emotional well-being. His research is particularly interesting because he not only wanted to describe the effects that he witnessed, but he also wanted to find ways of improving children's outcomes, even if the bond between mother, or primary caregiver, was not ideal.

Working with Bowlby, Mary Ainsworth designed the 'strange situation' experiment (Ainsworth and Bell, 1970). This is specifically to observe children's reaction to mum (or caregiver) leaving the room and leaving the children with a stranger. The experimenter generally watches the children's reaction through a one-way glass, so their presence does not affect the outcome. Ainsworth found that there was a range of reactions and behaviours displayed by children, which she theorised demonstrated different attachment behaviours. From this, and subsequent research, four types of attachment have been described. Note that these may vary according to the exact situation (children are in the real world, not in an experimenter's studio!).

1   Secure attachment. Typical for the majority of children and is described as emotionally healthy. Child is in distress after a brief separation, but can be comforted and settled by the caregiver reasonably quickly.
2   Anxious/avoidant. Child will not readily return to the main caregiver after the separation. In more extreme cases, may even prefer to go to the stranger.

3   Anxious/resistant. A more complex set of behaviours, with the child sometimes going to the caregiver, but also resisting contact. Occasionally this is seen with violent behaviour, but overly passive behaviour may also be seen.

4   Insecure/disorganised (or sometimes known as disoriented) attachment. The child has indiscriminate responses to separation from the caregiver, displaying a range of resistant, avoidant and apprehensive behaviours.

Schaffer and Emerson (1964) investigated both physical contact and 'social attachments in infancy' in a group of mums and children in Glasgow. They found that attachment was not a single event, but occurred in rough stages through a baby's development:

*   Asocial. From birth to six weeks old. Attachment can be formed with any other person.
*   Indiscriminate. Between six weeks and six months babies show little fear of strangers, although they can usually discriminate between close family and others.
*   Specific. From six to seven months babies start to show fear of strangers and will cry when their primary attachment person leaves them.
*   Multiple. From around 10 months onwards, babies are likely to have at least one good attachment with primary caregiver(s) and will start to make attachments with extended family and other caregivers (such as practitioners).

McLeod (2009) explains how Harlow's experiments in the 1950s found that baby monkeys would prefer the security of a fluffy mother substitute with no milk to a wire frame mother substitute with milk. When scared, they would resort to the fluffy 'mother' rather than the food provider. By removing the baby monkeys for different lengths of time, he concluded that attachment had to be made as early as possible. If good attachments are not made by the first year of life, for monkeys, then they are unlikely to bond at all.

There are obvious flaws, ethical issues and interpretation problems with all these experiments, but a core message is that it is important for babies to be able to attach to *someone*, that may be a key person, a family member or someone else. The crucial element is to experience that feeling of being kept in mind, of having someone care for you. If this has not been experienced by age five (Dollard and Miller, 1950), then it can be very difficult to establish good emotional bonds with anyone, though not impossible (see Perry and Szalavitz (2006), who describe some children raised in very poor emotional environments, with very little emotional stability, but who are helped to overcome these difficulties, even at much older ages).

The attachment of babies and young children will affect almost every other facet of development – not just personal, social and emotional development. For example, a toddler needs to feel emotionally secure before taking a risk on the obstacle course – there has to be someone to trust to catch him or her before attempting that climb or balance. It is vital to be aware that children's development and progress may be undermined by attachment complications and that these will need to be addressed before moving onto higher order learning. Page, Clare and Nutbrown (2013: 36) theorise that recent research demonstrates two key messages with relation to attachment:

1   High-quality caregiver relationships are central to emotional development and learning in infants and toddlers.
2   Relationships take time to develop, so the key person must be given that time and opportunity to become attached to their key baby or key toddler.

In the most extreme cases, secure attachment plays 'an important role in [the] prevention of abuse and neglect' (Cuthbert, Rayns, and Stanley, 2011: 5). Intervention can make a difference in the prevention of abuse, particularly when the wider issues are addressed, families are considered and the intervention has a wider scope than purely a medical model (Cuthbert, Rayns, and Stanley, 2011).

Recognising secure attachment

In practice, this means that there is a set of behaviours that would be expected from a securely attached baby. If a baby displays significantly different behaviour, over a long period of time (not just a 'one-off' when he or she is feeling a bit poorly, for example), then closer observations should be made.

You would expect the following behaviour from a securely attached baby:

*   Protest or crying when left with stranger or left alone.
*   Will give a stranger a dazzling smile *if* safely snuggled in your arms.
*   Baby smiles or lifts arms or crawls to you to be picked up when you come back into the room.
*   Baby snuggles on your body when held.
*   Baby calls, crawls, runs, or clings to you *if* tired, worried, stressed and needing reassuring murmurs, hugs, chants and cuddle time.
*   Baby engages in earnest coos and intimate 'talks' with you.
*   Baby ignores you and crawls away with vigour to explore when you are present.

adapted from Sterling Honig, 2016

Reflective Questions

Attachment

What would be the first signs you would look for in a baby that was securely attached? (See some of the ideas from Dr Alice Sterling Honing on p. 24.)

How has Attachment Theory affected your curriculum?

Key person

The key person role is a statutory requirement in the EYFS, based on the vital importance of attachment and emotional environments for children, and especially so for babies and toddlers. As already indicated, this must be more than a tokenistic gesture; practitioners must be fully committed to the children and families in their care. This bedrock of love, genuine involvement, emotional availability and care is essential for a baby's development in all areas. It is when children are 'safe and secure' (Elfer, Goldschmied and Selleck, 2011: 25) that they can enjoy and be involved in all the activities and experiences available to them in the setting. Obviously, the quality of the relationship between baby or children is as important, or more important, than simply ensuring that every child has been assigned a key person (Dowling, 2014) and practitioners need to be cued into their key children's emotional needs as well as their physical needs.

Reflective Questions

Key person

Practitioners and setting managers should appreciate that time is needed to get to know the babies and their families. This should be constantly reviewed to ensure it is happening. Practitioners also need to have a good understanding of how this development impinges on all other developments.

If you are working under the EYFS, or have a mandatory requirement for a key person, how are the children allocated? Or are the children allowed to choose their own key person? (Think how you would feel if you were 'allocated' friends and not allowed to choose your own friends.)

What challenges do you have with the key person system? (Think of drop off and pick up times, holidays.)

Social development

Stages of relatedness

As children grow from babies to toddlers, their social relationships develop and flourish with them. Lynne Murray has described the way that children relate to others during this time, through five core stages of relatedness. These are: newborn, core relatedness, topic-based relatedness, connected-up relatedness and cooperative relatedness (Murray, 2014).

The following is adapted from Lynne Murray's *The Psychology of Babies: How Relationships Support Development from Birth to Two* (2014):

- **Newborn/first month:** initial attraction to people, predisposition to respond to social signals. Relatedness is mainly through holding and touch.
- **2 months:** core relatedness – the predisposition towards social interaction increases and babies are highly motivated. This can be seen through longer eye contact, first smiles and prolonged face-to-face interactions. During this age they start to build up a range of gestures, expressions and vocalisations to use during social interactions.
- **4-5 months:** topic-based relatedness – objects, making funny sounds or body games replace face-to-face interactions. These are called 'topics'. Babies' vision improves and they begin to reach and grab things.
- **9-10 months:** connected-up relatedness – babies 'connect up' their interests in the world with their communication skills, and they communicate directly with others about their shared interests.
- **18 months:** cooperative relatedness – babies recognise themselves in mirrors, developing theory of mind. Social interactions can be genuinely cooperative, with shared goals and cultural values. Social development and a sense of other.

Babies have to discover that they are distinct beings, separate from their environment, other people and their main caregiver. This is called having a sense of self. Gradually realising a sense of 'others' is developed during the critical birth to three-year-old age, with babies becoming more aware every day that their actions have resultant consequences on their environment. For example, when they move their legs they can see their toes, or waving a jingle bell makes a noise (Veale, 2013). It is not a coincidence that around the same time that children start to realise that the reflection in the mirror is, in fact, themselves, around 18-24 months, that they also start to 'assert their own wishes' (David *et al.*, 2003: 63).

The basis of the 'social brain' may appear in newborn babies (Farroni *et al.*, 2013). This had previously been found in babies as young as four months old, but the research completed by Farroni *et al.* (2013) found that there was brain activity when the baby looked at a dynamic face (a face playing 'peek-a-boo') but there was no activity to just a moving human arm. They concluded from the research that even very limited face-to-face interaction with other human faces is enough to activate the 'social brain' in newborn babies. Between two and three years of age, positive 'prosocial behaviour' starts to emerge (Brownell, Nichols and Svetlova, 2014: 385) and develops rapidly. Initially this is social awareness, with behaviours such as pointing and bringing objects to show. Children aged three years will 'help, comfort and cooperate' as well as recognise some expected social behaviour. This is most likely to be between the parent and child, only becoming common between children at around three and a half years old (Ninio, 2016). These early experiences are 'cumulative' (National Association for the Education of Young Children, 2009: 12), so very early positive and affirming social experiences will lead to confidence to try new social experiences, creating a virtuous cycle of social competence and confidence. As David *et al.* (2003: 54) note: 'It would be impossible for a child to develop a sense of self without feedback and recognition from those with whom they spend their lives, so they are dependent on those people for a positive view of themselves'.

From this, it can be concluded that babies are born with a desire to react to social stimulus, such as a smiling face, and that this develops rapidly in the birth to three age range. It is imperative to build on these social skills for the benefit of future social competence.

Bronfenbrenner Social Ecological theory

Bronfenbrenner (1979) suggested that children are influenced by a number of systems or social circles, normally depicted as concentric circles with the child at the centre. These start at the centre with the microsystem (immediate family, peer group). The next circle out is the mesosystem (for example, school), then the exosystem (social services) and the macrosystem (cultural ideologies) and finally to the chronosystem (time-related, such as starting school). The closer the circle to the centre, the greater the influence on the child's life and development (Gray and Macblain, 2012), with particular significance placed on the social interactions. Bronfenbrenner's theory is particularly interesting because it identifies not only the types of social influences that a child may have, but also the extent of the influence. Obviously, as a baby, there will be limited contact with the wider social community, so this will have less influence. As a toddler attending a playgroup, there will be more community influence as he or she comes into contact with other children and families. Once at school, there will be regular and frequent contact with both adults and children outside of the immediate family, so the social influences have been expanded. Remember, though, that the wider social context will always have some influence – for example, the global economy is likely to have some impact on most families.

Quick Summary

Learning theories

There are many theories about how babies and children learn, some based on behaviours, some on social context and some on environment. A few of the major theorists are listed here.

Bandura proposed a social learning theory. Bandura showed that children learn by imitating what they see other people doing in their own environment. The actions of others become the model that children will copy.

Vygotsky hypothesised that children's learning is within a social context and the two cannot be separated, and that language (and use of language) is central to cognitive development.

Piaget believed that children 'interiorised' (David *et al.*, 2003) actions, so their cognitive ability was a series of assimilations and accommodations to build up their knowledge and beliefs.

Skinner theorised that children repeated actions that were positively reinforced (e.g. praised or got a reward) and undesirable behaviour could be ameliorated by punishment.

For much more detailed information and links to the EYFS (as well as to other curricula in the UK) see Featherstone (2016).

Gender identity

Kohlberg (1966) theorised that gender identity occurs in three steps, up to the age of six or seven years old. Initially there is basic gender identity, where children know there are girls and boys. This will usually be between the ages of 18 months and three years. However, children may not realise that gender is considered to be constant from birth in most cases. They may assume that when a boy grows his hair long he becomes a girl, for example. By age three, they will be aware that gender is constant, and that boys will be men and girls will be women. Finally, by age six or seven, children will know that appearances do not change the gender of a person and that there are certain 'norms' associated with each gender – for example, girls wear skirts. At this stage children will have stereotype views of gender roles and behaviour. Up to the age of three, children seem not to be concerned about the gender of their playmates, although this starts to change after the age of three, but can usually identify stereotypical 'boys' toys' and 'girls' toys' before this age, possibly as early as nine months (Todd, Barry and Thommessen, 2016).

 Reflective Questions

Gender stereotypes

Watch Anthony Schullo from TEDxNorthCentralCollege on YouTube: www.youtube.com/watch?v=6O9BKRJDqNA

He talks about fluidity of gender and different possibilities, concluding that we need to think about how we communicate gender identities to our children in positive ways for a more diverse, just world.

How could you do this in an Early Years setting? (Think about resources and books available to the children.)

What challenges are there? (Think about parents, other practitioners.)

Why would this be preferable to conforming to gender stereotypes?

Emotional transitions

Often transitions are only referred to in terms of 'moving up' to school or moving up a room in a larger setting. However, there are micro-transitions happening all the time for babies and young children: for example, being dropped off at the setting, settling down for a nap, waking from naptime, when the key person goes for lunch and so on. Babies and young children may also see other children being picked up and dropped off, while waiting for their parents. These are all transitions that babies and children have to cope with emotionally. In her Summit interview (Brodie, 2017), Dr Suzanne Zeedyk spoke about drop-offs and pick-ups of babies and young children at Early Years settings. It is something that happens all the time around the country, and yet there are no universal guidelines, good practice guides or support. These are likely to be the most emotionally charged transitions during the day, but they are sometimes treated as a minor distraction during the day. For these reasons, it is highly advisable to have the key person available to both receive the babies or children into the setting and to be there at home time, wherever possible.

Children and babies construct their own social norms and childhood based on their own experiences, social interactions and emotional disposition. Each setting is unique, and even when comparing settings to the same number of children in the same geographical area with a similar ethos, there will be differences in care, practitioners and pedagogy. Therefore, children will develop their social abilities and skills in different ways. It is to be expected that there will be highly significant differences in socialisations when this is extended to consider different types of settings. For example, the experience of being at a childminder's, or in a home setting, with different-aged children will be very different to that of being in a baby room with other babies and maybe several practitioners doing the caring. Transitions and their emotional impact will be different as babies 'move up' and others stay behind in larger day care settings, whereas babies who go to a childminder could be in the same place with the same childminder for a number of years, possibly only transitioning at statutory school age. Similarly, social interactions of children who attend a preschool, or stay and play, for a few hours will be different to those of children who attend full day care for five days a week.

 Reflective Questions

Emotional transitions

In the case study on pp. 180/181 in Page, Clare and Nutbrown's *Working with Babies & Children* (2013), the authors discuss transitions and micro-transitions (smaller transitions, such as the practitioner leaving the room and returning) throughout the day. They explain how a toddler, named Simon, goes from being dropped off at nursery, then moves through to the toddler room, experiences 11 other toddlers arriving, as well as four other staff arrivals, with his key person being the last to arrive that morning. This all occurs before his core hours at nursery even start. The changing of staff and children continues over lunchtime and throughout the whole day until mum comes to pick him up in the evening.

This would be a reasonably common experience for many babies and young children in nursery settings, especially those who stay for the whole day. If a longer view is taken over the whole week or longer, there will be days that the key person will not be at the setting at all, due to holidays, sickness or shift patterns.

Some of these transitions are not about babies moving from one place to another, but are emotional transitions as their friends arrive and leave, and as the key person arrives.

Count how many emotional transitions, including micro-transitions, which your key baby may have in one day. How might this ebb and flow affect the babies in your care? (Think about how different babies may respond differently.)

Being independent

A significant part of growing from a baby to a young child is a sense of independence and agency. Most toddlers at some time will utter the words 'Me do it' as they want independence to put on their boots or do up their zip or pour their own water. Turning to traditional theorists, there is a wide range of ideas of how to encourage and support independence in the best interest of the child. Susan Isaacs felt that providing choices and appropriate opportunities encouraged children's own independence. Piaget and Inhelder (1969) suggested that children become independent at certain ages. Vygotsky believed that children became independent within their social context and that this is dependent on the social construct. Finally, Bruner theorised that children become independent with help and support, and scaffolding, from a more knowledgeable other (who is usually an adult). Undoubtedly there is some truth in all these theories, and independence will depend on the unique personality of the child and the unique circumstances in which they grow. It is generally from age two onwards that children really start to enjoy their independence, and adults can start to really see their children's personalities shining through. Children will start to express themselves in a variety of ways, including speech, behaviour, movement and attitudes.

Self-regulation

Self-regulation is being able to control (or regulate) your own emotions and behaviour appropriate to the situation. For example, if you are in the middle of playing your game but you have to tidy away the table for lunchtime, good self-regulation would be to accept this and tidy up.

The first stage in being able to regulate emotions is to recognise an emotion – for example, babies crying when they hear or see other babies cry (even if there is nothing wrong with themselves). At 12 months, babies are emotionally labile (have fluctuating moods) and they should not be expected to self-regulate this until much older. Children will begin to self-regulate by the age of three, but are unlikely to be able to self-regulate effectively and consistently until they are around four or five years old. Self-regulation is achieved through an environment of nurturing; secure attachment, positive relationships and supportive experiences. Whitebread (2013: 25) notes that 'a number of studies have shown that early secure attachments are strongly associated with [emotional, social and motivational] self-regulation abilities'. He also presents a table that details the development of social-emotional regulation, which is summarised below:

0-12 months old: regulation of arousal, sleep/wake cycles

                       responsive interaction with others

                       begins to anticipate and participate in simple routines.

12-36 months old: increasing voluntary control and voluntary self-regulation

                       growing ability to comply with requests and situational demands

                       increasing assertiveness and desire for independence

                       increasing awareness of others and empathy

                       some spontaneous helping, sharing, comforting

                       increasing awareness of social rules and sanctions

                       increasing ability to inhibit prohibited activities and delay upon request.

                                                       abridged from Whitebread, 2013: 25

It is critical that children can self-regulate, so they can build friendships and negotiate social situations; problem solve in a thoughtful manner and transition effectively from activity to activity – for example, wait for their lunch, even if they are very hungry. Self-regulation is a 'process of executive function' (Winter, 2010: 23), which is essential later on for children to be ready for school. Self-regulation enables children to focus on cognitive skills and persevere, even if they have to keep trying (Florez, 2011: 47).

Theory of mind

Theory of mind (ToM) is understanding that you have your own thoughts, knowledge, beliefs and intentions but that these may be different to other people. At around one year old, children begin to appreciate concepts such as being 'fair', which needs children to understand that others may be upset, even if the baby is not upset himself or herself (Goswami, 2015). This type of behaviour is termed socio-moral cognition and is linked to mirror neurons in the brain. 'Mirror neurons' (Goswami, 2015) are fired in the brain when watching someone else and your brain 'mirrors' the action in your brain, even if you are not performing the action. For example, when a monkey watched another monkey tearing or grasping, the same areas of the brain that would be used to do those actions were also fired in the watching monkey. Interestingly, these neurons are only activated if it is a person doing the action – a robot grasping did not trigger the mirror neurons.

An observable indication that babies have started to understand that not everyone is thinking the same, and that they can influence this as well, is imperative pointing. This is when babies point at something that they want, prior to them being able to convey this thought through speech. This can be to draw joint attention to something (the cat has just walked into the room) or is more usually because they want something or they want the adult to do something for them (Brinck, 2004).

By about 18 months of age, as interactions with other children 'redesign' the child's brain, ToM develops and most children will begin to realise that others have different thoughts and ideas to their own (David *et al.*, 2003: 15). This knowledge comes from experiences such as socialising and watching others socialise, and understanding that communicating with others is important (Jones, 2016). This is an important building block for building further relationships, social interactions, as well as self-confidence, self-awareness and self-esteem.

Empathy

Empathy is being able to put yourself in someone else's place and see the world from their point of view. For babies in particular it includes:

*   recognising emotions in others
*   having compassion for others
*   refraining from harming others
*   sensitivity - being able to intuit how people are feeling from their tone and body language
*   giving people the same concern and respect as we give ourselves.

Weare and Gray, 2003: 79

Around 18 months old, babies realise that others have different tastes to themselves. Alison Gopnik demonstrated this using the broccoli/crackers research (Gopnik, 2009: 55). The researcher lets the toddler try both broccoli and crackers. The toddler prefers the taste of the crackers. Then the researcher tries the food - her facial expressions shows *she* prefers the broccoli. When asked to give the researcher her favourite food, by 18 months the toddler will give the researcher broccoli, even though it wouldn't have been the toddler's own choice. This demonstrates how, at 18 months, that toddlers can put themselves in someone else's position and understand they may have different likes and dislikes.

Attunement

Attunement between adults and babies or young children is more than adults just being 'in tune' with their children's needs - for example, that they need a nappy change. It involves an emotional interaction between adult and child, a feeling of being in harmony together - for example, knowing that the baby is feeling uncomfortable and irritable because their nappy needs changing. Attunement has been described by Stern *et al.* (1985) as:

*   An empathic responsiveness between two individuals which subtly conveys a shared emotion
*   Attuned adults will be able to acknowledge the infant's current emotional state and symbolise it in verbal and non-verbal interaction
*   Attuned interactions help the infant develop emotional regulation.

Attunement helps babies and young children feel like they 'belong', have a place, are kept in mind. 'Effective interpersonal relationships and secure attachments' (David *et al.*, 2003: 126), as well as developing a feeling of belonging, security and safety, depend on effective emotional attunement. Babies are born already looking for that connection, even though they have never seen or experienced another face before and are engaged, rational beings (Zeedyk, 2017).

Attunement is letting babies and children know that their 'voice' is being heard, from answering a cry to soliciting ideas or opinions on activities. For babies this could be knowing how to hold the baby in their preferred position, how they like their bottle presented, coming round to the

front and speaking to babies before picking them up – 'body language can say so much more for young children than the actual words' (Dowling, 2014: 45). For older children, knowing about their comforter, putting up family pictures or ensuring you ask about their weekend activities support attunement.

Resilience

Resilience is generally defined as the ability to 'bounce back' when you hit a problem or life throws you a challenge. Healy (2014) argues that 'the ability to bounce back or recover is important, but it's not the whole picture. A resilient child recovers from challenges, but they've learned to do more than that. They actually hold a different mindset. A mindset of resiliency that deeply believes: I am not my mistakes, I can try again, things will get better, and I am not alone'. It is no surprise, then, that attachment and resilience are often discussed together, because being attached to one, special person means that there is someone to turn to in times of need (David *et al.*, 2003) and to help babies and young children to know they are not alone.

Moral development

Kohlberg proposed a six-stage, three-level model of morality through which children progress, at their own pace (McDevitt *et al.*, 2013: 590). Most children under the age of three will be at the first level – pre-conventional morality – of one of the two stages within this level. The first stage is punishment avoidance and obedience, which means that children consider behaviour that is punished to be wrong. The converse of this is that behaviours that are not punished (or children are not 'caught' doing) are right. Others' feelings, needs or rights are not a consideration during this stage, and children's morality is based on what is right for themselves at that point in time. The second stage, exchange of favours, is where children become aware that by following rules or desired behaviour there may be some rewards – for example, getting a sticker for clearing up. Some children may start to understand that meeting the needs of others is also desirable and brings rewards (both intrinsic and extrinsic), although most children under three years old will still justify behaviour in terms of consequences to themselves rather than altruistic reasons. Obviously children's moral reasoning at this age is highly dependent on the words and actions of the adults and children with whom they come into regular contact, as well as the influences of TV and books. Children will often want to clarify who is the 'goody' and 'baddy' in a story as they begin to analyse the behaviour traits in different people.

Holistic links in this chapter

- *PSED and early physical development*
- *PSED and physical development as children become mobile*
- *PSED and physical development outdoors*
- *PSED and communication development*
- *PSED and cognitive development*
- *Sense of self, narratives, links with literacy.*

PSED and early physical development

The very first type of physical engagement that a baby will have with his or her mother is skin-to-skin contact. It has been shown that there is 'strong evidence for mother/baby bonding' (Koller Kologeski *et al.*, 2017: 94) through skin-to-skin contact, so this physical engagement is an important start for children's secure attachment and attunement. Emotional well-being is also closely linked to touch (O'Connor and Daly, 2016) and forms part of the good emotional environment in which babies will thrive. Babies communicate through physical activity with signs such as leg kicking and arm waving when they are happy and, later on, smiles. They are 'programmed' to be social, turning towards voices in preference to just sounds (which forms part of social bonding) and faces (Murray and Andrews, 2005). Similarly, when babies want a break, they will give physical signals such as turning away or have distressed facial expressions.

Baby massage

Baby massage is a great way to enjoy skin-to-skin contact in a relaxing and calm environment. There are many benefits, including:

- Becoming attuned with your baby and bonding
- It is a positive interaction between baby and adult, including extended family and siblings
- Baby may sleep and settle better as the levels of oxytocin rise in his or her body.

NCT, 2017

Review Your Practice

How do you initiate touch and picking up babies in your setting? (Think about saying baby's name first and getting his or her attention.)

Investigate baby massage classes in your area and consider how this might help the babies in your care.

Case Study

Babies know when a cuddle is coming

In this amazing piece of research by Professor Vasu Reddy at the University of Portsmouth, you can see that even young babies (two to four months old) anticipating being picked up by their parent.

Watch this video and discuss with a colleague how this could change or reinforce your practice when picking up babies.

http://uopnews.port.ac.uk/2013/06/25/babies-know-when-a-cuddle-is-coming/

PSED and physical development as children become mobile

As babies become mobile (creeping, crawling and walking) it is important that they have unrestricted movement and are allowed to test their physical abilities. Being held in 'containers', such as car seats, prams and buggies, and not being allowed to fall, run, balance or take 'risks' affects both their physical development, and also their attitudes towards movement and play (Goddard Blythe, 2005). If children are not allowed to practise their balance by cruising around the furniture, for example, then they will have less confidence when walking. Ironically, keeping toddlers 'safe' by not allowing them unrestricted movement will make them more liable to accidents because they haven't built up the physical skills, which could then affect self-confidence and self-esteem.

Movement to support PSED

Simple 'obstacle' courses for children just walking – for example, a rope laid on the floor to balance on, hoops to step in and out of, wooden blocks to step onto and off of. This helps self-confidence in children. Be sure to include tunnels or crawling exercises as well.

Review Your Practice

Read the article on container baby syndrome on 'Move Forward', the website of the American Physical Therapy Association: www.moveforwardpt.com/symptomsconditionsdetail. aspx?cid=53d90264-1846-4b86-891f-0facc63db3e8

Here both the short- and long-term, physical, emotional and cognitive effects of a baby spending long periods of time in a 'container' are described.

 Case Study

Climbing

Climbing is a skill that children need, from walking up stairs to climbing up a ladder for the slide. A combination of abilities is required, including, but not restricted to, hand-eye coordination to confident movement and a sense of balance.

Would you allow children to use a climbing frame?

How do you feel about children climbing trees?

Would you be alright with children climbing on chairs or the table?

How do these three situations differ?

What different skills are needed in each case?

What would be the determining factor in all cases?

PSED and physical development outdoors

Children need to learn to be independent - in fact, independence is crucial to children's well-being and a toddler's time spent outdoors will give him or her opportunities to be independent and explore their interests (White, 2011). Outdoors usually gives more opportunity for risky play and using large pieces of equipment, such as the climbing frame or bikes. This type of play necessitates physical skills (walking, running, climbing, jumping, sliding, pedalling) and a good level of social skills (waiting to go up the slide, taking turns with the bikes, running with other children in the space) to work at its best. There is likely to be an element of self-regulation and emotional control needed too, as the bikes get shared and the digging area fills up.

Activities outdoors

Mud kitchens have gained popularity, with areas for making mud pies and potions, using old pots, pans and wooden spoons. Playing with mud can also simply be stirring a puddle with a stick, or pressing thick mud concoctions onto the trunk of a tree and adding stone 'eyes', a stick 'mouth' and leaf 'hair'.

Collecting, sorting and categorising stones have strong mathematical links, and can increase social interactions if done as a group.

The Forestry Commission, England has some excellent ideas for things to do in the woods, from using stepping logs and a play path through the trees, to exploring and using your imagination in roots of trees that have fallen over or planting willow dens.

Find out more at: www.forestry.gov.uk/forestry/infd-7lsehw

Review Your Practice

How do babies benefit from being outdoors? (Think about the different emotional reactions to a new environment.)

How do we encourage children to self-regulate outdoors? (Think of modelling negotiations.)

How might being outdoors encourage social engagement between children? (Think of children who like to play as groups, for example football.)

PSED and communication development

Babies start their verbal communication journey with non-verbal and body language communication. Social referencing is a large part of non-verbal communication. This is the way that babies take cues from the emotive displays of adults, to inform and modulate their responses to events, their environment or other people. This can be facial expressions (a smile or a frown), an encouraging remark ('Go on, you can touch the toy') or body language (a nod or a shake of the head). Social referencing starts to build the skills for babies to make decisions and choices within a particular social context.

Quick Summary

Stages of language development

- Birth to six months: Babies will turn towards sounds, watch faces and start to make a range of noises.

- Six to 12 months: Babies will babble and hold proto-conversations.
- 12 to 18 months: Understand words, simple instructions, gesture and use a few words themselves.
- 18 months to 24 months: Children will understand 200 words or more and be using 50 or more words of their own.
- Two to three years: Use around 300 words and create sentences.

Activities

Be a good role model for babies. For example, be consistent with your reactions and check that you are not giving any unintended emotional communication, such as screaming at spiders.

Check that your body language mirrors your language and your facial expression. Sarcasm, for example, is very confusing for young children because the words, tone and body language are at odds with each other. So when a drink is spilt across the table, saying 'Oh, that's good!' in a cross voice, with folded arms, is sending very mixed messages to children.

Encourage joint attention, where you point at something (a bird on the tree; a mobile in the baby room) and encourage baby to look and share. When babies start to do this for themselves (usually around 8 months old), make sure to respond positively and encouragingly.

 Review Your Practice

Read the article on container baby syndrome on 'Move Forward', the website of the American Physical Therapy Association: www.moveforwardpt.com/symptomsconditionsdetail. aspx?cid=53d90264-1846-4b86-891f-0facc63db3e8

Here both the short- and long-term, physical, emotional and cognitive effects of a baby spending long periods of time in a 'container' are described.

PSED and cognitive development

Cognitive development is closely linked to dispositions and the willingness to learn. Dowling (2014: 120) describes them as: 'Dispositions vs feelings is long lasting habits vs brief emotions'. For example, many children are able to read, but not all of these children will want to read or are willing to read for the pleasure of the activity. Therefore, it is important to foster a disposition or lifelong desire to learn at an early age. It is becoming more and more apparent that 'the relationship between emotional and social factors and children's academic competence' (National Association for the Education of Young Children, 2009: 11) is critical. Developing mastery dispositions and children's belief in themselves (self-efficacy) are good foundations on which to build further learning and cognitive abilities. These are expressed well through the Characteristics of Effective Learning in the *Development Matters* guidance from Early Education.

Quick Summary

Characteristics of Effective Learning (CoEL)

The Characteristics of Effective Learning are divided into three broad areas:

Playing and exploring: engagement (skill)

- Finding out and exploring
- Playing with what they know
- Being willing to 'have a go'.

Active learning: motivation (will)

- Being involved and concentrating
- Keeping trying
- Enjoying achieving what they set out to do.

Creating and thinking critically: thinking (thrill)

- Having their own ideas
- Making links
- Choosing ways to do things.

Although these areas are not strictly hierarchical, there is a certain logic to them working from 1. through to 3., i.e. it is unlikely that a child will be curious and have creative thinking if they are unwilling to get involved with play or exploration (Early Education, 2012: 5).

These are sometimes referred to as Characteristics of Effective Teaching and Learning, because there are some areas where practitioners will be teaching to achieve children's learning.

Activities

Build mastery dispositions for learning in all areas, by presenting activities for babies and children that they will be able to achieve with the smallest amount of help and encouragement.

 Quick Summary

Integration of mathematics

Using mathematical language while doing everyday things around the setting helps young children to both learn a wider range of vocabulary, and also to understand the specific, meaningful mathematical terms heard in the correct context (Hutchin, 2012). For example, including 'I wonder how much this jug will hold – what is its capacity?' or the 'symmetry' of a pattern or the 'orientation' of a shape. After all, if they know there is a dinosaur called 'Tyrannosaurus Rex', the 'capacity' of a jug is pretty tame!

Review Your Practice

How often do you stretch and challenge the babies and children in your care? (Think how often you did things that they may have been able to do, with a little support.)

Case Study

Carol Dweck: 'Developing a growth mindset'

Carol Dweck: 'Developing a growth mindset'. In this video Carol Dweck describes how children react differently to cognitive difficulties and cognitive challenges. Some children rise to the challenge, others are 'devastated' or avoid the challenge. The 'growth mindset' processes and corrects errors, a closed mindset doesn't, which sets up problems for the future. See how Carol Dweck advises how to handle this situation: www.youtube.com/watch?v=hiiEeMN7vbQ

Sense of self, narratives, links with literacy

Storytelling has been part of humanity for a very long time and narratives are still used in many areas of life today. For children, telling stories and narratives may serve a particular developmental purpose – for example, to 'generate a person's sense of self' (David *et al.*, 2003: 65) or to internalise an emotion or to reminisce. This starts with the parent or practitioner 'story telling' (and this may be simply sharing an experience together, such as going outside in the snow). By around two or two and a half, the toddler will join in and add the bits they remember ('My red hat, boots') and by three they are likely to be able to tell a brief (sometimes inaccurate!) story themselves.

Often some of the first stories told by young children will be about superheroes and 'goodies' and 'baddies'. This is often discouraged or diverted into something more 'suitable'. However, consider the messages you are sending the children with this – that your choice of play is not suitable or desirable. Penny Holland's 2003 book *We Don't Play with Guns Here*, which was underpinned by her Masters research, is the seminal text. There has been much written about superhero play since then, especially since the expansion of films with comic book characters, and it is worth investigating the latest research.

Activities

Have a range of culturally and personally sensitive materials, such as books and stories for different family groupings, different cultures, a range of ethnicities, so children can find a representation of 'themselves'. These should be freely available.

Story *telling* sessions are an excellent way of incorporating children into the story and showing how special they are. You can use props and encourage children to suggest what might happen next or how the story ends.

Have photo albums available and pictures up on walls for children to look at themselves, and have videos on a tablet or computer. Discuss these with the children if they show an interest, to remind them of the day or when it was, so they have a sense of stories happening at a certain time and place.

Discuss and demonstrate how the different superheroes move or fly, super-powers, special moves or special pieces of equipment. How do these affect the story?

 Review Your Practice

Listen to children's storytelling abilities as they grow and become more proficient. Are there common themes? (Think how these might mirror the stories you choose to share with the children.)

Gather 'family' stories from parents, which you can discuss with the children to support the home-setting relationship.

How does your setting view superhero play? Are there policies or is it on an 'ad hoc' basis? How does this fit with your personal perspective?

 Quick Summary

Why incorporate 'neuroscience' into Early Years practice?

Neuroscientists affirm that 'billions of synaptic connections are made within the first five years of life' (Conkbayir, 2017: 22) and that practitioners are part of this process, through planning environments, developmentally appropriate activities and sensory experiences.

The process of incorporating neuroscience into Early Years settings with practitioners may have challenges (including a proliferation of 'neuromyths'), but is worthwhile because it vindicates good practice based on science (causation not correlation) and adds another layer of knowledge to understanding about how young children think, learn and develop.

Challenges

There are many challenges to securing PSED. For example, parents with English as an Additional Language can be a challenge when dropping off and picking up or when trying to explain the ethos or activities at a setting. This can be reduced by the sensitive use of translators (either official or friends and family helping).

Parents with post-natal depression (Hobcraft and Kiernan, 2010), both mums and dads, are likely to be less responsive to baby's first attempts to communicate or enjoy social exchanges at an early age. This is exacerbated by some taboos around mental health and not wishing to admit that it is difficult to raise a baby. However, this does seem to be slowly improving in the UK, with more encouragement and support being given to help parents during this stressful time.

Babies and children themselves may be processing very complex emotional feelings. A range of examples could include migrants, refugees or displaced families, witnessing domestic violence and bereavement. It may be that adults at home are not aware of how much children have seen or heard, and so they may not mention it to practitioners as they don't feel it is relevant. Or parents may be in denial or fear themselves and don't yet have the emotional reserves to be able to support their children. Therefore, having a secure emotional environment at the setting will help children to regulate their feelings and possibly share with practitioners, who can then support and help parents at this difficult time.

Opportunities

Supporting babies and young children's PSED lays down good foundations for all other learning and development, from a sense of identity to mastery and communication.

Settings are well placed to support many areas of PSED, especially social interactions with other babies, children and adults outside of the immediate family.

Early physical development and outdoors play may be much easier at a setting than at home, especially if the setting has access to a forest or beach school.

Conclusion

Babies and young children need love and care to thrive. As newborns, babies are totally reliant on more able others, usually adults, for every need, from food to shelter to nappy changes. In the past, it was felt that babies were only learning very rudimentary things from their environment, such as light and dark or hot and cold. However, with the advent of better recording equipment (both video and neuroscience) and more powerful computer analysis, researchers (e.g. Gopnik, 2010 and Goswami, 2015) are finding that babies have very complex thought processes, are social and are much more emotionally aware than previously assumed.

Personal, social and emotional development is hugely complex, and this chapter has only touched on some of the core concepts, such as attachment, resilience, well-being and self-regulation. It is strongly advised that the readings and reflections are actioned to gain more insights into this prime area of learning and development.

Further Reading and Research

David Whitebread's chapter, 'The importance of self-regulation for learning from birth', in Helen Moylett's book *Characteristics of Effective Early Learning* is an excellent examination of both metacognition and self-regulation. He also includes cognitive development as well as personal, social and emotional development.

Emotional well-being: children

Read the discussion on comforters, their role in emotional stability and how practitioners may respond on p. 111 of *Working with Babies & Children: From Birth to Three* (Page, Clare and Nutbrown, 2013).

Compare that to your practice in your own setting.

How do you manage comforters? Why do you do it this way?

What effect do you think this may have on the children's emotional well-being?

Watch this YouTube video from November 2016 with Professor Ferre Laevers talking to Early Years Scotland about his thoughts on well-being, involvement and the improvements in children's outcomes. He states: 'Well-being and involvement can be improved in a short time' and explains why and how this is the case: www.youtube.com/watch?v=5RZDYK 8tsvk&t=10s

Emotional well-being: practitioners

How do you know when YOU 'belong' as a professional or person; what little things make you feel comfortable? (Think about your picture on the board in the entrance hall, with your name spelled correctly and the correct qualifications, or is it more subtle than that?)

Is your birthday remembered? Do you have a special space in the staff room? (Do you have a staff room?) Do you share meals together?

How do you de-stress after a day's work or a tough encounter at work? (See Sonia Mainstone-Cotton's interview in *Personal, Social and Emotional Well-being in Young Children* (Brodie, 2017: 223–39 for ideas and inspiration.)

References

Ainsworth, M. and Bell, S. (1970) Attachment, exploration, and separation: Illustrated by the behavior of one-year-olds in a strange situation. *Child Development* Vol. 41 Iss. 1, pp. 49–67.

Bowlby, J. (1969) *Attachment and Loss*. New York: Basic Books.

Brinck, I. (2004) The pragmatics of imperative and declarative pointing. *Cognitive Science Quarterly* Vol. 3 Iss. 4, pp. 429–46.

Brodie, K. (2017) *Personal, Social and Emotional Well-being in Young Children: Summit Transcripts*. Wilmslow: Rainmaker.

Bronfenbrenner, U. (1979) *The Ecology of Human Development: Experiments by Nature and Design*. Cambridge, MA: Harvard University Press.

Brownell, C., Nichols, S. and Svetlova, M. (2014) Converging developments in prosocial behavior and self-other understanding in the second year of life: The second social-cognitive revolution, in M. Banaji and S. Gelman (eds) *Navigating the Social World: What Infants, Children, and Other Species Can Teach Us*. Oxford: Oxford University Press.

Conkbayir, M. (2017) *Early Childhood and Neuroscience: Theory, Research and Implications for Practice*. London: Bloomsbury.

Cuthbert, C., Rayns, G. and Stanley, K. (2011) *All Babies Count: Prevention and Protection for Vulnerable Babies*. NSPCC.

David, T., Goouch, K., Powell, S. and Abbott, L. (2003) *Birth to Three Matters: A Review of the Literature Compiled to Inform The Framework to Support Children in their Earliest Years*. London: DfES.

Department for Health (2009) *Healthy Child Programme: Pregnancy and the First Five Years of Life*. DCSF.

Dollard, J. and Miller, N. (1950) *Personality and Psychotherapy*. New York: McGraw-Hill.

Dowling, M. (2014) (4th edn) *Young Children's Personal, Social and Emotional Development*. London: SAGE.

Early Education (2012) *Development Matters in the Early Years Foundation Stage (EYFS)*. London: Early Education.

Elfer, P., Goldschmied, E. and Selleck, D. (2011) *Key Persons in the Early Years: Building Relationships for Quality Provision in Early Years Settings and Primary Schools*. Abingdon: Routledge.

Farroni, T., Chiarelli, A., Lloyd-Fox, S., Massaccesi, S., Merla, A., Di Gangi, V., Mattarello, T., Faraguna, D. and Johnson, M. (2013) Infant cortex responds to other humans from shortly after birth. *Scientific Reports* 3, Article number: 2851.

Featherstone, S. (2016) *An Anthology of Educational Thinkers*. London: Featherstone Education.

Florez, I.R. (2011) *Developing Young Children's Self-Regulation through Everyday Experiences*. National Association for the Education of Young Children. Available from: www.naeyc.org/files/yc/file/201107/Self-Regulation_Florez_OnlineJuly2011.pdf. Accessed 21 May 2017.

Gerhardt, S. (2004) *Why Love Matters*. Hove: Routledge.

Goddard Blythe, S. (2005) *The Well Balanced Child: Movement and Early Learning* (2nd edn) Gloucestershire: Hawthorn.

Gopnik, A. (2009) *The Philosophical Baby*. London: Bodley Head.

Gopnik, A. (2010) How babies think. *Scientific American* Vol. 303, pp. 76–81.

Goswami, U. (2015) *Children's Cognitive Development and Learning*. York: Cambridge Primary Review Trust.

Gray, C. and MacBlain, S. (2012) *Learning Theories in Childhood*. London: SAGE.

Halle, T.G. and Darling-Churchill, D.E. (2016) Review of measures of social and emotional development. *Journal of Applied Developmental Psychology* Vol. 45, pp. 8–18.

Harms, T., Cryer, D., Clifford, R. and Yazejian, N. (2017) (3rd edn) *Infant/Toddler Environment Rating Scale (ITERS-3)*. New York: Teachers' College Press.

Healy, M. (2014) *The Resilient Child: Can Your Child Bounce Back from Failure?* Available from: www.psychologytoday.com/blog/creative-development/201407/the-resilient-child. Accessed 21 May 2017.

Hobcraft, J. and Kiernan, K. (2010) *Predictive Factors from Age 3 and Infancy for Poor Child Outcomes at Age 5 Relating to Children's Development, Behaviour and Health: Evidence from the Millennium Cohort Study*. York: University of York.

Hutchin, V. (2012) *The EYFS: A Practical Guide for Students and Professionals*. Abingdon: Hodder Education.

Jones, M. (2016) *Talking and Learning with Young Children*. London: SAGE.

Kohlberg, L. (1966) A cognitive-developmental analysis of children's sex-role concepts and attitudes, in E.E. Maccody (ed.), *The Development of Sex Differences*. Stanford, CA: Stanford University Press.

Koller Kologeski, T., Strapasson, M., Schneider, V. and Renosto, J. (2017) Skin-to-skin contact of the newborn with its mother in the perspective of the multiprofessional team. *Journal of Nursing UFPE* Vol. 11 Iss. 1, pp. 94–101.

Laevers, F. (ed.) (1994) *Well-being and Involvement in Care Settings. A Process-oriented Self-evaluation Instrument.* Leuven: Leuven University.

Mainstone-Cotton, S. (2017) *Promoting Young Children's Emotional Health and Well-being.* London: Jessica Kingsley.

McDevitt, T., Ormrod, J., Cupit, G., Chandler, M. and Aloa, V. (2013) *Child Development and Education.* French's Field: Pearson Australia.

McLeod, S.A. (2009) *Attachment Theory.* Available from www.simplypsychology.org/attachment.html. Accessed 5 September 2016.

Murray, L. (2014) *The Psychology of Babies: How Relationships Support Development from Birth to Two.* London: Hachette.

Murray, L. and Andrews, L. (2005) *The Social Baby: Understanding Babies' Communication from Birth.* Richmond: CP Publishing.

National Association for the Education of Young Children NAEYC (2009) *Developmentally Appropriate Practice in Early Childhood Programs Serving Children from Birth through Age 8.* NAEYC.

National Strategies (2008) *Social and Emotional Aspects of Development (SEAD).* Nottingham: DCSF

NCT (2017) *Baby Massage.* Available from: www.nct.org.uk/parenting/baby-massage. Accessed 21 May 2017.

NICE (2012) *Social and Emotional Well-being: Early Years NICE guidelines* [PH40]. Available from: www.nice.org.uk/guidance/ph40. Accessed 10 June 2017.

Ninio, A. (2016) Bids for joint attention by parent–child dyads and by dyads of young peers in interaction. *Journal of Child Language* Vol. 43 Iss. 1, pp. 135–56.

O'Connor, A. and Daly, A. (2016) *Understanding Physical Development in the Early Years: Linking Bodies and Minds.* Abingdon: Routledge.

Page, J. (2017) *Professional Love in Early Childhood Education and Care.* Available from: http://professionallove.group.shef.ac.uk/. Accessed 18 May 2017.

Page, J., Clare, A. and Nutbrown, C. (2013) (2nd edn) *Working with Babies & Children: From Birth to Three.* London: SAGE.

Page, J. and Elfer, P. (2013) The emotional complexity of attachment interactions in nursery. *European Early Childhood Education Research Journal* Vol. 21 Iss. 4, pp. 553–67.

Perry, B. and Szalavitz, M. (2006) *The Boy who was Raised as a Dog.* New York: Basic Books.

Piaget, J. and Inhelder, B. (1969) *The Psychology of the Child.* New York: Basic Books.

Schaffer, H.R. and Emerson, P.E. (1964) Patterns of response to physical contact in early human development. *Journal of Child Psychology and Psychiatry* Vol. 5 Iss. 1, pp. 1–13.

Siraj, I., Kingston, D. and Melhuish, E. (2015) *Sustained Shared Thinking and Emotional Well-being (SSTEW) Scale for 2-5 Year Olds Provision.* London: IOE.

Sterling Honig, A. (2016) *Secure Attachment Promotes a Positive Emotional Life for Infants and Toddlers.* Available from: www.earlychildhoodwebinars.com/wp-content/uploads/2015/12/Slides-4-per-page_Nurturing-secure-attachments-for-infants-and-toddlers_March_9_2016.pdf. Accessed 16 May 2017.

Stern, D.N., Hofer, L., Haft, W. and Dore, J. (1985) Affect attunement: The sharing of feeling states between mother and infant by means of inter-modal fluency, in Field, T.M. and Fox, N.A. (eds) *Social Perception in Infants.* Norwood, NJ: Ablex, pp. 249–68.

Todd, B., Barry, J., and Thommessen, S. (2016) Preferences for 'gender-typed' toys in boys and girls aged 9 to 32 months. *Infant and Child Development.* Wiley online. Available from: http://onlinelibrary.wiley.com/doi/10.1002/icd.1986/abstract. Accessed 21 May 2017.

Veale, F. (2013) *Early Years for Levels 4 & 5 and the Foundation Degree.* Abingdon: Hodder Education.

von Hofsten, O., von Hofsten, C., Sulutvedt, U., Laeng, B., Brennen, T. and Magnussen, S. (2014) Simulating newborn face perception. *Journal of Vision* Vol.14 Iss. 16.

Weare, K. and Gray, G. (2003) *What Works in Developing Children's Emotional and Social Competence and Well-being?* London: DfES.

White, J. (2011) *Outdoor Provision in the Early Years.* London: SAGE.

Whitebread, D. (2013) The importance of self-regulation for learning from birth, in Moylett, H. (ed.) *Characteristics of Effective Early Learning.* Maidenhead: Open University Press.

Winter, P. (2010) *Neuroscience and Early Childhood Development.* Department of Education and Children's Services, South Australia.

Zeedyk, S. (2017) *Babies.* Available from: http://connectedbaby.net/babies. Accessed 10 June 2017.

3 Physical development

Through playful movement and physical activity the child can explore who they are, how the world works and how they fit into it.

White 2008: 68

Introduction

Physical development is identified as one of the prime areas in the Early Years Foundation Stage (EYFS), meaning that it supports learning in all other areas and is widely recognised as an essential foundation from which to build. O'Connor and Daly (2016: 159) state that 'physical activity and movement play are fundamental to brain development and children's learning potential' and that we need an 'abundance of opportunities for spontaneous movement' to increase brain development. Bruce (2004: 75) encourages a 'sense of embodiment' as part of good child development and positive links to children's physical environment. Although these would appear to be self-evident statements, physical development can sometimes be considered to simply happen, but more thought needs to be given to both quality and quantity of physical development, especially during the critical formative years from birth to three years old.

In this chapter, children's physical development is loosely subdivided into the three age groups: birth to one year; one year to two years; and two to three years. This is because physical development varies in each of these age ranges, with an associated change in children's physical requirements. The senses are also included in this chapter, as well as comment on health, nutrition, oral health and being outdoors.

Physical growth and development

Physical development is measured against 'typical development' and 'norms' more frequently and exactly than any other area of children's development. Even before birth, babies are measured for length and size to estimate growth rates. At birth the baby's weight, head circumference measurements and length may be recorded on predetermined centile charts so that he or she can be compared and measured against statistical averages. This often continues well beyond three years of age, into school life. The disproportionate amount of measurement for physical growth could be because physical growth is easily measurable and easy to track, whereas other areas of development are more difficult to quantify.

Physical growth and development are often put together as if both happen as a matter of course, with little external input, excepting possibly nutrition. However, it should be made clear at the very beginning that there is a difference between 'physical growth' and 'physical development'. Growth is simply the process of getting bigger, determined largely by genetics and in a very predictable sequence. Physical development is the use of body and skills – for example, for the muscle coordination and strength needed to control a baby's head; hand-eye coordination; and finger strength. Physical skills that a three-year-old child has acquired will have started when he or she was a newborn baby, and have been developed, coordinated and grouped in order to perform complex physical feats such as kicking a football or climbing a ladder. If young children's learning and development is only focused on the so-called academic aspects of development, such as maths and literacy, this will result in 'disembodied children' (O'Connor and Daly, 2016: 162) where children don't know about their bodies, where they start and end or how to exercise efficiently.

A recurring theme throughout this book is that there are significant changes from a newborn baby to a three-year-old child, in all areas of development. This is just as awe inspiring in physical development as anywhere else. Although every child will develop in a unique way, depending on many factors, including nature and nurture, there are some common patterns that you would expect to see in a child's physical development. Physical growth is continuous and sequential, which is determined by the nervous system. This explains why babies and children have predictable cephalo-caudal growth patterns (fastest growth at the top of the body and gradually working downwards) and proximo-distal growth patterns (from the centre, or trunk, of the body out towards the extremities). This can be thought of as 'downwards and outwards' (Tassoni and Beith, 2000: 108).

There are different muscle groups developing during this time, at a rate unique to the child. Those muscles that are not controlled cause 'involuntary' movements, such as recoiling when you have a fright. Other muscle groups start in babies as involuntary, but then children start to gain control as the nervous system matures and grows. Bladder and bowel control fall under this category, which is why potty training or toilet training can only be achieved when children both understand the concept and have conscious, physical control of these muscle groups. Young children are constantly on the move because 'their muscles contain a greater percentage of water than ours, so they tire more easily' (O'Connor and Daly, 2016: 151), which explains why children 'fidget' and are constantly changing positions, even if they are sitting on the carpet or the sofa.

Growth of the newborn baby to one year old

Babies are born with involuntary reflexes, which are body movements over which they have no control – for example, grasping an object placed into their palm. They start to lose their reflexes as they grow up, although some are maintained into adulthood, such as jolting when there is a sudden loud noise. The best known of these reflexes is the Moro reflex (Sharma and Cockerill, 2014), which is where the baby's arms are flung open in response to a falling sensation.

Muscle tone at birth is not universally the same throughout a baby's body. Newborn babies have more muscle tone in their limbs than in their trunk and neck, as witnessed by a baby's inability to support his or her own head initially. If you support a baby in a standing position, it will look as if he or she is trying to stand, but this is a reflex reaction. At around two months, baby will start to smile and by three months you will see 'obvious pleasure to friendly handling' (Sharma and Cockerill, 2014: 13). Social interactions will be more purposeful by around 12 months, when baby may have favourite games, such as peek-a-boo, and may initiate these with others.

Quick Summary

Tummy time

Tummy time (putting babies on the carpet on their tummies) is key for neck strength and trunk control (try doing a jigsaw yourself on the floor!). Tummy time builds up core stability in the trunk, which is needed before children can have secure arm and leg movements, as they develop physically from the centre of their bodies outwards. Archer and Siraj (2015) explain how babies using their arms to push up from the floor give the strength and alignment in the spine that will be needed for an upright posture. Interestingly, lots of tummy time stimulates the pelvic area, helping to support toilet training when the time comes. Good core stability is essential for children later on when writing or doing other activities sitting at a desk, because they need to be able to support their bodies sufficiently to support their arms, elbows, wrists and finally finger movements. Babies should be on their tummy from 10 weeks old until seven months (unless sleeping or being held).

From around five months onwards, and generally by nine months, a baby's muscles are sufficiently developed to be able to support his or her own head, and they may also be able to roll over from front to back or back to front. This develops into the baby being able to sit independently by around 7-11 months. By seven to nine months, baby will start to pull him- or herself to standing, and 'cruise' around furniture, using this as a support. Soon after cruising is mastered, you will probably see baby start to take his or her first steps and by around 12 months may be fully walking, although he or she may need some support for a while.

Therefore, the first physical development is the neck and head control (top) moving down through sitting (trunk) and then walking (legs). Similarly, development is from sitting (trunk) outwards to control arms, movement and finger grasp, simultaneously developing control of legs and head movement. A child needs to go through all stages, from gross motor skills to fine motor skills, to form and train the 33 muscles of the hand. They need to do the 'fiddly' things such as peg boards, threading and finer threading. This can also give challenging and individualised learning in one activity (big pasta for threading, smaller pasta and small beads). This tactile feedback helps children to write effectively later.

There are two groups of reflexes. First there are primitive reflexes such as the rooting, sucking, grasping and step reflex. Second there are the postural reactions, which support control of posture, balance and coordination at a pre-conscious level. 'Persistence of primitive reflexes and/or under-developed postural reactions above the age of three and a half years provide evidence [and signposting] of immaturity in the functioning of the neurological pathways involved (NMI)' (Goddard Blythe, 2017: 18). Therefore, by observing and understanding physical development, particularly reflexes, there is an indication for the neural readiness of children to learn. There is a book recommendation in 'Further Reading' at the end of this chapter which has an excellent chapter on reflexes.

The senses

Babies have poor sight when born, but are sensitive to changes in light. Newborn babies can see faces and facial expressions at around arm's length (30 cm), but they are unable to see any further than this (von Hofsten *et al.*, 2014). They can hear and be startled by loud noises as well as recognise familiar voices and tunes. As newborns, babies are very sensitive to touch and initial skin-to-skin contact has been shown to be very beneficial (Royal College of Midwives, 2012). Gradually 'gaze' is developed, where a baby will intentionally follow an object with the eyes and will make eye contact with other people around one month old. By six months he or she will be showing an awareness of depth (Sharma and Cockerill, 2014) and will be very interested in the visual world around them.

Preferences in tastes will develop around six months as baby is weaned onto solid foods and different flavours are presented. As baby's limb control starts to improve, he or she will bring things to his or her mouth to explore them. This is known as 'mouthing' and is a good way for baby to find out about the world, as the mouth is very sensitive, so gives good sensory feedback. By about 12 months, baby will still be bringing things to the mouth, but less often and he or she will be using the other senses to investigate objects.

The physical growth that takes place from almost helpless newborn baby to independent toddler in just over a year is astounding. It is from the basis of this physical growth that the toddler can start to develop physical skills and his or her senses.

One to two years old

By around 12 months the baby will probably be a toddler, seeking independence and actively exploring the world around. There will still be physical growth as children grow up, but now there is also deliberate and determined development as well. For example, once walking has been achieved, running, skipping and climbing will follow.

Between one and two years old, children will develop both their large motor skills and fine motor skills. Gross motor skills can be locomotive (i.e. to do with movement of the body through space) or skills that involve the whole body or large muscle groups – for example, kicking or throwing a ball. Fine motor skills can be manipulative or skills that involve small, precise, controlled body movements such as picking up a jigsaw piece or a pencil.

At around two years old, young children will start to develop hand-eye coordination so they can confidently reach for something on the floor and grasp it. This enables children to build towers with even small bricks, feed themselves using a spoon and hold a pencil reliably. At the same time, foot-eye coordination will also be developing, which means that children can kick a football without standing on it, climb without having to look down and manoeuvre around objects even when running.

The senses

Binocular vision (using both eyes) is developed, giving stereopsis vision, where the image from each eye is combined in the brain to produce depth perception or a 3D image. Tastes will start to develop and children will express a preference for the type of foods that they like and don't like. Sense of touch will take over from mouthing and your toddler will investigate new objects by feeling, looking and smelling.

Two to three years old

By the age of three, although there is still physical growth, many of the basic skills are now in place and children move into the physical development phase.

For example, although children have developed many of their fine and gross motor skills, co-ordination may still be a challenge, using scissors will still need practice and combined skills such as catching a ball will still be variable.

Coordination of the body is developing rapidly, so more complex activities such as riding a tricycle or bike are now possible. Fingers can be controlled much better, a tripod grip may be more frequent and a knife and fork may be used. At around two years of age, a key milestone is the two-foot jump from the ground (Evangelou *et al.*, 2009).

Children develop, master and refine their skills through a range of play activities, for example:

- locomotor skills (such as throwing, climbing, kicking, striking, sliding)
- manipulative skills (such as throwing, catching, kicking, bouncing)
- stability skills (such as banding, stretching, swinging).

Evangelou *et al.*, 2009: 71

The senses

The senses will continue to develop, with the sense of smell continuing to develop up to eight years old. There is a tendency to prefer sweet and fatty foods (reminiscent of breast milk) into puberty (Fleming, 2013).

The other two senses

In addition to the five senses already discussed (touch, smell, taste, sound and vision) there are two other senses, both of which are vital for good physical development: proprioception and vestibular.

Proprioception

Proprioception is defined as the perception of stimuli relating to position, posture, equilibrium or internal condition. This means knowing where your body is in relation to the external environment. For example, in gross motor skills this means being able to sit in a chair without turning round to look, or walking up stairs without having to look where to put your feet. For fine motor skills you use proprioception when picking up a cup, both to reach out for it but also to hold it with enough strength that it doesn't slip through your fingers or get crushed in your grip.

Vestibular

The vestibular sense is the sense of balance and spatial orientation, named because it is sensed in the 'vestibulum' system in the inner ear. This sense helps us to walk on moving surfaces, such as on a boat, as well as navigate movement such as escalators or balance on top of a log.

Proprioception and vestibular senses underpin all other physical movement development. Imagine trying to walk without knowing where your feet are in relation to the rest of your body, or being able to balance vertically.

 Reflective Questions

Proprioception and vestibular movement

What plans do you make for children's full body, vestibular and proprioception movement?

How could you improve this for children who are just walking?

Chief Medical Officer's guidelines to physical activities for babies

Physical activity is essential from birth, and the time spent in 'containers' such as car seats or prams should be minimised, so babies have free movement to use their whole bodies. Water-based activities are also good for whole body movement. For non-mobile babies, suggested activities include:

- 'Tummy time' – this includes any time spent on the stomach including rolling and playing on the floor
- Reaching for and grasping objects, pulling, pushing and playing with other people

- 'Parent and baby' swim sessions
- Children to sit on your knee with their heads supported by you.

Floor- and water-based play encourages infants to use their muscles and develop motor skills. It also provides valuable opportunities to build social and emotional bonds.

Chief Medical Officer's guidelines to physical activities for toddlers

It is suggested that these activities should occur through 'unstructured activities', i.e. free play, but they could also be incorporated into a physical development programme. The recommended amount of time that toddlers should be active is 180 minutes (three hours) – this improves the physical health of children, such as cardiovascular health and bone health. In addition, their coordination (hand-eye, foot-eye, whole body) will improve and provides opportunity for social interactions.

- Activities that involve movements of all the major muscle groups, i.e. the legs, buttocks, shoulders and arms, and movement of the trunk from one place to another
- Energetic play, e.g. climbing frame or riding a bike
- More energetic bouts of activity, e.g. running and chasing games
- Walking/skipping to shops, a friend's home, a park or to and from a school
- Minimising sedentary behaviour may include:
  - Reducing time spent watching TV, using the computer or playing video games
  - Reducing time spent in a pushchair or car seat – this can also help to break up long periods of sedentary behaviour.

> adapted from the Chief Medical Officers guidelines to physical activities
> (Chief Medical Officer, 2011)

Healthy eating, nutrition, food and eating habits

Dr Patricia Mucavele (2016) advises that the early years affect children's eating habits throughout life and that the Early Years setting is a vital route to encouraging healthy eating. Her recommendations to ensure that Early Years settings are providing the best possible eating habits are:

1 Guidance: encourage childcare providers to use evidence-based, age-appropriate nutrition guidance
2 Training: encourage LAs to increase access to accredited training
3 Funding: ensure nurseries, pre-schools, children's centres and childminders delivering free childcare schemes have the resources they need to provide good food.

The national guidance would include:

- Voluntary food and drink guidelines for Early Years settings in England
- Accredited training to help childcare providers use the guidelines
- Evaluation tools to monitor the outcome and impact of training

• Practitioner's knowledge and confidence
• Approach to and provision of food
• Family eating habits.

adapted from Mucavele, 2016

There is an Early Years code of practice for food and drink available from the Children's Food Trust (2016) that has seven principles for good practice:

1   Having a food policy
2   Communicating with families about their child's diet
3   Planning varied menus for snacks and meals in advance
4   Planning meals and snacks to meet the new national food and drink guidelines
5   Catering for the dietary requirements of all children
6   Having a positive and welcoming eating environment to encourage children to eat well
7   Ensuring staff are appropriately trained.

Even as older babies, children should be involved with their food preparation and knowing about where foods are grown or come from. As children get older, it is very beneficial for them to both get used to helping to prepare some foods as well as eating healthy foods. Even before the age of three, this can be coupled with understanding how this affects the body, building healthy bones and muscles, giving energy and so on.

Environments for healthy living

'Every child has the right to grow up in a healthy environment – to live, learn and play in healthy places' (World Health Organization, 2003: 1). Although this quote is applied globally, i.e. it is referring to contaminated drinking water, severe air pollution and environmentally related diseases, this also holds true for anywhere that children are growing up. In a UK home, for example, this could be in relation to having a smoke-free environment wherever there are children (DfH, 2009). This should start at the antenatal stage with good care of mothers, such as weight management, smoking cessation and preparation for parenthood (Burton, 2015: 18).

For practitioners in a setting, this will include supporting parents with information about healthy environments and healthy habits. Some settings share their food menus, which have been nutritionally balanced for babies and young children with parents, for example.

Oral and dental health

Looking after babies' teeth is incredibly important for a number of reasons, even though the 'baby' teeth will naturally drop out. If the baby teeth are not looked after, decay can affect the growing adult teeth underneath. If teeth have to be removed because they are decayed and/or are painful, the ability to make speech sounds is impaired. If this is at the young age when speech and vocabulary is being developed, it makes speech development much more difficult. Children may become aware of looking and sounding different, which could affect their self-esteem and self-confidence, both in speech and other areas. Loss of teeth can affect healthy eating and further physical growth.

For detailed advice about babies and young children's dental health and care, including tooth-brushing, amount and type of toothpaste and healthy eating advice, see the Public Health Document *Delivering Better Oral Health: An Evidence-based Toolkit for Prevention*, which can be found at: www.gov.uk/government/uploads/system/uploads/attachment_data/file/605266/Delivering_better_oral_health.pdf.

For information about the Smiles4Children project (2016) run by 4Children, go to: www.foundationyears.org.uk/files/2016/12/Toothbrushing-Report.pdf

For further information from Public Health England on targeted toothbrushing and more, go to: www.gov.uk/government/uploads/system/uploads/attachment_data/file/605266/Delivering_better_oral_health.pdf.

Reflective Questions

Oral and dental health

Do you ask parents about their baby or young child's dentist on registering?

How could you introduce children's toothbrushing into your setting?

If you already have a toothbrushing routine, how could you liaise with parents to ensure this is carried on at home as well?

Being outdoors

Playing outdoors has many benefits, from using large spaces in which to run and manoeuvre, to small hidey-holes; from branches to swing from and hills to roll down. It provides the 'ideal context to encourage children to explore, experiment, move and be active' (Evangelou *et al.*, 2009: 72). However, there are risks and hazards associated with some activities. A hazard is something that has the potential to cause harm or danger. For example, having a muddy puddle outside is a hazard, because children might slip in it. The risk is defined as how likely this is going to cause harm. In this example, if all the children are competent and confident walkers, dressed with boots, it is a low risk that there will be harm. If the children are only just learning to walk and have unsuitable footwear, then this becomes a much larger risk of harm. Therefore, doing a risk assessment is a judgement on how likely the harm is going to happen and whether this is unacceptably high, either reducing the risk or removing the hazard. In this example, it could be that the more confident walkers are allowed in the puddle, but the less confident children are steered away from it. If this is still too big a risk, the puddle could be swept away altogether. For an Early Years setting, this has to be weighed against the benefits for the children splashing through a puddle.

Quick Summary

Is the environment suitable?

There are a number of assessment tools available to help to determine the suitability of the environment. For the physical environment there is the US-based ITERS – Infant/Toddler Environment Rating Scale (ITERS-3) (Harms *et al.*, 2017) and the Early Years Quality Improvement Support Programme (EYQISP) (National Strategies, 2008). In addition there are the Leuven scales (Laevers, 1994) and the Sustained Shared Thinking and Emotional Well-being scales (SSTEW) (Siraj *et al.*, 2015) for the emotional environment.

How do you know whether the environment is suitable for babies, toddlers and young children for this area of learning and development?

Is it an enabling, a creative and a learning environment?

Think about how this group of babies or children may have grown and developed since the environment was last reviewed.

On any risk assessment or analysis, it is good practice to start with the benefits of the play area or equipment first. This helps to focus on the positive and reduces the temptation to make the area so 'safe' that there are no challenges or opportunities left. It is entirely possible that in an outdoor area with few challenges that the children simply create their own challenges – for example, dragging all the giant outdoor wooden blocks over to the fence and piling them up to make a staircase over into the field next door. Knight (2009: 35) says that 'I believe that we are taking away from children the right to learn about dangers. We need to take risks to discover the consequences'.

There are a number of commercially available risk assessment sheets, but there is a comprehensive one, with good explanations in Sara Knight's *Forest Schools and Outdoor Learning in the Early Years* (2009), which has photo-copiable sheets to use as well.

A robust risk management system helps to ensure the benefits and risks are correctly balanced. White (2008: 82) recommends:

- Checking the outdoor area regularly for repairs, e.g. broken fences
- Knowing your children's capabilities so you are enabling play rather than limiting opportunities
- Teaching children from the very beginning how to keep themselves safe; to use swings, slides and other equipment safely
- Helping children become aware of the impact of their play on other children in the area.

Any risk management system will only be as good as the practitioners using it and completing the analysis form. Practitioners need to be aware of their own perspectives and bias that may sway their pedagogy – for example, if a practitioner is used to being with very able pre-schoolers but then moves to working with toddlers, he or she will need to review their own practices and pedagogy to ensure these are developmentally suitable.

Quick Summary

Pedagogy

Pedagogy is the combination of the methods of teaching, the ethos, the interactions between baby or child and practitioner, the learning environment and the curriculum. It is the *way* teaching is conducted, considered as a whole with the content. It could be considered to be the holistic methods by which teaching and learning occur.

Research is also beginning to show that there may be additional benefits of being outdoors for children who have a special educational need (SEN), in particular children on the autistic spectrum:

1   There is strong evidence that outdoor activities can benefit children in general.
2   There is considerable evidence that outdoor learning is particularly helpful for children with SEN, who often face more difficulties with classroom learning and greater barriers to accessing the outdoors.
3   There is some evidence showing autistic children benefit from initiatives such as gardening projects, summer camps, field visits and animal therapy.

Natural England, 2013: 5

The outdoors prepares children for learning, prompting curiosity and discovery, for example. The environment is naturally suitable to build proprioception and vestibular abilities, from balancing on uneven surfaces to climbing trees and using stepping-stones. There are also natural hiding corners and places to go for quiet reflection or to watch the clouds go by.

Reflective Questions

Time outdoors

Reflect on your own views about risk and benefits of outdoor play. How has this been affected by your own experiences?

Share your thoughts with a colleague. How are your views similar or different?

Consider how your own perspectives affect the way that you encourage children to play outdoors. (Think about whether you are more or less cautious than other practitioners.)

Holistic links in this chapter

- *Physical development and its effect on social development*
- *Effects of sensory (physical) development on cognitive development*
- *Physical development and its effects on communication*
- *Effects of physical development on literacy development*
- *Effects of physical development on emotions and attention.*

Physical development and its effect on social development

Even before being mobile, babies' purposeful movements can be social. Being able to take a toy or pass a toy to their key person; dropping a spoon from the high chair and having a practitioner pass it back; grasping the maracas and waving them; watching the childminder's smile of joy in return. These small social interactions are building up the social world of the baby, but are equally dependent on being able to control their grasp and movements, as well as to act with purpose.

Once babies start to crawl, shuffle or cruise around the furniture, they are deemed to be 'mobile'. A mobile baby has more independence, which means that he or she can now choose who to interact with socially – whether that is other adults, children or the pet dog. It will become more obvious what their favourite social interaction is, and with whom, as children begin to self-choose.

As older children, their social interactions may be determined by their physical ability. For example, being able to pick up the large blocks or being able to put together the train tracks are skills that friends will appreciate and will make them 'socially valued' (White, 2008: 70)

 Quick Summary

Key person

A key person in a setting is a named person who has special responsibility for their key children, their family and any other agencies involved with the family. This good practice is the practical application of Attachment Theory, which says that a baby's emotional well-being is greatly improved if he or she has at least one adult to whom they can 'attach' or bond with.

The key person role includes emotional support, keeping the child in mind, observing (and acting on, where necessary) any changes in mood, health or behaviour, liaising with parents and being a special person for their children.

This includes all areas of development, and often the key person is the first to notice progress or problems with their key children, in all areas of learning and development.

Social activities

Babies

Tummy time can be social time, especially if you have a few babies of similar age together in the setting, or if you are a childminder and you have some older children who would like to join in.

Toddlers and older children

Activities outdoors often forge social connections as there is usually more freedom to move from group to group and it is generally less structured, so friends can make up games together.

Games such as Ring-a-ring-a-roses and Farmer's in the den, where there is cooperation needed, help to embed social norms.

 Review Your Practice

Are the babies allowed to play together on the floor, for example during tummy time?

How often are siblings allowed to play together?

How often do you reflect on the social groupings outdoors? Are they different to the ones inside?

 Case Study

Batman and Robin

While working in a children's centre with young children who had communication difficulties, I came across a boy called Michael (aged almost three years old) who had little confidence with his speech and consequently spent a lot of his time out in the garden, running around the climbing frame.

Soon after a new boy, Frederic, joined the centre; he was aged two years and eight months, and had English as an additional language. He was shy and looked a little overwhelmed by the size of the centre – all the noise and movement and the general novelty of being there.

Frederic wandered around all morning and didn't engage with any other children or any activities. He was just working out his surroundings and the routines.

After a few days of still not engaging meaningfully, Frederic braved going outside, where he encountered Michael, who was busily climbing up a small incline, leaping off and running round to do it again. Frederic watched for several minutes, then simply said 'Batman', to which Michael replied 'Yeah! Batman! C'mon'.

Frederic followed him round and leapt off, arms outstretched and imitating Michael. They spent most of the morning doing this, with very few words exchanged, simply shrieks and squeals as they got more adventurous and the leaps got higher and higher.

At the beginning of the following session, Frederic went and found Michael outside immediately and their game resumed. It was the beginning of a lasting friendship, and although much of their talk was about Batman, goodies, baddies and various characters, they did converse occasionally. However, they mainly communicated through shared physical activities.

How could you support this flourishing friendship?

How does this fit with your policies on superhero play?

Effects of sensory (physical) development on cognitive development

Sensory integration is when all of the senses (including vestibular and proprioception) work together to interpret the external world so you can take appropriate action. For example, catching a ball means seeing it, knowing where to put your hands and how hard to grasp when you catch it. This typically happens without you having to consciously think about it, but is as a result of previous experience and practice, sometimes called muscle memory.

White (2008: 69) states that 'movement activates the brain to make it ready for new information and learning' and emphasises that the development of the brain and body is 'completely intertwined'. Greenland (2013: 180) extends this, asserting that there is 'considerable evidence' to suggest that the way that a unique child's movement pattern develops influences their capacity to learn and their life chances.

Experiencing different physical weight, capacity, height, etc. lays the basis of mathematical development. So-called 'concrete' experiences make connections that can then help to clarify ideas in maths. When children are involved with schematic play, they are using their whole bodies to learn these concepts. Schematic play is deep-level learning, so children are more likely to remember and build on these experiences than simply being told 'this is heavy and this is light'. A child investigating transporting (carrying or things being carried) will need to be physically strong enough to pick up a bag. These types of feedback loop are evident for all of the senses – for example, Sacrey *et al.* (2012) explain how visual attention and movement are closely linked.

Activities for the senses

A word of warning before you embark on these activities – do be aware that baby's senses may be hypersensitive and they will experience things differently to adults. It may be a beautiful lavender smell in the water tray for you, but it may be an overpowering stench for baby!

Five senses

For sense of smell, add food essences (lemon, chocolate) to play dough, or add drops of oils onto a piece of cotton wool and seal in small plastic jars with pierced lids, so the babies and young children can smell them but not come into contact with them. Use small, sealed mesh bags with dried or fresh herbs and spices or strong-smelling items such as fresh cut grass or flower heads.

For visual perception, have shape sorters of all types and sizes, and use them - lots! They make 2D shapes out of 3D.

For spatial awareness, copy the shape or outline of a Lego construction; try obstacle courses; or spot the differences between similar objects. Visual figure ground or being able to isolate a shape or object from a group or busy background can be aided by pictures such as 'Where's Wally'.

A sense of touch can be fostered through using materials dry and wet - for example, dry sand, damp sand and wet sand *or* uncooked rice, dry pasta, dry porridge followed by cooked rice, pasta, damp porridge. Sticky stuff can be particularly useful for developing finger control, as children have to judge how hard to squeeze, push and pull to manipulate the material.

Activities for proprioception and vestibular development

Any activity that gives the feeling of weightlessness is good for developing the vestibular system, such as being on a swing or being raised into the air. Note that when helping children to balance, hold onto the back of the coat or jumper, not hand or arm because this pulls the child off balance.

Babies

* Gentle swinging or rocking in a practitioner's arms
* Dancing to different types and beats of music with baby in your arms.

Toddlers

* Using swings and slides to get the feeling of movement
* If the children are comfortable with this, try merry-go-rounds or spinning on the spot (you will usually see when children are ready for this, as they will spin on the spot by themselves, experiencing the sensation).

Three-year-olds

* Musical statues, musical bumps, those games where children have to stop on demand and control their movements (both proprioception and vestibular)
* Any weight-bearing activities, such as pushing, pulling and lifting are good for proprioception. For example:
  - Carrying bags with toys in them
  - Lifting large wooden blocks
  - Pushing weighted walkers (such as a block carrier)
  - Pushing boxes or baskets with toys in them
  - Pushing a wheelbarrow.

Crawling through tunnels, squeezing into dens and small spaces and moving around obstacles gives sensory feedback on where the body is. Similarly, negotiating irregular surfaces, such as slopes, dips and muddy patches helps both proprioception and the vestibular system.

For proprioception, children also need to know where their feet are, so activities which put weight through their feet, from supporting babies to taking the weight on their feet, right through to children climbing stairs, are good ways of developing how children know where their bodies are in space.

Learning is occurring all the time and certainly not 'only' when sitting at the table. In fact the self-control and concentration needed to sit at a table may be a distraction from the learning, because all of the toddler's efforts are focused on sitting still. To counteract this, rough-and-tumble type play is beneficial for both learning and proprioception/vestibular systems.

 Case Study

Baby Liv rolls over

Watch baby Liv start to find parts of herself and then roll over: www.youtube.com/watch?v= D9Ko7U1pLIg

Compare her first attempts to roll over (tempted by a toy giraffe) to her confidence at the end. Note the look on her face and how much more fluid her movements are.

What parts of her body had she used to roll over?

How has her coordination improved?

What do you think her next movement will be?

What has she learned from this experience? (Think of both physical and self-confidence and learning about own movements.)

Physical development and its effects on communication

Being able to communicate both verbally and non-verbally depends very much on the correct sensory integration and physical development. For example, hearing has to both be accurate and carry a meaning when processed in the brain, so babies will turn towards the sound of their caregiver's voice. When this is integrated effectively, and the physical movement is perfected, babies and young children can then make eye contact and hear the silence for when it is their turn to vocalise. In addition to these obvious physical developments, the vestibular system and vocalisation are linked. An improved vestibular input has reportedly improved speech and language, because the limbic system, responsible for emotional behaviour, depends on 'the vestibular system to help modulate the input from the senses' (O'Connor and Daly, 2016: 114). Interestingly, O'Connor and Daly (2016) go on to say that children have become more sedentary and there is currently an increase in speech and language problems, implying that the two phenomena are linked. A well-developed vestibular system is also necessary in order to have the motor control for speech (O'Connor and Daly, 2016: 115). It should also be remembered that babies and children enjoy movement and moving in different ways – some may enjoy dancing, others swinging and some running. Greenland (2013: 177) suggests that children's movement, even from a very young age, is 'as unique as their fingerprint', so practitioners will need to consider each unique child when planning movement activities.

 Quick Summary

Stages of language development

- Birth to six months: Babies will turn towards sounds, watch faces and start to make a range of noises.
- Six to 12 months: Babies will babble and hold proto-conversations.
- 12 to 18 months: Understand words, simple instructions, gesture and use a few words themselves.
- 18 to 24 months: Children will understand 200 words or more and be using 50 or more words of their own.
- Two to three years: Use around 300 words and create sentences.

Activity ideas for physical communication

Babies and pre-verbal children only have their bodies to communicate with. Practitioners need to respond to babies' physical communication to encourage the two-way flow that will turn into conversation.

If a baby points to an object, name the object, wait for baby to point again and then get the object – 'milk' wait 'milk'.

Review Your Practice

Do you have a quiet time, when babies can just listen to the noises going on around them, in their environment?

To be able to hear individual phonic sounds, there needs to be a 10-decibel difference in background noise compared to speech sounds.

Are unnecessary background noises at a minimum? if you have music playing constantly, babies cannot distinguish clearly between that and your voice.

Case Study

British sign language

I worked with a young child who was profoundly deaf. We used British sign language to communicate as this was being used at home as well. This relies on the person signing to be able to convey emotions facially, so you can't look down at your hands or else you would lose the eye contact and facial expressions.

As an adult, this proved incredibly difficult for me because I wanted to watch that my hands were in the correct positions all the time.

However, this young child picked up the signs very quickly and rarely had to check, because she had physically adapted to this at such a young age.

How else do we physically communicate? (Think of gesture and non-verbal communication.)

Effects of physical development on literacy development

Sharing books in an enjoyable manner from a very early age will foster a love of books for a lifetime. Babies and young children need to experience turning pages of books, stimulation from pictures, sharing with a loving and caring adult while 'snuggling in' (Sharma and Cockerill, 2014: 99), which requires physical closeness from an adult. When children are much older, their core strength, fine motor skills and hand-eye coordination will all support writing. Eye tracking is an essential skill for reading, and this is an even more important skill when considering the looking up and down action required to read from a vertical surface (white board in a classroom, for example) and transferring this onto a horizontal surface (in an exercise book).

Physical activities for literacy

Crawling gives babies both the strength in their arms and upper body and core strength ready for writing. In addition, the tracking motion (looking left to right and back again) of the hands on the floor is the skill that will be required for reading. In addition, it is at exactly the correct focal distance for children.

Fine motor skills, such as peg boards, picking up smaller blocks and small world play are ideal, ready for turning pages and handling books.

Review Your Practice

How often do you allow children who can walk go back to crawling?

Do you encourage time spent on their tummies, such as going through tunnels?

Case Study

Writing recovery

Early in my career I spent time in a Reception class, doing 'writing recovery' with children who were unable to moderate the pressure they were using with their pencils, both pressing too hard and not hard enough. This was usually during their break time, so they could still take part in the main class activities.

I cringe at this now. On reflection I am sure that these children would be much better outdoors, improving their core strength so they could control their trunk, shoulder, arm, elbow and wrist. Their physical development needed taking right back to the Early Years stages to create the right foundation for these later skills.

In addition, the children's body language was actually telling me this as well. They were often the children who chose to put their arm on the table and rest their heads while writing and who tended to fidget if asked to sit for longer periods. So the signs were already there.

How often do we look at the symptoms and not stand back to look at the whole picture?

How are children using their bodies? What does this tell us about their development?

Effects of physical development on emotions and attention

Rocking a baby in a practitioner's arms helps to develop the vestibular system right from the start. The limbic system produces emotionally based behaviour, which 'depends on the vestibular system to help modulate the input from the senses'. Therefore, ensuring a good vestibular system will help to support behaviour as your baby gets older. Interestingly, feeling grounded, termed 'gravitational security', supports emotional good health (O'Connor and Daly, 2016: 114), so babies need both the feeling of movement and that of safe, secure ground.

Conversely, lacking in physical ability and skills, especially as children get older and more aware of the ability of their peers, can impinge on children's self-confidence, self-esteem and social and emotional well-being (Evangelou *et al.*, 2009). In addition, self-confidence, self-regulation and well-being can be fostered when children are outside, playing in the mud or the sand or following their own agenda (Solly, 2015: 26).

Pointing is a physical development, but is also about shared joint attention skill and forms part of the roots of empathy and understanding other people's point of view, a vital skill for personal, social and emotional development.

A retained Moro reflex may impact on emotional development, by affecting emotional regulation and a tendency to sudden outbursts when this is no longer possible. Similarly, inner ear dysfunction, affecting the vestibular system, can impact on the emotional systems (Goddard Blythe *et al.*, 2017). Crawling is incredibly important for coordination of the left and right halves of their bodies, as babies have to move their arms and legs in coordination so they can move forward.

A steady sense of balance is critical for everyday activities. Often we think about physical development as being only movement. Sitting still, standing still and stopping on command are very different and underrated skills. This can be encouraged with a number of traditional games, such as musical statues or musical bumps.

Treasure baskets for babies who are able to sit securely as this promotes the other senses, while also encouraging balance and investigation.

The benefits of baby massage

Baby massage is becoming a regular feature of many parent and baby groups and is offered in many children's centres. The value of baby massage has been recognised for some time – for example: 'A ten-minute massage, two or three times a week helps create a more confident mother-infant relationship, babies love it and it can help alleviate baby ailments too' (Literacy Trust, 2005). Other benefits include becoming attuned with your baby and bonding, and baby may sleep and settle better as the levels of oxytocin rise in his or her body (NCT, 2017).

Somatics is the study of body experienced from within, the internal physical perception and experience. Greenland (2013: 172) explains how somatics describes the 'movement patterns in the developmental sequence underpin every aspect of our lives, our feelings and our capacity to think about things'. She goes on to explain how an increase in touch stimulation can lead to a greater progress in physical development, such as weight gain, more efficient metabolism and a stronger resistance to disease.

Activities

Part of communication is the non-verbal, physical signals that are conveyed through body language and facial expressions.

Encourage babies and young children to watch for facial clues to language – for example, any listening games, where children have to watch and wait for the 'Go' before acting (letting go of a car, blowing bubbles, pressing a button).

For older children, discuss facial expressions and use a continuum of faces (from very cross to very happy) for them to choose their own feelings.

Encourage expression of feelings through full body movement, such as a 'happy' dance.

Persona dolls and empathy dolls can help embody feelings for young children.

Review Your Practice

Sally Goddard Blythe's book, *Attention, Balance and Coordination: The A.B.C. of Learning Success* (Goddard Blythe *et al.*, 2017) has some fascinating analysis of how physical development affects emotions, including hormones, biochemical changes during pregnancy and the effects of the vestibular system (and how to use it to 'calm' emotions).

How do you use movement to regulate emotions in your setting? (Think of rocking a baby, 'burning off some energy' outdoors.)

What further activities could you include? (Think how the activities affect the body, e.g. balance, movement.)

Challenges to physical development

As we are considering development holistically, we should also consider the challenges to good development holistically. For example, childhood obesity affects gross motor movement, which will delay skills and which could in turn potentially affect self-confidence and social interaction. This is an obvious example, but not all challenges to physical development are that easy to identify.

If physical development is lacking in very young children, you will observe behaviours such as having to look down when walking in a straight line, not crossing the midpoint of the body when writing (occasionally you may see children pass the pencil from hand to hand, rather than write across in front of themselves) and not be able to sit up at a table for longer periods of time.

There is growing evidence that poverty, particularly persistent poverty, affects children in many areas of growth and development. The seminal Field Review (2010) found that poverty in the early years put children at a higher risk even later in life of ill health, unemployment and criminal activity. It also states that by age three the socio-economic gaps are obvious and persistent, as 'later attainment tends to be heavily influenced by early development' (Field Review, 2010: 37).

It could be that the baby's senses are developing in line with typically development norms and that they are experiencing a rich and dazzling array of experiences. However, there may be hidden sensory integration problems that are not yet apparent in such young children. In the Ayres sensory integration (ASI), Ayres (2005) talks of 'hidden sensory challenges', those that cannot be easily seen – for example autism, dyspraxia (now termed developmental coordination disorder or DCD) and therapies that can be used to help children.

If the furniture is too big for the toddlers, there is additional strain put on the knee joints when their legs are left to dangle, rather than being supported by the floor or a footstall. Even on a seat that is the right height, with a foot support, children still need to use their core strength to be able to sit upright and comfortably, which takes concentration and may even distract from the activity on the table.

When children do sit on the floor, encourage them to have their legs stretched out in front of them, possibly supported from behind by a wall. When children sit in a 'W' position, with their legs doubled under and splayed out, they risk damaging their hip alignment.

Opportunities

Consider whether poor physical development needs to go right back, even to tummy time, if they are struggling. A really quick and easy way to assess children is to ask them to do a simple physical activity, such as walking on a line or walking forwards and backwards. By observing different-aged children, and their different stages, you can see how physical development is occurring through the group. You can then start to determine what stage in ability each of the children are at, regardless of their age, and then plan suitable activities.

Practitioners have a good opportunity to help to support parents (where needed) with information on nutrition, exercise and dental issues – for example, toothbrushing in settings is becoming much more common.

Conclusions

It cannot be assumed that physical development will simply occur and needs no further thought – babies will grow into children whatever we do. Although there is some truth in this, we are finding more and more that good physical activity and supported physical development is vital for all other areas of development.

The development of physical skills such as balance (vestibular system) can literally make children 'feel good' as it helps to regulate the body. The embodiment of concepts, such as carrying something heavy gives a feeling of weight, helps children with deep-level learning of these concepts. Babies and young children are constantly moving, because they know that this is the way that they will learn.

Further Reading and Research

Sharma, A and Cockerill, H. (2014) (4th edn) *Mary Sheridan's from Birth to Five Years.* Abingdon: Routledge.

This is a classic text that has been updated to include online links. It is an excellent reference book that takes the reader clearly through each stage of growth and development, including speech and social interactions. It has been used here with a focus on physical growth and development, but it is equally useful for other aspects of children's growth and development.

Anne O'Connor and Anna Daly's book, *Understanding Physical Development in the Early Years*, has an excellent chapter on the role of reflexes, what they are and problems that may occur if they are retained. This includes a very useful section on 'Playful ideas to help inhibit or release primitive reflexes' (p. 90 onwards), which covers the Moro and palmar reflexes, among others.

References

Archer, C. and Siraj, I. (2015) *Movement Play and Benefits.* London: SAGE.

Ayres, J. (2005) *Sensory Integration and the Child.* Los Angeles: Western Psychological Services.

Bruce, T. (2004) *Cultivating Creativity.* Abingdon: Hodder Education.

Burton, A. (2015) *Supporting the Best Start in Life.* PHE.

Chief Medical Officer (2011) *Start Active, Stay Active: A Report on Physical Activity for Health from the Four Home Countries.* London: NHS.

Children's Food Trust (2016) *Early Years Code of Practice for Food and Drink.* Available from: www.childrensfoodtrust.org.uk/childrens-food-trust/early-years/ey-resources/tools/

Evangelou, M., Sylva, K., Kyriacou, M., Wild, M. and Glenny, G. (2009) *Early Years Learning and Development. Literature Review.* Oxford: DCSF.

Field Review (2010) *The Foundation Years: Preventing Poor Children Becoming Poor Adults: The Report of the Independent Review on Poverty and Life Chances.* London: Cabinet Office.

Fleming, A. (2013) *Changing Tastes: Food and Ageing.* Available from: www.theguardian.com/lifeandstyle/wordofmouth/2013/jan/29/changing-tastes-food-and-aging. Accessed 31 August 2016.

Goddard Blythe, S. (2017) Assessing neuromotor readiness for learning. *Early Years Educator* Vol. 18 Iss. 12.

Goddard Blythe, S., Beuret, L., Blythe, P. and Scaramella-Nowinski, V. (2017) (2nd edn) *Attention, Balance and Coordination: The A.B.C. of Learning Success.* Chichester: John Wiley.

Greenland, P. (2013) Physical development, in F. Veale, *Early Years for Levels 4 & 5 and the Foundation Degree.* Abingdon: Hodder Education.

Harms, T., Cryer, D., Clifford, R. and Yazejian, N. (2017) (3rd edn) *Infant/Toddler Environment Rating Scale (ITERS-3).* New York: Teachers' College Press.

Knight, S. (2009) *Forest Schools and Outdoor Learning in the Early Years.* London: SAGE.

Laevers, F. (ed.) (1994) *Well-being and Involvement in Care Settings. A Process-oriented Self-evaluation Instrument.* Leuven: Leuven University.

Literacy Trust (2005) *The Benefits of Baby Massage.* Available from: www.literacytrust.org.uk/talk_to_your_baby/news/2523_the_benefits_of_baby_massage. Accessed 10 June 2017.

Mucavele, P. (2016) *Future Priorities for Children's Nutrition: Presentation for Inside Government.* Available from: www.insidegovernment.co.uk/uploads/2016/03/patriciamucavele.pdf. Accessed 10 June 2017.

National Strategies (2008) *Social and Emotional Aspects of Development (SEAD).* Nottingham: DCSF.

Natural England (2013) Commissioned Report NECR116. Engaging children on the autistic spectrum with the natural environment: Teacher insight study and evidence review.

NCT (2017) *Baby Massage.* Available from: www.nct.org.uk/parenting/baby-massage. Accessed 21 May 2017.

O'Connor, A. and Daly, A. (2016) *Understanding Physical Development in the Early Years: Linking Bodies and Minds.* Abingdon: Routledge.

Public Health England (2017) *Delivering Better Oral Health: An Evidence-based Toolkit for Prevention.* London: PHE. Available from: www.gov.uk/government/uploads/system/uploads/attachment_data/file/605266/Delivering_better_oral_health.pdf. Accessed 10 June 2017.

Royal College of Midwives (2012) *Evidence-based Guidelines for Midwifery-led Care in Labour.* London: The Royal College of Midwives Trust.

Sacrey, L., Karl, J. and Whishaw, I. (2012) Development of visual and somatosensory attention of the reach-to-eat movement in human infants aged 6 to 12 months. *Experimental Brain Research.* Available from: www.ncbi.nlm.nih.gov/pubmed/22948738. Accessed 10 June 2017.

Sharma, A and Cockerill, H. (2014) (4th edn) *Mary Sheridan's from Birth to Five Years.* Abingdon: Routledge.

Siraj, I., Kingston, D. and Melhuish, E. (2015) *Sustained Shared Thinking and Emotional Well-being (SSTEW) Scale for 2-5 Year Olds Provision.* London: IOE.

Solly, K. (2015*) Risk, Challenge and Adventure in the Early Yea*rs. Abingdon: Routledge.

Tassoni, P. and Beith, K. (2000) *Diploma in Childcare and Education.* Portsmouth, NH: Heinnemann.

von Hofsten, O., von Hofsten, C., Sulutvedt, U., Laeng, B., Brennen, T. and Magnussen, S. (2014) Simulating newborn face perception. *Journal of Vision* Vol. 14 Iss. 16.

White, J. (2008) *Playing and Learning Outdoors.* Abingdon: Routledge.

World Health Organization (WHO) (2003) *Healthy Environments for Children.* Available from: www.who.int/features/2003/04/en./ Accessed 10 June 2017.

4 Language development

Those around them need to value, interpret and respond to babies' and young children's early attempts to converse.

David, 2003: 12

Conversation is the place where children develop as talkers - through learning about language, themselves, the world and their place in that world.

Jones, 2016: 30

Introduction

Language development is a complex and complicated process that children appear to do almost effortlessly, given a suitable environment. There is a diverse range of theories of the mechanisms for this development, which are constantly being updated and revised - particularly as neuro-science starts to give new insights into brain development and language development.

This chapter starts with an overview of the major theories about language development in the birth to three age range, followed by the types of typical developments that you would expect to see as children mature. Then the ways in which language development is part of holistic development are explored.

Language development theories

Noam Chomsky (1975) suggested that all children have a built-in 'device' when born, that allows them to pick up language as they grow and mature. He called this the language acquisition device (LAD), implying that language simply comes into being, rather than learned or taught. He goes on to say that the 'rules' of grammar are also already embedded, simply waiting to be used. He called this universal grammar. The corollary of this is that the environment and circumstances in which a baby grows up are largely irrelevant providing they hear some language, so grammatical rules can be honed and language skills practised, and language will develop. There is a logical rationale to this theory. Language is so complex and is used in many different ways by different people that it would seem almost impossible for a baby to make sense of all this input, and then be able to use that themselves, especially in such a seemingly short time period. The idea that language is inborn, or innate, is called the nativist theory.

Although this would seem reasonably logical, there are cases where children have not been exposed to language in the way that most children would be, but have subsequently not gone on to 'acquire' language, as the nativist theory would suggest. One of the best documented of these is the case of Genie, who was raised in California in the late 1950s. Due to her family circumstances she was locked in her room from 20 months old until the age of 13, with little or no exposure to language, when she was discovered. She had a vocabulary of around 15 to 20 words, including the phrases 'stop it' and 'no more'. This was obviously a highly complicated case, including physical abuse, malnourishment and a lack of physical movement among other circumstances, making it difficult to pin lack of language on one cause. However, it would seem to indicate that children do need to hear language, to engage in the social aspects of language development and to have reinforcement and repetition before they can use or understand language.

Conversely, Skinner (1957) had theorised that children learn language through the encouragement and positive reinforcement of people around them, rather than the skill being inborn and simply waiting to be 'activated' through maturation. There are also problems with this theory too. If children only repeat the language that they hear, and have positive reinforcement to help them to develop language correctly, how can they create new words? A typical example of this in English is the verb 'go'. For most past tenses, an -ed is added to the end of the verb – for example, walked, talked, skipped. However, the verb 'go' is irregular and changed to 'went' in the past tense. Yet, a large proportion of children, when learning English, will say 'I go-ed to the park yesterday' rather than the correct version, 'I went to the park yesterday'. Children are very unlikely to have heard adults, or older children, saying this, so will not have had either a role model or positive reinforcement. Somehow, children have worked out independently how to put this verb into the past tense.

Somewhere between these two theories are Bruner's theories of language acquisition support system (LASS) and Vygotsky's theories, both of which suggest that language is part of social development, through interactions. Bruner posited that children learn language from interested and interactive adults, who scaffold good language development. In addition, children have an innate LASS that supports this way of learning. Similarly, Vygotsky proposed that children learn to talk by having language scaffolded for them so they can move through their zone of proximal development (ZPD), i.e. progress from their current level of knowledge to the next level by being helped by others. Therefore children acquire language from more knowledgeable others, whether that is parents, peers or practitioners. David *et al.* (2003: 77) suggest that the foundations for competent use of language are the social relationships that children make, so they can 'share emotions and experiences'.

It has been suggested that if children have not acquired language by the age of 12, that it may be impossible to acquire language at all (Bernicot, 2014). However, neuroscience research is beginning to show that the brain has much more plasticity than has been previously thought, so it may be that supporting language development in the future will be possible, even for older children.

This is a complex but very interesting area of young children's development. See the end of the chapter for further information and reading recommendations.

Typical language development from birth to three

In order to help understand the progress of language development, an overview of the typical types of behaviours from birth to three years old is outlined here. These are the building blocks

for language development. This is very general and children will vary within the suggested age limits.

Birth to six months

- Turn towards a sound when they hear it and be startled by loud noises.
- Watch your face when you talk to them and recognise your voice. You can encourage this by copying the sounds and holding them so they can see your face. You can also keep a running narrative, where you talk about what you are doing while baby listens.
- Smile and laugh when other people smile and laugh.
- Babies will make sounds to themselves, like cooing, gurgling and babbling and will make different noises, like squeals, to get your attention. They are likely to have different cries for being hungry, tired and uncomfortable or having fun.

At around two months old, babies will start the 'serve and return' exchanges, where first the parent or practitioner speaks, then waits. Baby vocalises, but then waits for a response from the adult. Obviously at this stage these will be babbling or noises and the adult's response may simply mirror those noises, but the importance is that is a shared understanding of the 'serve and return' rules.

Six to 12 months

- Babies will start to listen, turning towards speech sounds and will pay attention when they hear their own name.
- Babble will increase to strings of sounds, like 'no-no' and 'go-go'.
- Getting and holding another person's attention is important, so babies will make noises, point and look at you, smile at people who are smiling at them. Pointing out the source of noises, whether that is a person, an airplane or the doorbell will help babies to cue into environmental sounds and make them more aware of their environment.

- At this age, babies will start taking turns in proto-conversations, babbling back and forth to an adult. It is helpful to encourage babies to watch you and look at your face, so they can see lip formations and facial expressions.
- Start to understand words like 'bye-bye' and 'up', especially when a gesture is used at the same time.
- Recognise the names of familiar objects, things like 'car' and 'daddy'.
- Action songs and rhymes can link words, actions and meanings, especially if props are used too. Singing songs together helps with concentration.

12 to 18 months

At this stage, children will start to use language in a more recognisable way and those in the immediate family may begin to understand some of their utterances. Children will also become more sociable. Although children develop skills at different rates, by 18 months usually children will:

- Enjoy games like peek-a-boo and pat-a-cake as well as action songs and toys that make a noise.
- Start to understand a few simple words, like 'drink', 'shoe' and 'car'. Also simple instructions like 'kiss mummy', 'kick ball' and 'give me'. You can help this by talking about what you are doing all the time and naming objects, such as toys, clothes, parts of their body or animals.
- Point to things when asked, like familiar people and objects such as 'book' and 'car'.
- Gesture or point, often with words or sounds to show what they want.
- Copy lots of things that adults say and gestures that they make.
- Start to enjoy simple pretend play, for example pretending to talk on the phone.

At this age, babies will use up to 20 simple words, such as 'cup', 'daddy' and 'dog'.

18 to 24 months

At this stage, children try out new things and explore the world around them more actively. They will often choose their own activities and will become more independent in their choices. Children develop skills at different rates, but by two years, usually children will:

- Concentrate on activities for longer, like playing with a particular toy, sitting and listening to simple stories with pictures.
- Understand more simple questions and instructions – for example, 'where is your shoe?' and 'show me your nose'.
- Copy sounds and words a lot, so it is important to keep talking to children.
- Use a limited number of sounds in their words – often these are p, b, t, d, m and w. Children will also often miss the ends off words at this stage. They can usually be understood about half of the time.
- Giving options helps children have a sense of independence and also increases their vocabulary, especially if you have the objects as well – for example, 'red jumper or blue shirt?'

- Read books together, looking at the pictures and describing them. 'Lift-the-flap' books also help concentration.
- Repeat and expand on what a child says. If a child says 'juice' you can say 'more juice', 'juice please' or 'juice gone'. This shows your child how words can be put together to make short sentences.
- Children learn speech sounds gradually. It is better to say the whole word back to a child rather than correcting them. It also helps them if they can see your face when you are talking to them. This helps them to watch and copy the movements of your lips.
- Encouraging a child to use gestures or actions for objects can help reduce their frustrations.

Children will understand between 200 and 500 words and use 50 or more single words. These will also become more recognisable to people not in the immediate family. They will also start to put together short 'sentences' with 2-3 words, such as 'more juice' or 'bye nanny'.

Two to three years

Children develop skills at different rates, but by three years most children will usually:

- Listen to and remember simple stories with pictures, understand longer instructions, such as 'make teddy jump' or 'where's mummy's coat?'; and understand simple 'who', 'what' and 'where' questions.
- Start to ask lots of questions. They will want to find out the name of things and learn new words, including action words as well as nouns, such as 'run' and 'fall'.
- Start to use simple plurals by adding 's' – for example, 'shoes' or 'cars'.
- Use a wider range of speech sounds; however, many children will shorten longer words, such as saying 'nana' instead of 'banana'. They may also have difficulty where lots of sounds happen together in a word, e.g. they may say 'pider' instead of 'spider'.
- Often have problems saying more difficult sounds like sh, ch, th and r. However, people that know them can mostly understand them.
- By adding words to children's sentences, we can show them how words fit together. For example, if a child says 'dolly hair' you can say 'brush dolly's hair'.
- Often children enjoy helping. Sharing daily jobs gives a chance to talk about objects and actions.
- Use puppets, props and pictures to help children listen to stories. Repetition helps children to understand and remember words.
- Give children the correct example for sounds and words. This helps if they are having problems saying a certain word or sound. If you correct them or make them say it again, you can make them feel anxious. Simply repeat what they have said using the right words and sounds.

Children are likely to use up to 300 words and be able to put four or five words together to make short sentences, such as 'want more juice' or 'he took my ball'.

adapted from www.talkingpoint.org.uk

Quick Summary

Stages of language development

- Birth to six months: Babies will turn towards sounds, watch faces and start to make a range of noises.
- Six to 12 months: Babies will babble and hold proto-conversations.
- 12 to 18 months: Children will understand words, simple instructions, gesture and use a few words themselves.
- 18 to 24 months: Children will understand 200 words or more and be using 50 or more words of their own.
- Two to three years: Children will use around 300 words and create sentences.

There will be many individual differences in the rate and the way babies' and young children's language develops – for example, some children may not attempt new words until they feel very confident, but other children may be willing to try out new words the first time they hear them. These differences should be noted through sensitive observations and used to support the unique child.

The development of language and a two-way conversation starts from birth, with the inter-actions between baby and adult. Initially these are short periods of baby gazing, with vocalisations following. For effective two-way conversation, there have to be the backwards and forwards exchanges, where one waits for the other, until the 'conversation' is finished.

This is called the 'dance of reciprocity' and is characterised by the following stages:

- Initiation
- Orientation
- State of attention
- Acceleration
- Peak of excitement
- Deceleration
- Withdrawal or turning away.

Hassett, 2016

To be a successful encounter, both the baby and the adult need to be active in the process, so they are both affected and able to affect the other. When even very young babies are ignored or if the adult's attention is distracted, then the baby can get upset and distraught. These social proto-conversations (Trevarthen and Delafield-Butt, 2016) or interactions with babies are essential building blocks in developing successful conversations later on in life.

Reasons for learning language

The theories about the reasons for children learning a language are closely linked with their holistic development. Halliday (1975), for example, suggests that language and speech is a set of social functions. He identifies some of these functions as:

- Group interactions. This type of language both defines and consolidates the group
- A method for accomplishing a need or a want
- A way of expressing an imaginative or pretend world
- Heuristic or enquiring, exploring and discovering, such as 'I wonder why . . .'
- Representational, so a message needs to be conveyed
- Regulatory. This is language that directs or controls behaviour, for example
- Language that represents how children's personality is developing.

Many of these underpin children's personal, social and emotional development as they begin to use language to define themselves, control and participate in social situations and explore their environment.

From birth, the adult's role in a baby's life is a critical part of the holistic development of children's language. For example, Infant Direct Speech (IDS) is the way that parents and carers talk differently to children, often in a higher register, exaggerated tone of voice and with made-up words (this can be referred to as 'motherese' or 'parentese'). When infants start to use their first words, this moves towards a more recognisable conversation, called Child Directed Speech (CDS), which is simpler in vocabulary, length and syntax (Jones, 2016). It is important to engage in both IDS and CDS, as these are the interactions that form 'a positive emotional bond' (Jones, 2016: 26) that is vital for children to enjoy communicating, interacting and talking with others.

Nursery rhymes and singing

Singing or saying nursery rhymes (such as Twinkle, twinkle little star; Baa, baa black sheep; Incy wincy spider) with babies from an early age enables them to hear 'specifically pitch interval, meter, phrase length, contour, and harmony, also contribute substantially to the development of language' (Gonzalez, 2016: 1).

They are short enough to remember and usually predictable with repetition, so children feel confident joining in. For older children, when they begin to understand the words and their meaning, nursery rhymes can build children's imagination, storytelling skills (follows a narrative of beginning, middle, end), vocabulary and word awareness. An additional benefit is that singing nursery rhymes together creates 'a dynamic learning environment through which learners can enthusiastically benefit from peer interaction in chorus' (Pourkalhor and Tavakoli, 2017), often with actions that support their physical development as well.

Nursery rhymes and singing can support many other areas in a subtle and unobtrusive way, such as:

- Mathematics with number songs (1, 2, 3, 4, 5, once I caught a fish alive; Five little ducks went swimming)

- Physical, gross motor skills (3 little monkeys jumping on the bed) and physical, fine motor skills (Twinkle, twinkle – including using alternate hands to 'twinkle', Incy wincy spider actions)
- Social as they are shared at circle time and in small groups.

By three years of age, children are likely to have a favourite nursery rhyme, which can be shared and recited with new friends or in new social situations as a common experience. There are some recommendations for further reading about singing and movement at the end of this chapter.

Challenges with language development

The children's communication charity, iCan, subdivides the learning of children's language into four distinct areas: listening and attention; understanding; speech sounds and talk; and social skills (iCan, 2017). This gives an indication of the many different facets of language development and how the communication chain works. This is a way of describing the way that speech is understood and processed in the brain, and is called a chain because it is only as strong as the weakest link. The three main areas of the communication chain are receptive language, expressive language and speech.

Receptive language is being able to understand the language that is being spoken to children. Challenges in this part of the chain may include hearing problems (including distinguishing speech over a noisy background), interpreting body language, short-term memory problems and understanding both the words and their combined meaning (for example, 'Shall we tidy up?' - is this sentence a question? Or is it an instruction?). This equates to listening and attention, and understanding in the iCan model.

Expressive language is the language children use and includes choosing a suitable response and then finding the words to formulate the response. If adults have problems with this, we sometimes say it is 'on the tip of your tongue', but adults have a number of strategies learned over time to retrieve words, such as rhyming words, similar words or linked words. Children do not have these strategies yet, and some may simply not have the words available - for example, some may not yet have the vocabulary or children with English as an additional language (EAL). As children become more fluent and socially aware, there is also the social context of which words to select before talking. This is part of the understanding and speech sounds and talk in the iCan model, as well as the social skills.

Finally, speech is attempted once the speech muscles have been coordinated. Children may be able to say an individual word, but once it gets into a sentence there may be stammering or dysfluency. This is the main area of speech sounds and talk difficulties.

There can be disconnects in any part of the communication chain, resulting in problems with language development. The initial assessment has to identify where the problem lies, whether that is from not being able to hear language to being able to understand, to vocabularise or being able to physically express an answer.

It is important to note that during routine activities are among the ideal times to talk to babies and young children. However, research has shown (Goouch and Powell, 2013: 6) that sometimes these routines were accompanied by talk that is 'more instructional and less affectionate than the talk that occurred in observed playful (non-routine) interactions'. This is possibly because the opportunities to use these times have not been explained to practitioners or well role modelled in the past.

There are some recommended sources of further information about speech and language at the end of this chapter.

Holistic links in this chapter

- *Communication, attachment and building first relationships*
- *Language and social interactions*
- *Language and personal/emotional development*
- *Physical development and language*
- *Cognitive development and language development*
- *Language, problem solving and understanding about the world*

- *Language, dialect and cultural identity*
- *Language laying the foundations for future literacy.*

Communication, attachment and building first relationships

Babies communicate with their parents and others before recognisable spoken language is established. Sensitive, responsive adults use babies' cries, coos and gurgles and indicators of communication, whether that is to meet a physical need (such as being fed or changed) or to gain attention to start a conversation. These first noises, sounds, babbles and attempts at language cement the relationships between adult and baby, helping to build lasting bonds and attachment for the future. Secure attachment and a positive response between baby and another adult (most often a parent) will encourage more attempts at communication, so building the foundations for a good relationship. Babies very quickly start to distinguish between different types of language, possibly by rhythm (Ramus, 2002), and by 12 months old infants know that specifically speech sounds convey meaning from one person to another, as distinguished from not non-speech sounds, e.g. coughing (Vouloumanos and Waxman, 2014).

Quick Summary

Secure attachment

Secure attachment is typical for the majority of children and is described as emotionally healthy. It is characterised by a child who is in distress after a brief separation, but can be comforted and settled by the caregiver reasonably quickly.
  Page, Clare and Nutbrown (2013: 36) theorise that:

1 High-quality caregiver relationships are central to emotional development and learning in infants and toddlers.
2 Relationships take time to develop, so the key person must be given that time and opportunity to become attached to their key baby or key toddler.

Activities

The distance that very young babies can see is approximately arm's length, so any activities should be within that space. All these activities encourage babies to look at the adult's face, notice facial expressions and take turns. Do be mindful of baby's enjoyment and continue at their pace, following their lead in games.

Pulling tongues

Make faces at baby, like pulling tongues and over-exaggerated facial expressions.

Peek-a-boo

Hide behind a cloth or blanket and then pull it away so baby can see your face. As babies become more confident with this game, you can also say 'boo.

Say my name

Use baby's name while chatting to them, at the beginning of sentences to gain their attention and during play.

Naming body parts

Naming objects and actions is good practice in general, and naming body parts is a good way to build both vocabulary and baby's awareness of their own body being different to yours. For example, counting and naming toes as you put on socks, talking about head, ears and nose as you put on their tee-shirt, and naming left and right legs as you pull on their tights.

Finger and body activity games

Finger games, where you use fingers to illustrate a rhyme, such as Incy-Wincy Spider, are good for language building, body awareness and building turn taking. Similarly, games such as Wind the Bobbin Up or The Wheels on the Bus Go Round are good for awareness, language and following visual cues.

Reflective Questions

Language and first relationships

The foundations for bonding, which is the two-way emotional attachment between baby and adult, are partly built on the same requirements as those for early language development, which are responsive, sensitive, quality interactions.

What would be the defining factors of a 'quality' interaction for a young baby?

What would this look like in practice?

Language and social interactions

The relationship between language and social development tends to be mutually beneficial. It is suggested that social relationships, such as forming friendships and sharing experiences, lay the foundations for competent language use (David *et al.*, 2003). Correspondingly, those children who are able to express themselves confidently and clearly are more likely to form new friendships, be invited into play and interact with adults. However, it should be remembered that it takes self-confidence to risk speaking to others, to be understood and to make your intentions clear. Most adults who have learned a new language in a class will recognise the feeling of anxiety as they try out the sentences 'for real' with a native speaker of that language. Thus it is essential to be patient with children and allow them to take the risk when they feel ready to do so, and bear in mind that talking to a close family member is much less risky than talking to an unfamiliar adult, such as a practitioner from another room.

In addition there is now more neuroscientific evidence that mastery of language is achieved within a social context and that this may be why children with autism have both social and language challenges (Kuhl, 2011). It is theorised that the quality of the mother-child interaction is an influence on both the time at which children start to speak and also the development of their phonological system (Elsabbagh *et al.*, 2013). However, it is also important that children watch and experience other social interactions. This becomes vitally important if there are challenges present during the child's formative time for early language. The types of challenges could include post-natal depression, domestic violence, trauma, parenting style, cultural considerations and ill health.

 Quick Summary

Why incorporate 'neuroscience' into Early Years practice?

Neuroscientists affirm that 'billions of synaptic connections are made within the first five years of life' (Conkbayir, 2017: 22) and that practitioners are part of this process, through planning environments, developmentally appropriate activities and sensory experiences.

The process of incorporating neuroscience into Early Years settings with practitioners may have challenges (including a proliferation of 'neuromyths'), but is worthwhile because it vindicates good practice based on science (causation not correlation) and adds another layer of knowledge to understanding about how young children think, learn and develop.

Activities to support these skills

Babies

Even if babies are not even babbling yet, hold them so they can see your face clearly (be aware of not having bright light behind your head) and start a 'conversation' by talking or just babbling. Wait for a response and repeat.

Play games where babies have to stop and watch your face before their turn. For example, have some bubbles and say 'Ready, steady . . . (pause) go'. Increase the length of the pause so babies have to look at you and are aware of the turn-taking element.

Toddlers and older children

Model good conversations, where adults clearly take turns and listen to one another. Play lots of turn-taking games, such as board games, and listening games.

Reflective Questions

Social interactions and language

There are some instructional YouTube clips and videos where the adult is initially interacting with his or her baby. When instructed, the adult stops responding and turns away. You will see the baby get very agitated, quite quickly.

What are the implications of this for a baby whose parent doesn't interact? For example, if it is a chaotic household or there is post-natal depression? (Think about how you would feel if you got no reaction from someone – would you 'give up'?)

Watch Dr Edward Tronick's 'Still Face Experiment' videos on adults not responding to babies. How does this make you feel? What is your instinct?

Look for YouTube clips on proto-conversations – search for 'Pre-birth to Three: Professor Colwyn Trevarthen'. What are the similarities in these early conversations? How do they vary by parent/infant dyad? (Watch some different ones and compare.)

Case Study

Twins talking

Watch this adorable video of twins 'talking' to each other: www.youtube.com/watch?v= _JmA2CIUvUY

Look for the 'serve and return' as they wait for each other.

What other indicators of a conversation can you see? (Think about body language, use of hands, facial expressions.)

What do you think they start discussing? What does the conversation end on? (Think about the shared attention and the body language.)

How would you support this in the setting?

Language and personal/emotional development

A baby's early emotion is usually associated with crying, whether that is a hungry cry or distressed (such as wet nappy or too warm). It is also their first communication and is their 'only tool to manipulate their immediate environment' (Hayes, 2016: 53). Often parents will start to tune in to the different types of cry and will be able to identify their baby's need from the cry that they can hear.

As babies become more aware of the world around them, they are more likely to pick up on emotions from others. If you have ever worked in a baby room, you are likely to have experienced one baby crying setting the other babies crying, even if they were quite calm up to that point. This is thought to be caused by 'mirror neurons' (Goswami, 2015), which are fired in the brain when watching someone else and your brain 'mirrors' the action in your brain, even if you are not performing the action. For example, when a monkey watched another monkey tearing or grasping, the same areas of the brain that would be used to do those actions were also fired in the watching monkey. This can be linked with understanding how others feel even if you have different feelings, which is called theory of mind.

 Quick Summary

Theory of mind

Theory of mind is realising that others people may have different views and perspectives to yourself. At about one year old, young children start to appreciate that other people are different, with different ideas.

Up to this point of realisation, babies and young children will always assume that everyone else will have had the same experiences, have the same knowledge and are experiencing the same emotions as they are.

As children reach an age of growing independence, usually around two years old, they experience an almost overwhelming amount of emotional information. If they are unable to explain to others how they are feeling, this can result in frustration and emotional distress. It is the practitioner's role to help children to name those feelings, so children can express in words how they feel (Lindon, 2008). The practitioner can hold up a 'virtual mirror' (Gerhardt, 2004: 25) to reflect back the emotions, and then differentiate these into language children can use. For example, feeling 'cross' can be embarrassed, angry, tired or confused. Without this nuancing of feelings at an early age, it may be that children grow into adults who are 'alexithymic', i.e. who are unable to put their feelings into words (Gerhardt, 2004: 94), sometimes with very distressing outcomes.

Even if verbal language is still developing, being able to use 'sign language', whether that is British sign language, Makaton or baby sign, can often reduce frustrations and help to meet the toddler's needs. Research in this area is beginning to show that there is a 'significant, positive impact' on children's development when using baby signs (Mueller, Sepulveda and Rodriguez, 2014).

Activities

Persona dolls each have a distinct, unchanging background and 'persona' - for example, one of three children; lives in a flat just with mum; is scared of the dark. Originally developed to encourage respect and understanding for others, these dolls can be used to support children who maybe experiencing emotional difficulties, by being empathetic, 'talking' and 'listening' to the children (via the practitioner).

Similar to persona dolls, empathy dolls have a specific background and history, but they can be used all the time for any emotional support and can simply be used as a conduit for the practitioner to voice a child's feelings if he or she is too shy to talk. They are good for younger children or for mixed aged groups (say, at a childminder's) where older children are able to articulate, but younger children may need a surrogate to talk on their behalf.

Books

There are a multitude of books that explore the character's emotions in a way that young children can relate to. These can be used to extend vocabulary and language about emotions. For example:

Anthony Browne's books, particularly *How do YOU feel?*, are good for exploring feelings and starting conversations, with beautiful illustrations.

Jane Evans' set of books deal with emotions (particularly linked with trauma) that children may be finding difficult to explain or cope with, for example *Little Meerkat's Big Panic*.

For older children, Sally and Phill Feathertone's *50 Fantastic ideas for Exploring Emotions*.

Illustrations

Create a continuum of faces that go from sad to happy. Children can use this to indicate how they are feeling - where they are on the continuum. Practitioners can give children the language to describe the picture the children have chosen.

Songs

Songs that include emotions, such as 'If You're Happy and You Know It', can be altered to include a range of emotions, demonstrated by suitable facial expressions.

 Review Your Practice

Around two years of age, children can often experience very strong emotions that they may need support with. These are sometimes called temper tantrums.

However, if this is rephrased as 'an emotional need' or 'distressed behaviour' (both terms used by Dr Suzanne Zeedyk), then the dynamic changes and we can start to see the behaviour from the child's perspective - even if they can't explain it to us.

Think about the language that you use to describe children's emotions. Is it largely positive towards the child or negative? How could you ensure it is mostly positive. (Think about how the child might be feeling or trying to cope with.)

How can you reflect the children's feelings and let them know you are there to support them? (Think about the language you may use to talk to the children.)

How else could your use of language affect children's feelings and emotions?

Physical development and language

As babies become more aware of themselves as a separate person and begin to move independently, language to describe both body parts and actions becomes more meaningful. Describing body parts helps support children with vocabulary and can make them more aware of the different parts of the body. For example, children often need to be made aware that their fingers can move independently, as can their toes. Discovering a tummy button is often very exciting!

Language that describes actions will encourage children to move in different ways and to use their body in different ways. The skills needed to hop are very different to those needed to run or walk backwards. As children start to follow simple instructions, they will need to know the meaning of the words and any additional instructions, such as 'walk slowly'. This gives greater enjoyment of physical activity, greater confidence with movement and links the action with the words more firmly.

Another reason for children to use their hands with intent is while using sign language. Children need to be able to control their fingers, hands and arms to make meaningful signs, so their physical development and language development are mutually beneficial. The popularity of TV shows such as *Mr Tumble* shows how children enjoy using their bodies to communicate and have fun.

Physical activities with reinforcing language

Any game that uses instructions for movement will help children to recognise their own bodies, and understand how they can move. For example: 'Simon says'; 'Head, shoulders, knees and toes'; all finger games such as 'Peter pointer', 'Where are You?', '5 Little Ducks Came Swimming One Day', and '5 Fat Peas in a Pea Pod Pressed'.

If you are unfamiliar with any of these songs, most of them are on YouTube for you to watch before you do them with the children.

The *Let's Sign Early Years* range of books has nursery rhymes, songs and information that all have the signing directions with them.

 Review Your Practice

Think about the language that you use when doing physical activities with the children.

Instructions should be clear and precise, but how often do you use unusual words, such as creep, slither, tiptoe and sneak?

Do you differentiate language to encourage children who may be physically more able than others?

Case Study

Playing football

While watching a physical development programme with a group of young children, one of the older boys attempted to deliberately dribble with the ball. It became evident that he had been going to early football sessions, which he had enjoyed, and wanted to show some of his new skills.

'I can dribble!', he'd said proudly.

The leader of the session picked up on his use of language and encouraged him to say more about his football class, including using football-specific words such as 'dribble', 'score' and 'penalty'.

The little lad was really excited and chatted happily about his class and the other children in the class.

How could you extend this opportunity for language development?

What sort of links do you think this boy is making between language and physical development?

Cognitive development and language development

It has been hypothesised for a long time that cognitive development and language development are inextricably linked. Vygotsky believed that 'language mediated cognitive development' (Goswami, 2015: 22) and, as it becomes inner speech it then drives the child's cognitive development. However Goswami (2015: 13) also notes that cognitive development 'shows marked variations' depending on the quality and quantity of the interactions and conversations that children experience. More generally, Finnegan (2016: 8) states that 'Good language development and brain development are interlinked and mutually reinforcing', which supports David *et al.* (2003) who assert that language and thought both depend on each other but also promote each other, and that children's use of narrative also assists with making sense of the world around them.

Cognitive development and language development are both very complex areas of learning and development. Although research has found time and again that the two are linked, depend on each other and are reinforcing, it is very difficult to unscramble the two areas. Therefore, it is ideal for practitioners to support and promote language development, knowing that this will help cognitive development and vice versa.

Use of language and language development can also be an indicator of children's abilities later on in their childhood. For example Roulstone *et al.* (2011: 3) found that children's language at age two is 'very strongly associated with their performance on entering primary school'. They also mirrored the findings from the EPPE research (Sylva *et al.*, 2004), which found the communication environment (i.e. what parents did with children) was more important than their socio-economic status.

Activities to support cognitive development through language

Sensory activities give babies and children both the physical sensation and, when supported by a practitioner, the language to explain the sensation. For example: In the water tray, use cold water and say 'cold' to babies, then make the water warm and say 'warm'.

As children grow and their language expands, you can add words such as splash, ice, bubbles, pour, etc. When the language is linked to the sensation, children are more likely to remember it because it makes sense to them.

Simple sensory activities have enormous scope for learning opportunities.

- Sand (dry and wet). Good for texture words such as scratchy, gritty. Cognitive learning: how dry sand pours and moves differently to wet sand.
- Gloop (cornflour and water mixed). This is liquid until squeezed and then it goes firm, returning to liquid after the pressure is released (a non-Newtonian fluid). Good for words such as squeeze, pour, mix. Cognitive learning: can the children see how the gloop differs to normal fluids (such as paint) when squeezed?
- Paint. Good for babies to feel the paint, and even better if you can add texture or safe glitter for them, to increase the range of words – for example, wet, smooth, squash, rough, sparkly, shiny. Cognitive learning: cause and effect, how using hands can spread and mix paint, moving onto tools and finally mark-making.

 Reflective Questions

Cognitive development

It is debatable whether language precedes knowledge or whether knowledge precedes language.

Explain to someone how to make a cup of tea, but do not use the words for kettle, tea bag or cup.

How difficult is this? Could you find alternative ways of explaining the process satisfactorily? Was it frustrating? Did you give up trying if the person you are talking to didn't understand?

In this case, knowledge precedes language – although the assumption is being made that you know how to make a cup of tea, using a tea bag and boiling a kettle. This raises the question of whether children may simply never have had the right experiences to either have language or knowledge! 'Climb a tree' is meaningless if you've never seen a tree, don't know what one is, have never climbed and don't know what climb means.

How can you evaluate children's cognitive development if they have limited language or are at a pre-language stage? (Think about the things that babies and children do – for example, anticipating lunchtime from a practitioner putting on an apron.)

What else demonstrates knowledge and understanding? (Think about social situations where a baby may hand another baby their favourite toy, for example.)

Language, problem solving and understanding about the world

Sometimes, when observing young children, they will chat to themselves about what they are doing, what the toys are doing or who is going to be involved. This is known as 'self-talk' and is used to keep focus or to help solve a problem (Jones and Mason, 2017). It is a technique that we can use ourselves as adults (I've walked round the house saying 'keys, keys' before leaving for work!).

When observing children, this use of language can give an insight into their thinking about how they are problem solving and their view of the world. For example, if a child is building a tower and starts to use the last blocks up, if he or she says 'more' then it would be fair to assume that they know that more blocks means a higher tower. If they then look in the box and it is empty and he or she says, 'all gone', that could demonstrate that he or she thinks that is the only place where blocks come from.

Quick Summary

Sustained shared thinking

Sustained shared thinking is defined as:

> an episode in which two or more individuals 'work together' in an intellectual way to solve a problem, clarify a concept, evaluate activities, extend a narrative etc. Both parties must contribute to the thinking and it must develop and extend.
>
> Sylva *et al.*, 2004: 36

These are the two-way interactions that occur from birth and support babies and children's thinking processes and knowledge base.

Language approaches to support problem solving

Positive questioning

Rather than peppering children with questions to find out how they are thinking, there are a few other techniques than can be used which can be grouped under 'positive questioning':

- 'Tune in' not just to what is being said verbally, but also to the child's body language, tone, context and background.
- Respect children's choices, so they know there is no pressure to respond.
- Re-cap where the practitioner is simply repeating back your child's own thoughts, so he or she can help you to understand their thinking process – 'So you think that . . .'
- When problem solving, suggest a different method, but don't present it as the only solution: 'Would you like to try turning the box round to see if it fits on the shelf better?'
- Reciprocate or share common experiences or thoughts – 'My feet are soaking wet from the puddle. Thank goodness that you were wearing wellington boots when you jumped in. I hope they kept your feet dry'.
- It is far better to use How, What, When, Where, Who. Note that 'Why' questions can become judgmental and make children feel as if they have to justify their answers, so should be used very sparingly.
- Use silence! As practitioners, we can sometimes feel uncomfortable if there is a lull in the conversation, but for children this may be vital thinking time.

Active listening

Active listening is, as the name suggests, concentrating your whole person on listening, which can be a challenge in a busy setting or if you have a lot of other things to be thinking about.

- Make appropriate eye contact with the children, getting down to their level.
- Ensure your body language is open and encouraging.
- Have minimal verbal interruptions. If you are constantly jumping in with a comment, it shows you are thinking about the comments and not fully listening.
- Wait a fraction longer than normal to take your turn; your child may just be pausing for thought and you could accidentally interrupt this.
- Try very hard not to find an 'answer' or solve the problem. Sometimes the children may just be working through a problem 'out loud' to clarify their own solution.
- Paraphrasing back to the children and clarifying encourages more thinking and talking.

 Review Your Practice

When you are with the children, do you always 'solve' their problems, such as showing how duplo fits together or the train track? What could the children learn by trying different methods before you step in? (Think of orientation of pieces, manipulation of pieces, hand-eye coordination.)

How often do you discuss different methods with children first?

Case Study

Golden key

When my oldest son was learning to read, we would take it in turns to read a page of his school reading book until he became confident enough to read it all himself. The school used a reading scheme, where there was a magic golden key that would lead the children and their dog to all sorts of unlikely adventures.

There was one story (possibly the pirate one?) where the children are standing on a jetty next to the water's edge, ready to board the boat; however, the word used in the text for this was 'quay', which I had read aloud – so it sounded like 'key'.

When it came to read the next page, my son said: 'Where's the key gone?'

> Me: 'There's no key yet.'
> Him: 'Yes, there was, you said they were standing on the quay.'
> Me: 'That's "quay", not "key" (showing him the word). Why did you think they'd all be able to stand on a key?'
> Him: 'Because it's magic!'

My son had made sense of the words, as read to him, and had created a believable scenario given his knowledge of the book (it was a magic key) and his knowledge of language.

When you use words that may be ambiguous, do you always check the children understand? (See/sea; ate/eight; hear/here; knot/not; won/one; poor/pour; write/right.)

How could you improve children's knowledge of language using word games like this?

Language, dialect and cultural identity

Language can be a reflection and identification of cultural background, both with its use and also the dialect words that may be used. Vygotsky recognised language as 'the individual's internal-isation or appropriation of culture (French, 2007: 17). This is from babyhood and the way that parents and adults talk to babies (or, in some cultures *whether* they talk to babies), use parentese and the type of suitable talk. Babies will learn from the interactions of which they are part and will absorb accents, words and the use of words from their environment. Between the age of one year old and three years, young children will quickly learn culturally appropriate speech (David *et al.*, 2003), and some may even be aware that there are different contexts for different speech. Aitken and Beardmore (2015) give the example of Sarah, who had worked out at a young age that her 'Potteries' accent was acceptable at home, but not at her setting, so had modified her speech accordingly. Use of dialects is not detrimental to children's language development and it cements cultural identity, but it may become problematic if the dialect includes lots of non-specific words or reduces the richness of vocabulary that young children hear. For example, Michael Jones (2016: 89, 90) explains how the use of words such as 'thingy', 'whatnot' and 'ump' restricts the vocabulary of children, so practitioners should always try to use proper words.

Activities

Ask parents (or grandparents) to record regional variations of songs and rhymes, with any dialect words explained.

Explore different cultures, finding similar and different words for the same thing (e.g. bairn for baby).

Review Your Practice

How do you celebrate the local dialect or accent with the children? (Think of the words in the games you play.)

How could you combine cultural celebrations with language? (Think of traditional language that is used when presents are exchanged, for example.)

Language laying the foundations for future literacy

There are some predictable reasons for good language development laying the foundation for literacy development, such as knowing and understanding vocabulary and understanding that stories have a beginning, middle and end. However, it is likely that if you asked a practitioner in the baby room whether he or she is teaching literacy, that they would say no. Saracho (2017: 299) states that the 'early childhood years before introducing children to formal literacy instruction is viewed as critical in developing competent and literate children. All early childhood education teachers, at all levels, are considered to be literacy teachers, even before children participate in formal reading instruction'. This can be shown from research – for example, Kuhl (2011: 129) found that babies' phonetic learning not only predicted language skills between 18 months and 30 months, it 'also predicted language abilities and pre-literacy skills at the age of 5 years'.

The early childhood literacy skills that have been identified as strong predictors of later achievement include:

- Oral language
- Phonological awareness
- Alphabetic code
- Print knowledge/concepts
- Emergent writing or mark-making.

adapted from French, 2013: 37

So, for babies and young children, the start of literacy is hearing plenty of oral language, both quality and quantity; being made aware of environmental print and that it conveys a meaning; early mark-making can be pictures or words (note that swirling fingers in paint for a baby is a sensory experience, not early mark-making. The onset of early mark-making is when children know they are using their 'marks' to convey a meaning or word or idea – for example, 'This says my name, James').

Types of activity to support literacy skills

Early literacy will start with picture books, which can simply be illustrations without text. The illustrations can be supported by creative arts and discussing colours, patterns and shapes. These will be even more powerful if children can 'see themselves' in the illustrations, i.e. images of children and families that look like their own families or themselves.

Storytelling (oracy) games. These can start with really simple stories for babies. As children get older, retell the story making it longer and more complex. If the children are more confident, they can tell the story back to you.

Eye tracking or 'gaze' is the basic need for reading and is important for finding your place on a page or following a sentence on the board. Good activities for this are:

* Following torches in a dark tent
* Ball games and watching balls move
* Watching cars go down a click-clack track (backwards and forwards)
* Ribbons on sticks
* Drawing a route out of a maze, or use the ready-made maze with ball bearings and watch them roll in the maze.

Note that there are plenty of computer-based eye gaze games, but be aware that the children will not get the adult interaction or feedback with these.

Review Your Practice

With a colleague, think of the number of ways that you support literacy in the baby room. (Use some of the previous ideas as well as other activities you do with the babies.)

In the toddler room, do children have free access to books? Are they valued as a story-telling medium? (Think how the books are treated and cared for.)

How often do you share a quiet story time with just two or three children and really discuss the story, sequencing, differentiating between the words and the pictures? (Think how you could plan this into a day or a week with your colleagues.)

Case Study

Is this the right way?

It is very easy to assume that children know which way up a book is held and the difference between the illustrations and the text.

One game we would play with toddlers would be to sit with the group, but hold the book upside down or back to front (or both) and ask, 'Is this the right way?' At first the toddlers were a bit bemused (surely the practitioner should know?) but after a few times, they were eager to play with shouts of 'NO!' until you got it the right way round.

This was then extended to pointing to parts of the illustrations and asking, 'Are these the words?' until you got it right and finally pointed to the text.

This usually only took a few seconds at the beginning of story time, but it stressed the difference between text and illustration, and that direction of 'front to back' for English books.

Challenges to language development

Due to the complexity of language development and the environmental influences, there are many challenges. The disturbing statistic that one in every ten children will have long-term difficulties (in areas of poverty that number rises to over five in every ten children experiencing difficulties) demonstrates the need to ensure a good foundation for language development (iCan, 2017).

The focus here is on socio-economic status (SES), because this has an effect on holistic development, but there are a multitude of other challenges to language development in addition to this. It has been found (Tomalski *et al.*, 2013), using resting baseline EEG (electroencephalography, a measure of electrical activity in the brain using electrodes on the scalp) of six- to nine-month-old babies that there was significantly less activity in those from low-income families. Similarly, there was lower activity if the maternal occupation was of lower status. This shows that the effects of SES 'can already be detected in early infancy, potentially pointing to very early risk for language and attention difficulties' (Tomalski *et al.*, 2013: 676). This supports Kuhl's assertion that SES has an effect on learning, and 'the complexity of language input is a significant factor in developing brain areas related to language' (Kuhl, 2011: 128).

Socio-economic status affects other areas of development, such as physical development and health, literacy and numeracy, but the biggest impact on holistic development is likely to start with language and stem from there onwards. For example, storytelling and oracy are a basis for literacy and numeracy.

A sometimes overlooked challenge is that inexperienced practitioners may simply not know to talk to babies. After all, they can't talk back. Therefore the baby room leader, setting manager or childminder colleague should emphasise the importance of talking with babies to colleagues to ensure this is happening.

Opportunities for practitioners to support language development

From babies onwards, practitioners are able to provide a good environment for babies to listen to language; hear and see communications between adults and children; and to enrich children's vocabulary.

Practitioners are more likely to notice speech and language difficulties because they have specialist knowledge about language development and, with experience, will be aware of typical language progress.

Children will naturally be aware of each other's language. In settings where there are older children with more advanced language, such as a childminders, the children will benefit even more.

Conclusions

'Language is crucial for development' (Goswami, 2015: 25), which is why it is a prime area of learning and development. Language, communication, and personal, social and emotional development are closely related parts of a delicately balanced system. Helping one area of learning and development helps in all the areas, and trying to isolate one over another is not beneficial or desirable. Although the methods by which babies and children learn language are likely to be debated for some time, there is agreement that a language-rich environment is necessary.

Advances in neuroscience in the future may be able to pinpoint even more closely the types or styles of language that are the most effective for language development. However, currently it is well proven that good early language development provides an excellent foundation for children's development for years after their fourth birthday.

 Further Reading and Research

Language theorists

Find out more about Chomsky's work and ideas here: https://chomsky.info/

There are a number of texts that analyse the case of Genie: Curtiss, S. (1977) is entirely devoted to the story of Genie.

An excellent book that explores early childhood trauma and the resultant effects is Bruce Perry and Maia Szalavitz's book, *The Boy Who Was Raised as a Dog* (2006). Each chapter discusses and analyses a different child or children who have experienced trauma, how this has affected them and their subsequent transformations.

Steven Pinker's website has further discussion and ideas about the language instinct (as well as a range of other topics): http://stevenpinker.com/

While assessing a range of early interventions, their effectiveness and their efficiency, Asmussen *et al.* (2016) suggest that sensitive parenting, in a secure attachment relationship, facilitates both children's language and self-regulatory skills.

Singing and movement

For more information about the benefits of singing and of singing with movement, go to: www.britishcouncil.org/voices-magazine/why-song-and-dance-are-essential-childrens-development; or www.britishcouncil.org and search 'singing'.

For example:

> Singing is also an aerobic exercise that improves the efficiency of the cardio-vascular system, increasing the oxygenation of the blood and improving alertness. It is linked to stress reduction, longevity and general health. Improving airflow in the upper respiratory tract impedes the bacteria that can cause colds and flu.

For more information on singing with children in general, visit the Kodaly website: http://kodaly.org.uk/

Speech and language

You can find out more information about speech, language and communication needs from both of these charities: iCan (www.ican.org.uk) and Afasic (www.afasic.org.uk).

There is specialist training run by speech and language therapists at Elklan (www.elklan.co.uk).

Improving Early Child Development with Words, by Dr Brenda Fitzgerald at TEDxAtlanta (www.youtube.com/watch?v=y8qc8Aa3weE). Babies are hardwired to learn language and they do this from their parents and caregivers. 'Language is the interaction between caretaker and baby'. Dr Fitzgerald explains how the research shows that the amount and variety of language and vocabulary between baby and parents affect baby's ability to learn – and beyond – for the rest of their lives.

The Literacy Trust has an excellent set of resources, projects and research on its website, which include many resources and ideas for babies. Find more information here: www.literacytrust.org.uk/

References

Aitken, S. and Beardmore, K. (2015) Accent, dialect and phonics: Encouraging inclusion, in Brodie, K. and Savage, K. (eds) *Inclusion and Early Years Practice*. Abingdon: Routledge.

Asmussen, K., Feinstein, L. Martin, J. and Chowdry, H. (2016) *Foundations for Life: What Works to Support Parent Child Interaction in the Early Years*. London: Early Intervention Foundation.

Bernicot, J. (2014) Bases of linguistic development, in C. Fäcke (ed.) *Manual of Language Acquisition*, pp. 143-61 Berlin: de Gruyter.

Chomsky, N. (1975) *Reflections on Language*. New York: Pantheon.

Conkbayir, M. (2017) *Early Childhood and Neuroscience: Theory, Research and Implications for Practice*. London: Bloomsbury.

Curtiss, S. (1977) *Genie: A Psycholinguistic Study of a Modern-Day 'Wild Child'*. New York: Academic Press.

David, T., Goouch, K., Powell, S. and Abbott, L. (2003) *Birth to Three Matters: A Review of the Literature Compiled to Inform The Framework to Support Children in their Earliest Years*. London: DfES.

Elsabbagh, M., Hohenberger, A., Campos, R., Van Herwegen, J., Serres, J., de Schonen, S. and Aschersleben, G. (2013) Narrowing perceptual sensitivity to the native language in infancy: Exogenous influences on developmental timing. *Behavioral Sciences* Vol. 3 Iss. 1, pp. 120–32. Available from: http://dx.doi.org/ 10.3390/bs3010120

Evangelou, M., Sylva, K., Kyriacou, M., Wild, M. and Glenny, G. (2009) *Early Years Learning and Development Literature Review*. Oxford: DCSF.

Finnegan, J. (2016) *Lighting up Young Brains*. London: Save the Children.

French, G. (2007) *Children's Early Learning and Development*. National Council for Curriculum and Assessment (NCCA): Dublin.

French, G. (2013) Early literacy and numeracy matters. *Journal of Early Childhood Studies* Vol. 7, pp. 31–45.

Gerhardt, S. (2004) *Why Love Matters*. Hove: Routledge.

Gonzalez, A. (2016) *Music and Language Development: Traits of Nursery Rhymes and Their Impact on Children's Language Development*. Cal Poly. Available from: http://digitalcommons.calpoly.edu/musp/75/. Accessed 10 June 2017.

Goouch, K. and Powell, S. (2013) *The Baby Room. Research Summary 2*. Canterbury: Canterbury Christ Church University.

Goswami, U. (2015) *Children's Cognitive Development and Learning*. York: Cambridge Primary Review Trust.

Halliday, M. (1975) *Learning how to Mean*. London: Edward Arnold.

Hassett, A. (2016) *Brain Development and Impact of Trauma and Stress on Children*. Available from: https:// create.canterbury.ac.uk/15296/1/15296.pdf. Accessed 10 June 2017.

Hayes, C. (2016) *Language, Literacy and Communication*. Northwich: Critical Publishing.

iCan (2017) *Stages of Development*. Available from www.icancharity.org.uk. Accessed 23 April 2017.

Jones, A. and Mason, K. (2017) *The Impact of Childhood Deafness on Executive Function*. London: NDCS.

Jones, M. (2016) *Talking and Learning with Young Children*. London: SAGE.

Kuhl, K. (2011) Early language learning and literacy: Neuroscience implications for education. *Mind Brain Education* Vol. 5 Iss. 3, pp. 128–42.

Lindon, J. (2008) *What Does it Mean to be Two?* London: Practical Pre-School Books.

Mueller, V., Sepulveda, A. and Rodriguez, S. (2014) The effects of baby sign training on child development. *Early Child Development and Care* Vol. 184 Iss. 8, pp. 1178–91.

Page, J., Clare, A. and Nutbrown, C. (2013) (2nd edn) *Working with Babies & Children from Birth to Three*. London: SAGE.

Perry, B. and Szalavitz, M. (2006) *The Boy Who Was Raised as a Dog: And Other Stories from a Child Psychiatrist's Notebook*. New York: Basic Books.

Pinker, S. (2015) *The Language Instinct: How the Mind Creates Language*. London: Penguin.

Pourkalhor, O. and Tavakoli, M. (2017) Nursery rhymes and language learning: Issues and pedagogical implications. *International Journal of English Language & Translation Studies* Vol. 5 Iss. 1, pp. 111–16.

Ramus, F. (2002) Language discrimination by newborns. *Annual Review of Language Acquisition* Vol. 2, pp. 85–115.

Roulstone, S., Law, J., Rush, R., Clegg, J. and Peters, T. (2011) *Investigating the Role of Language in Children's Early Educational Outcomes*. London: DfE Research Report DFE-RR134.

Saracho, O. (2017) Literacy and language: New developments in research, theory, and practice. *Early Child Development and Care* Vol. 187 Iss. 3-4, pp. 299–304.

Skinner, B.F. (1957) *Verbal Behavior*. Acton, MA: Copley.

Sylva, K., Melhuish, E., Sammons, P., Siraj-Blatchford, I. and Taggart, B. (2004) *The Effective Provision of Pre-School Education [EPPE] Project Effective Pre-School Education: A Longitudinal Study funded by the DfES 1997-2004*. London: DfES.

Tomalski, P., Moore, D.G., Ribeiro, H., Axelsson, E.L., Murphy, E., Karmiloff-Smith, A., Johnson, M.H. and Kushnerenko, E. (2013) Socioeconomic status and functional brain development - associations in early infancy. *Developmental Science* Vol. 16, pp. 676-87.

Trevarthen, C. and Delafield-Butt, J. (2016) Intersubjectivity in the imagination and feelings of the infant: Implications for education in the Early Years, in *Under-three Year Olds in Policy and Practice*, pp. 17-39. London: Springer.

Vouloumanos, A. and Waxman, S. (2014) Listen up! Speech is for thinking during infancy. *Trends in Cognitive Sciences* Vol. 18 Iss. 2, pp. 642-6.

5 Play and holistic development

The importance of playful experiences for young children's holistic growth and development has been well documented over the years.

Dowling and Walsh, 2017: 102

Introduction

Babies' and young children's 'play' is notoriously hard to define, although it is generally acknowledged to be an effective way for most children to learn, solve problems, have social interactions and express their own personalities (Dowling and Walsh, 2017). However, a reflective practitioner will also know that play can 'be political and involves morals and ethics' (Grieshaber and MacArdle, 2010: 1) and that sometimes children's play can be at the expense of other children's well-being.

In this chapter, the role of play, including risky play and outdoor play, is explored in relation to how babies and children learn through play. It is too simplistic to state that 'children learn through play', so the question of what they do learn and the special aspects of play that enable this, is examined in more detail. The scope of the chapter is not intended to include everything possible for children to learn through play, rather to highlight the major components, especially for the birth to three age range, onto which other learning is then built.

Definitions of play

Play, by virtue of its breadth and depth, is truly holistic. However, for something so prevalent, so easy to see and with most people able to describe it, play is notoriously and dangerously difficult to define. One person's play is another's work and one person's fun is another's flippancy. It would be impossible and foolish to attempt to investigate the whole of 'play' in such a confined space. Consequently, some definitions and descriptions of play are discussed here, but with a focus on how play is holistic, supports all areas of development and is, ultimately, greater than the sum of its parts. Starting with Article 31 of the United Nations Convention on the Rights of the Child (UNCRC), it states: 'That every child has the right to rest and leisure, to engage in play and recreational activities appropriate to the age of the child and to participate freely in cultural life and the arts' (UNCRC, 1990). Interestingly, the comment on this Article defines play as:

 any behaviour, activity or process initiated, controlled and structured by children themselves. Play is non-compulsory, driven by intrinsic motivation and undertaken for its own sake, rather than as a means to an end. It may take infinite forms but the key characteristics of play are fun, uncertainty, challenge, flexibility and non-productivity.

French (2007: 20) suggests that 'what is clear is that young children learn through play in an integrated way. Using all modalities – the senses, physical activity, emotions, and representations, children indulge in and enjoy play'. Free play is described by Play England as:

> children choosing what they want to do, how they want to do it and when to stop and try something else. Free play has no external goals set by adults and has no adult imposed curriculum. Although adults usually provide the space and resources for free play and might be involved, the child takes the lead and the adults respond to cues from the child.
>
> Play England, 2007: xi

However, McInnes *et al.* (2013: 270) suggest that play should be viewed from the child's perspective, rather than the adult observations. This 'gives insight into the internal, affective quality of play which is important for learning, namely playfulness'. Playfulness is thought to promote 'enthusiasm, motivation, willingness to engage in an activity and flexibility of thought' (McInnes, *et al.*, 2013: 270), which are all foundations for holistic learning and development.

In everyday usage, 'play' is seen as something that is fun, and is sometimes used as the antithesis of 'work', but mainly that it is a freely chosen activity. Many theorists have defined play through the characteristics.

Huizinga (1949: 7–13) states that:

1   Play is a voluntary activity.
2   Play is a stepping out of 'real' life, into a temporary sphere of activity with a disposition all of its own, a 'pretend' world.
3   Play is distinct from 'ordinary' life both as to locality and duration.
4   Play creates order, is order. Play demands order absolute and supreme, or else the game is 'spoiled'.
5   Play has no material interest, and no profit can be gained from it.

abridged from Huizinga, 1949

Since then, other theorists have extended this list of features of play, with Bruce (2004a) most notably producing a 12-point list of features of free flow play, including some of Huizinga's points, such as play being a choice, it is in a world of pretend and children keep control in their play. However, Bruce extends this by defining some nuances of play, such as whether it is solitary or in parallel; with an adult or not; most importantly, the role of play to help children to 'test out' their feelings, competencies, relationships and culture in order to keep a balance to their lives. Alternatively, some define play through the different characteristics of the play itself; for example, Hughes (2002) defines 16 play types, from social to deep, to locomotor. As children get older, Santer *et al.* (2007: 24) suggest that their play can be subdivided into 'epistemic' (exploring the properties of materials), 'ludic' (which is imaginative and fantasy play) and 'games with rules'.

It is equally important to consider the reasons for playing. Again there are many theories and many pages of research, but Blaustein (2005: 4) explains the reason for sensory play well: 'they confidently test new knowledge in a relaxed atmosphere, relate it intuitively to existing knowledge, and store that information for future use'. There are some recommendations for further reading at the end of this chapter.

Reflective Questions

Defining play

How would you define play? Is this context specific? What other aspects might this depend on? (Think of other children present, toys available in the environment, adults/practitioners present, comfort of the baby or young child.)

[Handwritten note: Playing is engaging in an activity either solitary or with others. It can be structured or unstructured. Play can happen anywhere and with anyone – young or old]

Case Study

How may play be experienced differently?

Consider this quote about Gypsy, Roma and traveller children:

> There is a lack of safe play facilities on roadside sites ... girls' early involvement in domestic tasks and learning, which precludes time for play, play may be through manipulating real objects rather than toys.
>
> Cemlyn *et al.*, 2009: 121

How might this affect the play of a girl from a travelling family who attends a setting for the first time? *[Handwritten: Child may not know what to do with resources]*

How could you support her, while not singling her out from the other children?
[Handwritten: Choose playmate carefully. Allow her freedom to explore]
Consider the boys from the travelling family too; how do you think their play might differ?
[Handwritten: Will be rough. Short attention span. Unable to sit for long.]

Play and the emotional environment in the setting

The emotional environment will affect the type of play and play opportunities in which the baby or young child is playing. For babies and children who are not yet independent, and therefore depend on the adult's support to supply toys, books, music, etc., the play opportunities are almost exclusively in the control of the adult. Thus responsive, sensitive and caring adults, whether parent or practitioner, are necessary for good-quality play and opportunities. Their role will be to provide both resources and to ensure the environment is calm, relaxed, pleasant and supportive. To be most effective, this will require secure attachment between baby and adult.

Quick Summary

Secure attachment

Secure attachment is typical for the majority of children and is described as emotionally healthy. It is characterised by a child who is in distress after a brief separation, but can be comforted and settled by the caregiver reasonably quickly.

Page, Clare and Nutbrown (2013: 36) theorise that:

1 High-quality caregiver relationships are central to emotional development and learning in infants and toddlers.
2 Relationships take time to develop, so the key person must be given that time and opportunity to become attached to their key baby or key toddler.

There is ongoing research being done on play, how children of different ages play, the benefits and pitfalls of play. There is a special focus on the role that practitioners (in all types of settings) have to ensure that play is enriched and supported rather than interrupted or disrupted (Evangelou *et al.*, 2009; Fisher, 2016). For babies, learning will happen if play includes interest and unpredictability, and as children become more independent and lead their own play, they construct knowledge about their physical world, social world, language, conflict resolution and empathy (Evangelou *et al.*, 2009).

How physical development and abilities affect play

The way children's play is affected by their physical abilities and the changes in those abilities in the birth to three age range are highly significant. For example, babies go from having a reflexive grasp at birth to purposefully holding an object at about three months old. They go from not being able to support their bodies to being able to sit, stand, walk and run in those few years. These changes are not only going to affect the way that young children play, they will also affect the types of developmentally appropriate activities that practitioners need to provide for children so that they learn and are cared for appropriately.

Gradual change of 'play' activities from baby to three-year-old

For the age range birth to three years, there is considered to be a typical progression of play patterns and behaviours, from solitary play through to full socialising play. Parten's (1932) classic study of young children's play theorised that they moved through six stages:

1 Unoccupied – watching from the sidelines
2 Solitary (independent) play – happily playing by themselves
3 Onlooker play – watching, may comment but not a main participant in play

4   Parallel play or adjacent - playing next to other children; may copy or imitate others
5   Associative play - interactive, but not cooperative (necessarily), often each child trying to assert their own agenda
6   Cooperative play - organised and structured, negotiated and consulted.

It is important to note that this is a gradual transition from one stage to the next, and there are no fixed ages or time limits on any stage. Similarly, the play is going to depend on a wide range of situational factors, such as the circumstances, whether the other children are known, personality and mood, to name but a few. However, by three years old, children may be trying some associative play, cooperating and making up games together. This supports their social understanding, especially around social conventions and expectations or norms, as well as developing empathy (Evangelou *et al.*, 2009).

Play in practice

Children's play is usually full-bodied and has plenty of movement, so there are many holistic links between play, physical development and sensory experiences.

From the very beginning, parents and carers will be babies' first 'plaything'. Babies will gaze at parent's faces, turn to the sound of their voice and generally respond to parents and main caregivers (who may also be practitioners in a setting). These will mainly be interactions between adult and baby, including gazing, proto-conversations or singing together. For babies, tummy time and playing with parents and carers is an incredibly rich and rewarding play activity. As well as strengthening core muscles, the muscles in the neck and shoulder are strengthened as baby lifts his or her head. It encourages independence of movement and gives a whole new world for baby to watch.

 Quick Summary

Tummy time

Tummy time (putting babies on the carpet on their tummies) is key for neck strength and trunk control (try doing a jigsaw yourself on the floor!). Tummy time builds up core stability in the trunk, which is needed before children can have secure arm and leg movements, as they develop physically from the centre of their bodies outwards. Archer and Siraj (2015) explain how babies using their arms to push up from the floor give the strength and alignment in the spine that will be needed for an upright posture. Interestingly, lots of tummy time stimulates the pelvic area, helping to support toilet training when the time comes. Good core stability is essential for children later on when writing or doing other activities sitting at a desk, because they need to be able to support their bodies sufficiently to support their arms, elbows, wrists and finally finger movements. Babies should be on their tummy from 10 weeks old until seven months (unless sleeping or being held).

As vision develops, mirrors become a fascinating new plaything, and colourful or high-contrast (e.g. black and white patterns) objects are of most interest. Shaking a rattle on one side and then the other encourages the baby to turn towards the sound, as well as to cue into environmental sounds.

As hand-eye coordination develops, the baby's next toy is likely to be your hair, glasses and face. Very often, this type of exploratory play will include 'mouthing' (putting objects in the mouth to feel their texture and taste). If toys are put just out of reach, babies will have to roll and stretch, which helps physical development as well as an awareness of where the body is in space (proprioception).

When babies are able to sit securely, presenting toys such as treasure baskets will help to develop the exploratory urge and encourage stretching, reaching and turning. Repetition is still very important, as babies begin to discover and understand that their bodies are independent of the rest of the world and that they can control them.

Around four months old, a purposeful grasp is starting to develop (Hutson and Ward, 2015) and a common game to play will be to pick something up to drop again. At first this will be easy to grip items, but this turns into a more refined grasp so toys such as blocks and board books can be played with. Play becomes more exploratory as buttons can be pressed and handles turned to make things pop up.

Play takes a new turn as the baby starts to cruise the furniture and then turns into a toddler, and can now reach the 'toys' he or she wants. This may necessitate moving items to higher shelves and securing cupboards. Around the 12-month age, toddlers will start to 'play' in the more traditional meaning of the word, i.e. engage with toys, investigate books, imaginative play, sand and water play and outdoor games. Playtime is likely to become more physical as toddlers discover they can climb, run, roll and jump. Their social development may be based on common play interests with other children – for example, both playing in the sand pit together and splashing in the water.

At two years, a new era of play really takes off, with imaginative play, chat and more interactions with other children. Problem-solving skills help to make play more exciting and challenging, as children learn how to climb the slide steps or use construction toys. Imaginative play can flourish using props and open-ended dressing-up materials. Jigsaw puzzles, paint, pencils and play dough all take on a new fascination as children's physical skills mature. This is a time of exploratory and investigative play. By the age of three, children will be enjoying playing with other children and will be likely to seek out the company of others, especially as language starts to develop.

As play develops from an almost stationary one-to-one activity with parents to a very mobile social interaction with other children, all areas of development are being explored, experimented with and improved. Providing age-appropriate activities helps to develop cognitive, language and personal, social and emotional (PSE) aspects of child development. The importance of providing full sensory experiences for even the youngest babies cannot be overstated.

In conclusion, although older children's (and adults') play will vary with age, development and abilities, there are some similarities. However 'play' for a baby will look significantly and profoundly different to play for a three-year-old. The different terminology, numerous definitions and pedagogies of play can hinder the practitioner's understanding of the process of play. Rather than trying to encompass all definitions and nuances, it is preferable to have a pedagogy that *results* in purposeful play and meaningful play, as defined by the children, not the adults. It is the process and not the product that is the significant aspect of play - the playfulness of the activity.

Quick Summary

Stages of language development

- Birth to six months: Babies will turn towards sounds, watch faces and start to make a range of noises.
- Six to 12 months: Babies will babble and hold proto-conversations.
- 12 to 18 months: Will understand words, simple instructions, gesture and use a few words themselves.
- 18 to 24 months: Children will understand 200 words or more and be using 50 or more words of their own.
- Two to three years: Will use around 300 words and create sentences.

Schematic play

Chris Athey (2007: 5) led a five-year research study at the Froebel Institute in Roehampton that investigated all areas of children's play, interactions, model making and representations. From this, they identified certain repeated types of play or schema, which she defined as 'patterns of behaviour and thinking in children that exist underneath the surface feature of various contents, contexts and specific experience'. Among common schemas seen in play are:

- Transporting
- Enveloping
- Enclosing
- Rotational
- Trajectory
- Positional
- Connecting
- Going through a boundary
- Transforming.

For example, for a child with a transporting schema, carrying (transporting) objects is the most important or engaging part of their play. Typically, a 'transporter' will pack everything into bags, prams or buckets and carry them around the setting. Sand play may consist of carrying the sand to the water tray. The bikes outdoors will be used to transport toys. Bike wheels, windmills and spirographs will intrigue a child with a rotational schema.

There are many different identified schema, with more being defined as research continues. Athey (2007: 62) describes 10 graphic, 11 spatial and 9 dynamic schema. Understanding and knowing about schematic play helps to tune into and become attuned to the areas of interest that highly motivate a child, so the most suitable sort of experiences can be provided to support the child's development. Schematic play is likely to result in deep-level learning: the children will be highly self-motivated and are likely to have high levels of involvement while playing.

Although Athey's (2007) work was with a slightly older age range (two and a half years old upwards), it clearly demonstrates that children's seemingly random play may be very purposeful for them, and that close, detailed observation of children and their play is very worthwhile.

❓ Reflective Questions

Schematic play

[handwritten: Positional - lining up cars / connecting - trains / trajectory]

Have you already identified any children who are exploring schematic play? (Transporters are probably the most common, with envelopers, enclosures and rotational next.)

How do you support this type of deep level learning and play? (Think of both resources and interactions.) *[handwritten: offer tunnels and new routes. / slopes]*

How could you build on schematic play for further learning? (Think about combining schema, introducing variations and grouping children with similar interests.

[handwritten: enclosing - put houses and trees around cars and trains]

Risky play

Tim Gill states a number of reasons why risks in childhood are beneficial:

1 Help children manage risks – for example, learning to swim in case you fall in water
2 Children will always seek risks; by providing suitable environments these can be controlled a little
3 The benefits outweigh the risks – for example, playing in the woods may be risky but has health benefits, knowledge of the outdoors, etc.
4 Builds character, resilience, self-reliance.

The benefits of risky play are difficult to assess, identify and prove. It may be that only the child taking the risk would be able to qualify or quantify the benefits for that, but risks are easy to assess, identify and prove. For example, the number of children who hurt themselves on a slide is documented and known, but the benefits that the rest of the children get from the slide are not so easily known and are not captured centrally in the same way, so there is a call for common sense and balance (Gill, 2007). Toddlers (i.e. walking one-year-olds) are likely to engage in less risky play and, when they do, it is likely to be briefer than with two- and three-year-olds and consists of exploring their environment with their bodies (Kleppe *et al.*, 2017).

Outdoor play

Being outdoors is a full sensory experience, from the wind and the rain to the smell of the newly mown grass and the sound of the sparrows. The sunlight moves round during the day, casting interesting shadows and the dark is an opportunity to use torches. The outdoor environment is already fully populated with spiders, worms and birds, as well as the occasional visit from an unsuspecting cat. Even in the smallest of back yards there are likely to be plants, soil, puddles and interesting textures of brick, wooden fences and railings. The sheer difference and changing variety of things to explore outdoors makes it an essential play area for children to investigate, from babyhood onwards. As noted in the All-Party Parliamentary group, outdoor play 'complements and enhances all aspects of children's development and learning through its physical and open-ended nature' (2015: 29).

Case Study

'. . . they just want to go outside . . .'

Many years ago, when free flow play indoors/outdoors was just becoming established, the setting in which I was working implemented this by opening up the back doors after the welcome circle time, so the children could choose to go outdoors or stay inside.

Inevitably, every day the room would empty as the children all streamed outdoors, obliging practitioners to follow them out, even if they had planned on some lovely activities indoors. Consequently, there was a rule imposed where only a certain number were allowed outdoors at any one time. This just made the stampede even more desperate after circle time.

During planning time, one of the practitioners said, in exasperation, 'There's no point planning for their interests – they just want to go outside!'

How would you handle this situation? (Think about the children's interests – what are they telling you?) *You plan for outside activities!! and interests*

What reasons could there be for the outdoors being so fascinating? (Think of what might, or might not, be available at home. Think about the environment outdoors compared to indoors.) *Freedom, space, colour, autonomy risk taking*

How might the gender or attitudes of the cohort of children make a difference? *Boys and girls are more likely to play together. All abilities. Different interests. Inclusion for all. Personalities*

In summary, play is difficult to define but is an essential part of children's experiences. Undoubtedly there will be shifting, changing definitions as children's activities described as 'play' change, affected possibly by technology, attitudes (such as forest schools, the value of 'risky' play), society and the culture in which children are raised. It should be remembered that 'a playing child is a learning child' (National Strategies, 2008: 40).

Playful learning

For birth to three years, play and playful learning will always be central to children's agenda. The physical and mental foundations are made during these years and are then used in different ways as children grow, mature and develop. Through early playful relationships, babies and toddlers

are constructing views of themselves as individuals: that they are interesting, worthy of attention and can be partners in exchanges with those around them (Play England, 2007: 33). Singer (2015: 27) states that 'play experiences have a major impact on learning' and goes on to conclude that both 'play and playfulness are basic aspects of early childhood education' (Singer, 2015: 34) and that practitioners should be aware that play has benefits for learning, such as confidence and cultural identity. Play should be a shared pleasure and shared creativity, where the role of the practitioner is one of being 'playful', so children do not become overburdened. This can be through all types of creativity, including songs, dance, rhythm and humour. French (2013) also mentions playfulness and creativity, with respect to problem solving, and the All-Party Parliamentary group suggest that evidence points towards a playful approach being 'beneficial to children in early years' settings and has a lasting legacy on their later academic performance' (APPG, 2015: 23).

 Quick Summary

Playful learning

Playful learning can be child initiated, adult initiated, adult supported or adult led – any type of play where learning occurs through children's play. Typically the play will be exploratory, problem solving, discovery and experiential.

Pedagogy

Pedagogy= Method of 'how' learning occurs (handwritten)

Lindon and Brodie define pedagogy as 'a holistic approach to supporting children in learning, including the behaviour of practitioners and the learning environment they create' (Lindon and Brodie, 2016: 242). Pedagogy is the method or the 'how' learning and education occurs, which is very different to the content or 'what' is learned by young children – for example, learning that one plus one equals two. This is the 'what'. How this is done will depend on your pedagogy. This could be one apple and one apple – this makes two, using concrete objects; or using the symbols: 1 + 1 = 2; or using fingers to demonstrate how one digit plus one digit makes two. It is the method of doing this that becomes your pedagogy.

A practitioner's pedagogy will be influenced by all the experiences in life, social interactions, cultural heritage, family upbringing, knowledge and subsequent education. It may be that the setting has been chosen because it fits well with the practitioner's personal pedagogy already, or that the approach to teaching, learning and care has changed as a result of working within the current setting. Hopefully, a practitioner's pedagogy will change and become more effective as a result of learning about children's development – for example, reacting differently to aspects of children's play after learning about schematic play. The type and quality of pedagogical interactions between practitioners and children are the most significant factors for children's care and education. This is called the 'process quality' (Wall, Litjens and Taguma, 2015: 4).

Although there is not a specific pedagogy that is superior to others, some pedagogical practices, such as sustained shared thinking and a mix of child- and adult-led activities, are considered good practice in most settings. Consequently, there are also some pedagogical approaches that are considered to be better practice than others, with good developmental reasons – for example, only introducing a tripod grip when developmentally appropriate, when children have enough core strength, gross motor skills and fine motor skills.

Pedagogies have developed in different countries depending on their historical background, links with cultural norms and government policies. Sometimes the pedagogy may not be explicitly stated, but is implied throughout, such as the play-based nature of the Early Years Foundation Stage (EYFS) in England. Some theories are more influential than others on pedagogy – for example the Piaget theory of 'ages and stages' (Piaget and Inhelder, 1969) is very evident in many curricula, especially in the EYFS, as is Bruner's scaffolding (Wood, Bruner and Ross, 1976). Across many OECD countries, a child-centred and interactive approach is favoured (OECD, 2015), as a result of research findings. Research has found that there are three areas of pedagogical practice that have a positive and significant influence on children's development:

1   High-quality interactions between adults and children, where there is genuine interest and sustained shared thinking.
2   Play-based learning is valued and encouraged by adults in an appropriate way.
3   A balance of child-initiated, practitioner-initiated and practitioner-directed activities, managed in an appropriate way to support different learning outcomes. For example, some practitioner input gives better learning outcomes with phonics, but growth in vocabulary is more effective in child-initiated play.

OECD, 2015

Quick Summary

Learning theories

There are many theories about how babies and children learn, some based on behaviours, some on social context and some on environment. A few of the major theorists are listed here.

Bandura proposed a Social Learning Theory. Bandura showed that children learn by imitating what they see other people doing in their own environment. The actions of others become the model that children will copy.

Vygotsky hypothesised that children's learning is within a social context, that the two cannot be separated and that language (and use of language) is central to cognitive development.

Piaget believed that children 'interiorised' (David *et al.*, 2003) actions, so their cognitive ability was a series of assimilations and accommodations to build up their knowledge and beliefs.

Skinner theorised that children repeated actions that were positively reinforced (e.g. praised or got a reward) and undesirable behaviour could be ameliorated by punishment.

For much more detailed information and links to the EYFS (as well as to other curricula in the UK), see Featherstone, S. (2016) *An Anthology of Educational Thinkers* London: Featherstone Education.

Pedagogical documentation

A practitioner's pedagogy will also determine how children's learning is recorded and documented. This may be through the children's own creations, for example, in a Reggio Emilia approach, or it could be that practitioners scribe children's words. To be truly thought of as pedagogical documentation, it needs to be a process for 'listening to children, for creating artefacts from that listening, and for studying with others what children reveal about their competent and thoughtful views of the world' (Wien, 2013: 1). It can be thought of as a way of making children's thinking visible and accessible to adults' understanding. So, just recording what happened is not pedagogical. Documentation only becomes pedagogical when it also considers the why and how, when there is awe and wonder from the practitioner and active motivation to co-construct knowledge with the children.

The vast majority of curricula detail *what* it is that children are expected to know and understand by a certain age, not *how* they came to know it. This means that practitioners can choose how to educate young children using their own philosophy and ethos. This is important because practitioners must choose how to present experiences and information to children in a way that will make sense to those specific, unique children. This may be in an age-appropriate way or in a way that piques their interest. Research has shown that the interactions and experiences between children and adults are 'one of the most significant factors' (Wall, Litjens and Taguma, 2015: 4) when determining quality of care and education for young children. Similarly, it is important to know the reasons for documenting children's learning and how this then impacts on assessment, planning and environments (both physical and emotional). The co-construction from children, as well as sharing documentation with other partners, such as parents or multi-agency staff, is an important element of pedagogical documentation. There are some areas of learning and development that will be heavily influenced by a practitioner's pedagogy – for example children's attitude to 'risky' play. However, areas such as physical development (e.g. how tall a child will grow) will only be affected marginally (possibly by the foods offered in the setting). There are some further reading recommendations on the play cycle at the end of this chapter.

 Reflective Questions

Pedagogy and pedagogical documentation

Can you clearly explain your own pedagogy? (Think about how you manage situations differently to other practitioners you know.)

Where did this originate? (Think about your own childhood as well as any courses and childcare experience you have.) *Outdoor play. mix of Planned and free play*

How would others know about your pedagogy? *Teachers/TAs have similar pedagogies.*

Do the children co-construct their documentation? *No*

How do you share pedagogical documentation within your setting? With others?

UNCRC – RIGHT to play – what does this mean in reality? Is it only aspirational? *This would depend on provider*

A pedagogy of care recognises and celebrates 'that infants and very young children have agency; that they play an active role in their own learning' (Ionescu and Tankersley, 2016: 17). How does this fit with your personal pedagogy? *Children in EYFS are directed to an activity or given choice of activity laid out. No real agency to choose.*

Holistic links in this chapter

- *Play and understanding the world*
- *Environments for creativity*
- *Play and emotional development*
- *Play and social development*
- *Play and physical development.*

Play and understanding the world

Due to its ubiquitous nature, play supports every area of learning and development. It 'engages children's bodies, minds and emotions' (National Strategies 2009: 10) and 'is a process which fosters cognitive development' (David *et al.*, 2003: 9). It is a vital and core way of babies' and children's exploring, examining, analysing and knowing about the world around them.

Treasure baskets and heuristic play

Across the birth to three age range, play evolves from babies playing with parents and carers, to discovering their body is separate (and can be controlled) to mobility and independence. Throughout this transformation, there are developmentally appropriate games and toys. Obviously children may go back to using simpler toys, even if they are able to use more advanced toys, which helps them to consolidate learning through repetition (as well as being good for self-confidence). Treasure baskets and heuristic play have been singled out here, because many settings have both of these play opportunities for babies and children, but practitioners are not always confident in how to use them to their best advantage.

Treasure baskets for babies

The items in a treasure basket need to give baby a full sensory experience – touch, smell, colour, sound (and safe to taste!). For this reason, plastic toys are not encouraged, because they are generally smooth, have very little smell and tend not to be natural colours. It is much better to use natural materials, such as woods (including pine cones, chopsticks), loofa, sponges, pumice, cork and leathers. Think of the materials that may give several sensations, such as cold, heavy metal chains that clank together, or sets of metal measuring spoons or keys that make great musical instruments. Sense of smell can be met by using small muslin bags with herbs or spices such as lavender or cloves. Think carefully about the sensory experience that the babies will get from each item you include.

Once you have the sturdy, low-level basket assembled, sit the babies in a circle, with support if they aren't sitting confidently by themselves. The practitioners sit behind the babies, ready to intervene if necessary (for example, if something looks unsafe or if a baby gets distressed) and the treasure basket is put in the middle of the circle, within reach of the babies. The babies can then explore at their own pace, independently choosing items and playing with them in their own way.

Treasure baskets should be treated with respect. They are best used maybe a couple of times a week, no more. This means the babies stay interested every time they are used. It is possible to have different baskets, each with a theme such as shiny or wooden.

Heuristic play for toddlers and older children

Heuristic – from the same root as Eureka – means discovery or exploratory play. This is excellent for toddlers and those children who are investigating and experimenting with how to use different objects. As with treasure baskets, the heuristic items can be a wide selection of objects you may find around the home, such as empty kitchen rolls that will fit inside a crisps tube; small pans that stack; boxes that fit inside each other; whisks; and natural materials such as shells, wooden spoons, jamjar lids. Again, practitioners must be vigilant and ensure the children's safety with any items presented.

The extension of heuristic play from treasure baskets is the element of exploration and discovery. Find items that will fit inside or through each other (chopsticks through a colander); items that can be connected (ribbons wound round a willow ball); sealed tins that rattle when shaken; or paired items or sparkly things that catch the light.

Review Your Practice

Analyse some of the observations of the babies in your care. What sort of objects fascinate them? (Think of mealtimes – do they like to feel the cold metal of the spoon? Or are they fascinated with the material of their bib? Or the smooth feel of the table?)

How could you use this information to make a treasure basket to meet their interests? (Think of similar materials, similar touch sensations or similar shapes.)

How could you extend heuristic play? As well as developing toddler's sensory experiences, how can heuristic play aid practical skills? (Think of doing up buttons, fitting zips together.)

Case Study

Versatile hair rollers

Some while ago, I did some training on heuristic play bags in a 'baby room' in the West Midlands. The room had a mixture of very young babies, but there were also two boys who were toddling, due to move up in the near future. The practitioners wanted to stretch and challenge the toddlers and they felt it was getting 'boring' for them being with just the babies. Heuristic play is ideal for this, so I had taken along a bag of items that I thought they might want to try.

Through sheer luck, the babies all went to sleep after lunch, so the two boys were able to play independently with the heuristic play bag items. I had included two sizes of pink hair rollers, mainly because I liked the texture – a bit scratchy, but not too rough. One of the boys was fascinated by these and gradually became more confident in handling them and feeling them. He then amazed us all by pushing the smaller roller into the larger one, with no prompting or help, even though it was a snug fit.

His key person had not seen him do anything similar before, so his confidence and ability was astonishing.

How could you build on this? What other items could you add to the heuristic play to encourage and challenge him?

Stacking cups

Environments for creativity

It is difficult to imagine young children's play without creativity. Children are endlessly imaginative and creative with toys and objects they play with, their role-play and fantasy play. However, creativity still goes through stages of development as babies grow into more capable and independent toddlers.

Bruce (2004b: 73) describes the development of 'creativity' into three areas or aspects:

1   Emergent beginnings
2   Being a creative learner (process)
3   Making creations (product).

The emergent beginnings are the times when babies make connections in the cause and effect. For example, if I hold this rattle and move my arm, it makes a noise; if I push my fingers through this paint, it makes a stripe of colour. Bruce goes on to explain how emergent beginnings turn into toddlers becoming creative learners by an exploration of new experiences, but also variations on a theme. For example, paint can be used creatively by babies' finger painting, to toddlers using brushes to purposeful marks being made.

The creative process during play is a way for young children to explore their abilities and achieve a sense of embodiment, which will be necessary for future development. Bruce (2004b: 74) states that encouraging babies and young children to 'predict and anticipate' will also lay the foundations for creative ideas later on. Through the physical manipulation of materials, babies and children learn about the property of materials, which is the start of basic science and understanding the world around them.

Activities for creativity

Activities to encourage creativity need to be process based, that is, it is the processes that children use which are important rather than the product at the end. For example, it is more important that babies and children experience the texture, fluidity, smell and colour of paint than it is to paint a recognisable or beautiful image. Open-ended materials are generally the best type to provide for this, because they don't demand a finished product but require creativity and imagination to use.

For babies this can be as simple as paint or gloop on a tray, ribbons to wave or Velcroing bells to wrists and ankles.

For toddlers and older children, open-ended resources such as cardboard boxes, cardboard tubes, materials from the scrap stores and lengths of fabric encourage creativity and imaginative play.

Extend this by adding paint, colouring pens, string, masking tape or clothes pegs.

Review Your Practice

How are creative dispositions supported and encouraged rather than valuing the product over process?

How do the children know that you value their creativity? (Think about the wall displays. Does everybody's painting go up, even if it's 'not very good'?)

How do you encourage creativity in all areas of learning and development? (Think about your maths activities and use of creativity.)

Play and emotional development

Babies start to learn 'who' they are and that they are separate unique beings through the play activities that they enjoy with their key person or other practitioners. The quality of interactions, in a loving and caring environment, lets babies know that they are cared for and loved, providing good foundations for their emotional development. Young children use play to work through emotions, explore situations in a safe, play environment and re-enact situations. This is some-times called 'pretend play' and, although the situation may be pretend, it may feel very real to the children.

Occasionally, however, children's play with each other can be less emotionally supportive. In their thought-provoking book, *The Trouble with Play*, Grieshaber and MacArdle (2010) describe a number of situations where, for example, play is unfair (such as making one of their playmates 'the paper that catches the cinders from the fire') and may even reinforce negative and damaging social and emotional divisions. Therefore, it is important to have activities for children's play that support their emotional well-being, especially during free play.

Activities

- Provide plenty of different puppets and 'small world' figures, ensure that there is a range of ethnicities, disabilities and lack of stereotypes (e.g. all the doctors are male and all the nurses are female).
- Have cultural artefacts in the home corner or dressing up so children feel 'at home' and welcomed.
- Simple turn-taking games, or even when playing with the blocks or Lego, take it in turns to put a block on the tower.
- Have a quiet, withdrawn area – for example, a den, tent or sheltered corner, where children can go to reflect or just be with their own thoughts.
- Use empathy dolls, to 'model' sharing, being thoughtful about others or anything that you feel the children need some support with.

Review Your Practice

How do you support emotional development through play with all ages of children?

Do you have a procedure or clear guidelines for challenging sexist, racist or negative stereo-types in your setting?

Empathy dolls are slightly weighted, so when you hold them, they naturally turn towards your face, which helps to make the emotional connection. Find out more about using empathy dolls using Kirstine Beeley's book, *Using the Empathy Dolls Approach*, and you can get a range of dolls from: www.ascoeducational.co.uk/page.php?xPage=empathydolls.html

Case Study

Professional love

This is a concept formulated by Dr Jools Page to explain the love that practitioners feel for the babies and children in their care. It is the affectionate and caring behaviours that happen when you care for babies and children, even though it is part of your professional role. Dr Page's research started with a focus on babies, but the concept is equally applicable to older children.

How do you feel about 'professional love'? Is it inevitable that you love the babies and children in your care or not?

How does this support emotional development in babies and young children? How can your play reflect and support this?

Dr Page explains how professional love needs to start with the practitioner becoming self-aware, then de-centring until a reciprocal and authentic relationship leads to professional love. For more about this process, and the attachment toolkit, go to: http://professionallove. group.shef.ac.uk/attachment-toolkit/thinking-about-professional-love-tool/

Play and social development

Being social, understanding cultural and social customs, and using social skills are best developed through play, especially in the early years as social attitudes are formed. The supportive prac-titioners and adults around children will be very instrumental in the way that children interact and socialise with each other for the first time. Initially, toddlers may need some guidance with their social abilities – for example, encouraging turn taking – but as their skills develop, it is important for them to explore through play, to embed and learn the skills for themselves. Children play with their friends and friendship groups and pairs are likely to be made at the setting, so it is important to support this and observe any blossoming friendships.

Activities

Mealtimes and snack times are good for encouraging social development, such as saying 'please' and 'thank you', sharing round food or asking about preferences. You may find this reflected in children's own free play afterwards.

Discuss friendships and being friends.

Read and share books about friendships, discuss these with the children.

For the older children, have a couple of very simple 'rules', such as 'we use Kind Hands' to help their understanding of expected social behaviours.

Review Your Practice

How would you support a shy or new toddler who wants to play with a group of other children? (Think of the balance between 'imposing' a child onto a game and encouraging involvement.)

How do children resolve conflicts? Do they know when and how to request a practitioner's help? (Think – do practitioners always step in very quickly, or are children allowed to discuss their disputes first?)

How do you support friendship groups? (Think of how you seat children at mealtimes, consider transition into the next room.)

Case Study

Suzanne Axelsson and social development

During the spring 2017 Early Years Summit, I asked Suzanne Axelsson about how she supports children during play. She recommends giving children independence as well as emotional support, and that having your friends help is a powerful learning method, as this abridged excerpt shows:

Taking care of each other. When the children fall over, I'm always there, I always see. If it's a big fall or a big hurt I'm there, I'm on the spot. But when there's a smaller fall, instead of me rushing there and the children relying on the adults to help the child, I make sure that the children go over and ask 'What do you need? How can I help him now?'

I've got an absolutely amazing photo series of children – the whole group – running over to a friend that's fallen over. They pick him up. They check their knees, check how they are, they hug them they ask them how can I help, they move them to a bench. They sit down for a while say 'We can play again when you are ready to play', modelling exactly the same things that I had done with them when we were younger and when they still needed adult help. But it was amazing they could do it themselves, because I believed that they could do it.

It's the hardest thing you do. You literally put your hands in your pockets when you're standing, or you're sitting on your hands. You really, really want to go over and help. And yes, definitely the first time you feel like you got your heart in your throat the majority of the time. Sometimes they might come and say they're bleeding. We need a plaster and we'll go over and help them . . .

They realise that they don't have to depend on an adult to fix their problems. They can be resourceful themselves and fix an awful lot more than what they have been given the time and the belief that they can do.

How do you encourage friends to support each other?

Brodie, 2017: 135

Play and physical development

As previously discussed, play crosses all domains of learning and development, and children's play tends to be physical and uses all their senses. As well as the benefits of physical development on perceptions, spatial awareness, sensory experiences and keeping healthy, Mathers *et al.* (2014: 11) explain how 'through physical movement, babies and young children gain knowledge of their environments and become oriented.' Through exploratory play and being able to move away from their caregiver independently, they develop confidence and mastery.

Archer and Siraj (2015) describe this as movement-play and have explored the importance of this for young children, especially in the way that exercise can affect cognition and behaviour. They found that their intervention programme resulted in improvements, but most significantly they found 'consistently enhanced results in relation to the vital role of the adult at the two intervention settings' (Archer and Siraj, 2015: 21).

From being a newborn, babies engage with their environment using all their senses and full body movements, from stretching and grasping initially to rolling, creeping, crawling, walking and running. Their physical development is driven by an urge to play – to reach that toy, or get to the sand tray or to climb the step of the slide. Similarly, their play is driven by their physical abilities; being mobile means that there are many more 'toys' available to get to and being able to walk, run and climb opens up the world of social interactions, being able to choose friends, areas to play in and also those areas you'd prefer not to be in. The mutually reinforcing nature of play and physical development and ability means there is an array of activities that support both. In fact, it would be hard to find a play activity where an element of physical development is *not* being utilised as well, from gross motor skills, to fine motor skills and all the seven senses as well. However, the activities have been chosen because there is a special significance to each one.

Activities

Babies

Popping bubbles with their fingers. This is deceptively difficult; babies have to track the movement of the bubbles using their eye muscles, and then use gross motor skills (lift arm), fine motor skills to use a finger, hand-eye coordination to actually pop the bubbles.

Toddlers

When babies become mobile, their play tends to be highly physical, from running, climbing, swinging and jumping; toddlers enjoy their new-found skills. Activities that stretch and challenge these skills are climbing or walking on slopes, using climbing frames or clambering through woods – in particular, an obstacle course that includes climbing ladders, low balance beams (or walking along a rope), crawling through tunnels (or under a parachute) and changing direction when running (from side to side).

Older children

Older children need to hone some of their early skills – for example, running, but being able to stop in a controlled manner when asked to, manoeuvring around obstacles and being able to look forward when running (not watching the ground or their feet). Some of the children may also be able to use equipment, such as kicking balls or carrying a beanbag while running.

Obstacle courses, or games where children have to follow instructions (gallop like a horse, stop still like a tree) are good.

Depending on the children, superhero play may be emerging at this age too. This play naturally involves running, jumping and gross motor skills. The setting's policies around superhero play will need to be consulted and discussed.

 Review Your Practice

The Association of Play Industries (API) has a number of good publications for the birth to three age range and older. There are practical ideas (building a new play area), community links and the All-Party Parliamentary Group's report – Fit & Healthy Childhood: The Early Years. Find all these and more here: www.api-play.org/resources/publications

Quick Summary

The seven senses

The first five senses are well known:

- sense of smell
- sense of sight
- sense of hearing
- sense of touch
- sense of taste.

However, there are two other senses that we also rely on.

Proprioception is knowing where your body is in space, so that you can sit on a chair without looking behind you or pick up a plastic cup without squashing it or dropping it.

Vestibular is having a sense of balance and motion, so you can walk on a moving ship, balance on a log and spin round in a circle without falling over.

Challenges to play and creativity

One of the biggest challenges to play and creativity is having an understanding that it is not mutually exclusive to learning, and especially learning the 'academic' subjects such as literacy and mathematics. In fact, it could be argued that young children's learning should always be a subset of their play. Similarly, the idea that teaching does not belong within children's play is clearly nonsensical, because practitioners (parents, adults) are teaching children every day, through their actions, reactions and role modelling of everything from emotions to doing up a zip. A practitioner's presence is teaching babies and young children about expected behavior, and once the practitioner is involved in the play, either as a participant or someone to provide resources, there will be overt teaching in modelling language, manners or interactions, to name a few. It is unlikely that this challenge will be resolved, as the role of 'play' in learning and teaching has been debated for hundreds of years. However, taking a holistic approach, rather than trying to compartmentalise play, learning and teaching into discreet areas, would be a promising start.

There are still concerns about both the quality and quantity of play, including toys and games that limit imagination, health and safety fears, lack of access to nature play and play that is highly adult-directed so limiting creativity (for example, Bodrova, 2008).

Opportunities for practitioners and play

Practitioners in the baby room and onwards, as well as childminder practitioners, have a great opportunity to support play in all its forms. To optimise play opportunities, the pedagogy and methods to support play should be essential – 'as integral to both the initial qualification and ongoing professional development of the entire children's workforce' (All-Party Parliamentary Group, 2015: 48).

Practitioners are also in a good position to support, help and liaise with parents to explain the importance and relevance of play to their babies' and children's holistic development. This could be as practical advice – for example, that a large cardboard box is likely to be as much (if not more) fun than a computer game, or explaining how hanging from the climbing frame is building core muscles ready for writing.

Conclusions

Babies and young children play according to their level of development, physical abilities, motivation and PSED. Play is the all-encompassing and truly holistic manner in which children learn. This chapter has investigated a few of the individual areas of learning and development and the ways that play can support these.

The practitioner's role is to facilitate, stretch and challenge children's play and learning equally. Sometimes this may mean standing back while babies and children solve problems for themselves – for example, using a treasure basket or social support as Suzanne Axelsson describes. Sometimes this will be helping children to develop their physical abilities so they can achieve balancing or climbing by themselves.

Play should be valued and encouraged as *the* learning process for babies and children, with suitable support from sensitive practitioners.

Further Reading and Research

There are a range of books and journals on play. David Whitebread's book, *Developmental Psychology and Early Childhood Education*, has an excellent chapter on play and learning, which both reviews some seminal texts, such as Janet Moyles' book *The Excellence of Play*, and extends some of the concepts, such as the practitioner's role in play, in a clear and practical manner.

The National Strategies document, *Learning, Playing and Interacting* (2009), although a few years old, is an excellent resource for thinking about the basics of play and its role in the setting. In particular, the chart on page 5, which shows the continuum of unstructured play, through child-initiated play, focused learning to highly structured (i.e. no play), is very useful in helping to plan and evaluate the play within a setting. Rarely is an activity or experience totally child-initiated or adult-led – there is almost always some sliding along the scale as the children start to lead or the practitioner presents further guidance.

Agency and engagement are central to successful learning.

Eaude, 2011: 46

Agency is the child's own active, and proactive, exploration of the world and experiences. It is children's own ability to affect, influence or control their environment and thus direct their own learning.

It is useful to reflect on whether the babies and young children in your setting are passive receivers of knowledge, or whether they have more agency.

The play cycle

The play cycle is a way of describing a child's play process, used mainly by play workers to understand children's play better and how this can be supported. Find more information and description of the play cycle here: www.surreycc.gov.uk/schools-and-learning/childcare-professionals/playworkers/the-theory-of-play; and for a much more in-depth analysis, there is an excellent literature review here: www.gov.scot/Publications/2015/10/6809/5. Although written for play workers, it has some excellent links and resources about play.

Treasure baskets and heuristic play

Goldschmeid, E. and Jackson, S. (1994) *People under Three – Young Children in Day Care*. Abingdon: Routledge. This book is the classic book about treasure baskets and heuristic play, with theory to support the practice.

Hughes, A. (2006) *Developing Play for the Under 3's – The Treasure Basket and Heuristic Play*. Abingdon: David Fulton. This is a very practical book, with lots of ideas for putting together the resources and their use with babies and young children.

References

All-Party Parliamentary Group on a Fit and Healthy Childhood (2015). *Play*. Association of Play Industries. Available from: http://outdoorplayandlearning.org.uk/downloads/. Accessed 8 June 2017.

Archer, C. and Siraj, I. (2015). Measuring the quality of movement-play in Early Childhood Education settings: Linking movement-play and neuroscience. *European Early Childhood Education Research Journal* Vol. 23 Iss. 1, pp. 21–42.

Athey, C. (2007) *Extending Thought in Young Children* (2nd edn). London: PCP.

Beeley, K. (2009) *Using the Empathy Dolls Approach*. London: A & C Black.

Blaustein, M. (2005) See Hear Touch: The basics of learning readiness. *Beyond the Journal: Young Children on the Web*. Available from: www.naeyc.org/files/yc/file/200507/01Blaustein.pdf. Accessed 8 June 2017.

Bodrova, E. (2008) Make-believe play versus academic skills: A Vygotskian approach to today's dilemma of early childhood education. *European Early Childhood Education Research Journal* Vol. 16 Iss. 3, pp. 357–69.

British Educational Research Association (BERA) Early Childhood Special Interest Group and TACTYC (2017). *Early Childhood Research Review 2003–2017*. London: British Educational Research Association.

Brodie, K. (2017) *Personal, Social and Emotional Well-being in Young Children*. Wilmslow: Rainmaker.

Bruce, T. (2004a) *Developing Learning in Early Childhood*. London: SAGE.

Bruce, T. (2004b) *Cultivating Creativity in Babies, Toddlers & Young Children.* London: Hodder Education.

Cemlyn, S., Greenfields, M., Burnett, S., Matthews, Z. and Whitwell, C. (2009) *Inequalities Experienced by Gypsy and Traveller Communities: A Review.* Manchester: Equality and Human Rights Commission.

David, T., Goouch, K., Powell, S. and Abbott, L. (2003) *Birth to Three Matters: A Review of the Literature Compiled to Inform the Framework to Support Children in their Earliest Years.* London: DfES.

Dowling, M. and Walsh, G. (2017) *Playful Teaching and Learning.* London: SAGE.

Eaude, T. (2011) *Thinking through Pedagogy for Primary and Early Years.* Exeter: Learning Matters.

Evangelou, M., Sylva, K., Kyriacou, M., Wild, M. and Glenny, G. (2009) *Early Years Learning and Development: Literature Review.* Oxford: DCSF.

Featherstone, S. (2016) *An Anthology of Educational Thinkers.* London: Featherstone Education.

Fisher, J. (2016) *Interacting or Interfering? Improving Interactions in The Early Years.* Maidenhead: Open University.

French, G. (2007) *Children's Early Learning and Development: A Research Paper.* Dublin: National Council for Curriculum and Assessment (NCCA).

Gill, T. (2007) *No Fear: Growing up in a Risk-averse Society.* London: Calouste Gulbenkian.

Goldschmeid, E. and Jackson, S. (1994) *People under Three - Young Children in Day Care.* Abingdon: Routledge.

Goouch, K. and Powell, S. (2013) *The Baby Room. Research Summary 2.* Canterbury: Canterbury Christ Church University.

Goswami, U. (2015) *Children's Cognitive Development and Learning.* York: Cambridge Primary Review Trust.

Grieshaber, S. and MacArdle, F. (2010) *The Trouble with Play.* Maidenhead: Open University.

Hughes, A (2006) *Developing Play for the Under 3s - The Treasure Basket and Heuristic Play.* Abingdon: David Fulton.

Hughes, B. (2002) *A Playworker's Taxonomy of Play Types* (2nd edn). London: Play Education.

Huizinga, J. (1949) *Homo Ludens.* London: Routledge and Kegan Paul.

Hutson, M. and Ward, A. (2015) *Oxford Textbook of Musculoskeletal Medicine* (2nd edn). Oxford: Oxford University Press.

Ionescu, M. and Tankersley, D. (2016) *A Quality Framework for Early Childhood Practice in Services for Children under Three Years of Age.* International Step by Step Association (ISSA).

Kleppe, R., Melhuish, E., Beate, E. and Sandseter, H. (2017) Identifying and characterizing risky play in the age one-to-three years. *European Early Childhood Education Research Journal* Vol. 25 Iss. 3, pp. 370-85.

Lindon, J. and Brodie, K. (2016) *Understanding Child Development 0-8 Years* (4th edn). London: Hodder Education.

Mathers, S., Eisenstadt, N., Sylva, K., Soukakou, E. and Ereky-Stevens, K. (2014) *Sound Foundations: A Review of the Research Evidence on Quality of Early Childhood Education and Care for Children under Three. Implications for Policy and Practice Research.* London: The Sutton Trust.

McInnes, K., Howard, J., Crowley, K. and Miles, G. (2013) The nature of adult-child interaction in the early years classroom: Implications for children's perceptions of play and subsequent learning behavior. *European Early Childhood Education Research Journal* Vol. 21 Iss. 2, pp. 268-82.

National Association for the Education of Young Children (NAEYC) (2009) *Developmentally Appropriate Practice in Early Childhood Programs Serving Children from Birth through Age 8.* Washington, DC: NAEYC.

National Strategies (2008) *Social and Emotional Aspects of Development (SEAD).* Nottingham: DCSF.

National Strategies (2009) *Learning, Playing and Interacting: Good Practice in the Early Years Foundation Stage.* Nottingham: DCSF.

Organisation for Economic Co-operation and Development (OECD) (2015) *Early Childhood Education and Care Pedagogy Review: England.* Available from: www.oecd.org/edu/earlychildhood. Accessed 14 June 2016.

Page, J., Clare, A. and Nutbrown, C. (2013) (2nd edn) *Working with Babies & Children from Birth to Three.* London: SAGE.

Parten, M.B. (1932) Social participation among preschool children. *Journal of Abnormal and Social Psychology* Vol. 27 Iss. 3, pp. 243-69.

Piaget, J. and Inhelder, B. (1969) *The Psychology of the Child.* New York: Basic Books.

Play England (2007) *Free Play in Early Childhood.* York: Play England.

Santer, J., Griffiths, C. and Goodall, D. (2007) *Free Play in Early Childhood. A Literature Review.* York: Play England.

Singer, E. (2015) Play and playfulness in early childhood education and care. *Psychology in Russia: State of the Art* Vol. 8 Iss. 2, pp. 27-35.

United Nations Convention on the Rights of the Child (UNCRC) (1990) *Convention on the Rights of the Child.* London: Unicef. Available from: www.unicef.org/crc/files/Rights_overview.pdf. Accessed 7 May 2017.

Wall, S., Litjens, I. and Taguma, M. (2015) *Pedagogy in Early Childhood Education and Care (ECEC): An International Comparative Study of Approaches and Policies.* London: DfE.

Whitebread, D. (2011) *Developmental Psychology and Early Childhood Education.* London: SAGE.

Wien, C. (2013) *Making Learning Visible through Pedagogical Documentation.* Ontario: Queen's Printer.

Winter, P. (2010) *Neuroscience and Early Childhood Development.* Department of Education and Children's Services, South Australia.

Wood, D., Bruner, J.S. and Ross, G. (1976) The role of tutoring in problem solving. *Journal of Child Psychology and Psychiatry* Vol. 17, pp. 89-100.

6 Early mathematical development

In brief early childhood educators need to be informed about numeracy related concepts, to plan everyday experiences, communicate about those experiences, reflect on their practice and continually strive to improve their practice.

French, 2013: 41

Introduction

Mathematical concepts are far wider than counting and numbers. Very young children naturally experiment with the ideas of capacity, size, weight and length during their everyday play, even as babies.

The Early Years Foundation Stage (EYFS) 2008 referred to 'problem solving, reasoning and numeracy' rather than mathematics. As a name, this is a more accurate description of the activities that young children will be involved in, which will advance into primary school mathematics. However, in order to align with the EYFS, the word mathematics will be used here.

Mathematics is everywhere and is a vital part of children's learning. It is part of play, but it is also part of snack time, lining up, mealtimes, tidy-up time and outdoor play. In fact, everything that babies and children do will have a very real and evident element of mathematics. Reflective practitioners should grasp every opportunity to support, stretch and challenge children with their mathematical concepts - even if mathematics is not their favourite subject.

Children's mathematical development

Piaget theorised that children learned and re-learned their knowledge of the world, moving through identifiable stages (Pound, 2005). The age range from birth to three falls mainly within the sensorimotor stage and is usually defined from birth to the acquisition of language (or around two years old). During this stage, babies learn through their senses, the environment and movement. The senses gradually become more coordinated and start to work together. By the time the next stage, preoperational, has been reached, they will still be egocentric but will understand concepts such as object permanence.

Children's understanding of mathematical concepts during these stages is through their experiences. For example, children will start to learn about shapes, both 3D and 2D, through the handling of objects and the sensory feedback this gives through the coordination of the sense of touch and sight. By the age of three, children will usually be able to understand the concept of numbers and counting, so they will be able to count on their fingers, for example (Ojose, 2008). Mark-making is usually reserved for the beginnings of literacy or writing, but, of course, it is also the basis for written maths too. All the links with basic physical development, core strength, fine and gross motor skills are just as applicable to the simple recording of maths as well as the deeper-level learning of maths graphics and children's own representation of maths.

Quick Summary

The seven senses

The first five senses are well known:

- sense of smell
- sense of sight
- sense of hearing
- sense of touch
- sense of taste.

However, there are two other senses that we also rely on.

Proprioception is knowing where your body is in space, so that you can sit on a chair without looking behind you or pick up a plastic cup without squashing it or dropping it.

Vestibular is having a sense of balance and motion, so you can walk on a moving ship, balance on a log or spin round in a circle without falling over.

Research into mathematical development

Compared to early literacy and language, there is a scarcity of research on very young children's early mathematical development. Current research on babies' eye gaze experiments makes it obvious that they are viewing the world through a mathematical lens, with experiments on probabilistic reasoning showing this (Denison *et al.*, 2013). As research has advanced, it has been demonstrated that babies may be much more mathematically aware than was first realised. Although they might not be able to describe their experiences verbally, inferences can be made by observing how long babies stare or gaze at sets of objects. Izard *et al.* (2009) describe how newborn babies could discriminate between the ratio of 3:1 objects and by six months old could discriminate between 2:1 ratios. At nine months of age, babies could discriminate ratios of 3:2.

Case Study

Babies and ratios

In her YouTube video of a TED talk by Laura Schulz, she explores the 'magic' of children's learning by drawing rich inferences from sparse, noisy data (the sensory-filled world around them). She asks, '*how do babies learn so much from so little so quickly?*' This talk includes some fascinating videos from actual experiments, showing babies making logical inferences from random sampling: www.youtube.com/watch?v=y1KIVZw7Jxk

More recent research by Starr *et al.* (2013) has clearly demonstrated that number sense precedes children's verbal skills to explain the mathematical ideas. By testing a six-month-old baby's mathematical skills and then re-testing three years later, they found that there is close correlation between number sense at the two ages, i.e. a baby who demonstrated good number sense at six months old still had good number sense at three years plus, even allowing for other variables. In later research, Denison and Xu (2014: 335) suggested that their results provided 'strong evidence for a rich quantitative and statistical reasoning system in infants'. This demonstrates that children's number sense, even as a baby, is important and should be supported and incorporated into their holistic development from the very beginning.

Embodiment

Embodiment is the postulation that the body plays a role in shaping the mind and in aiding understanding of concepts. For example, young children will understand how 'heavy' something is (weight) by carrying and lifting heavy and light objects. Initially, they will discover that, in general, large objects are heavy (a big book) and small objects are light (a cloth book). As their learning progresses, they will become to understand that even very big objects (an empty cardboard box, for example) can be lighter than smaller objects (a bowling ball). Ideally, these concepts are reinforced in many different ways, with many different objects. Edwards *et al.* (2014) explore the ideas around mathematics being shaped by the body, through the fact that we all have physical experiences and basic biology in a material world. They go further than embodiment and examine gesture as well.

Mathematics in the EYFS

There is a large range of concepts that the 'mathematics' area of learning and development includes in the Early Years Foundation Stage (EYFS), from number recognition, to time to shapes to the physical world. In addition, there are numerous theories about how children's mathematical knowledge progresses and develops in each of these areas. There are some integrated theories in some areas. For example, Siegler (2016: 341) suggests that numerical development can be described as a 'progressive broadening of the types and ranges of numbers whose magnitudes are accurately represented'. However, on the whole, babies and children tend to progress at different rates in different areas, so some babies will have good spatial awareness and others will have good pattern recognition, for example.

In the EYFS (2017: 8), mathematics is a Specific Area of learning and development, so is an 'essential' rather than 'fundamental' skill. It is defined as:

> providing children with opportunities to develop and improve their skills in counting, understanding and using numbers, calculating simple addition and subtraction problems; and to describe shapes, spaces, and measure.

This is then subdivided into 'numbers', and 'space, shape and measure'. In the non-statutory guidance, *Development Matters* (Early Education, 2012: 32), in the 'Numbers' subsection, babies from birth to 36 months are expected to progress from:

- Notices changes in number of objects/images or sounds in a group of up to 3

to:

- Selects a small number of objects from a group when asked, for example, 'please give me one', 'please give me two'.
- Recites some number names in sequence.
- Creates and experiments with symbols and marks representing ideas of number.
- Begins to make comparisons between quantities.
- Uses some language of quantities, such as 'more' and 'a lot'.
- Knows that a group of things changes in quantity when something is added or taken away.

However, for the 'space, shape and measure' subsection, from birth to 11 months:

- Early awareness of shape, space and measure grows from their sensory awareness and opportunities to observe objects and their movements, and to play and explore.
- See Characteristics of Effective Learning – Playing and Exploring, and Physical Development.

This emphasises the holistic nature of the 'space, shape and measure' element of mathematical development. Similarly, the many different, and underpinning, areas of learning and development are mentioned in the expected development around 36 months:

- Notices simple shapes and patterns in pictures.
- Beginning to categorise objects according to properties such as shape or size.
- Begins to use the language of size.
- Understands some talk about immediate past and future, e.g.'before', 'later' or 'soon'.
- Anticipates specific time-based events such as mealtimes or home time.

In order, these are closely related to the following areas of learning and development:

- Creative arts and design
- Physical development experiences

- Communication and language
- Understanding the world.

Therefore, babies and young children need to have full access to the whole curriculum, including experiential learning, experimenting with objects and language development, to help formulate and create understanding about mathematical development.

 Quick Summary

Stages of language development

- Birth to six months: Babies will turn towards sounds, watch faces and start to make a range of noises.
- Six to 12 months: Babies will babble and hold proto-conversations.
- 12 to 18 months: Understand words, simple instructions, gesture and use a few words themselves.
- 18 to 24 months: Children will understand 200 words or more and be using 50 or more words of their own.
- Two to three years: Use around 300 words and create sentences.

Order of learning mathematics

Marmasse *et al.* (2000: 3) describe five principles that 'govern and define counting'.'These are:

1   The one-to-one principle (one number per object)
2   The stable-order principle (numbers always run in the same order)
3   The cardinal principle (the last number counted represents the total number of objects – it is the total quantity)
4   The abstraction principle (counting applies to any set of objects or even different objects put together – Apples AND oranges)
5   The order-irrelevance principle (counting the plates around the table clockwise will give the same number as counted counterclockwise).

In general, children will learn the number names first, so young children will chant 'one, two, three, four' with little understanding of the 'two-ness' of two cups. Then they will start to understand the one-to-one principle, but the cardinal principle will take longer to embed. Thus toddlers will count 'One, two, three' cups, touching one at a time, but then if asked how many cups there are in total, they won't know.

Babies are born with a 'number sense' (Goswami, 2015: 20), which in many ways is analogous to the Language Acquisition Device (LAD) of language, but children still have to learn the 'symbolic number'. For example, for small groups of up to four items, young children use 'subitising', or seeing at a glance the number of objects, which requires skills in the visuo-spatial working memory. Just as children need to be aware of phonics, rhymes, syllables, etc. to be able to read well, children's language development, perception, spatial development and working memory are all essential parts of their mathematical skills. It follows then, that a child whose spatial development is poor will have difficulties with mathematics.

Even as children get older, a more holistic approach is still advised. For example, Gifford (2004: 99) suggests that mathematics for three to five years should be 'based on holistic principles and considering children's mathematical learning in terms of cognitive, physical, social and emotional aspects'. There is some evidence that some pedagogical approaches, such as the Montessori approach, can demonstrate greater gains in mathematics, 'although the effectiveness is conditional on good implementation fidelity' (Wall *et al.*, 2015: 5). This would tend to suggest that it is the interaction of the practitioners with the children that results in the gains, rather than the presentation of the pedagogical methods.

Mathematics is everywhere

Practitioners are applying practical mathematics every day, every hour, from the obvious numerical calculations, such as working out the number of cups needed for lunchtime and how many children there are in the room, to less obvious calculations – for example, the ratios of adults to children in each area at a particular time or, as a childminder, whether a parent can have a particular day according to the ages of the other children in that day. Times and timings are a constant thought, such as how long until snack, when are parents coming, how long will story time be today. Managers will need to be able to prepare bills accurately and calculate the different levels of funded hours, 'extras' charged for and at what rate.

In addition, there is all the proactive mathematics that practitioners are doing all the time, such as spatial awareness (putting boxes and bikes away), capacity (how much milk to put in the jugs for snack) and trajectory (throwing and catching a ball). Practitioners should be aware that far from 'being bad at maths' they are using mathematical processes all day to support their practice. By being aware of this, they can start to encourage babies' and children's mathematical achievements as well.

 Quick Summary

Learning theories

There are many theories about how babies and children learn, some based on behaviours, some on social context and some on environment. A few of the major theorists are listed here.

Bandura proposed a Social Learning Theory. Bandura showed that children learn by imitating what they see other people doing in their own environment. The actions of others become the model that children will copy.

Vygotsky hypothesised that children's learning is within a social context and the two cannot be separated, and that language (and use of language) is central to cognitive development.

Piaget believed that children 'interiorised' (David *et al.*, 2003) actions, so their cognitive ability was a series of assimilations and accommodations to build up their knowledge and beliefs.

Skinner theorised that children repeated actions that were positively reinforced (e.g. praised or got a reward) and that undesirable behaviour could be ameliorated by punishment.

For much more detailed information and links to the EYFS (as well as to other curricula in the UK), see Featherstone, S. (2016) *An Anthology of Educational Thinkers* London: Featherstone Education.

Reflective Questions

Friedrich Froebel and developmentally appropriate resources

Friedrich Froebel was probably the most influential educationalist of the nineteenth century. He turned common sense upside down by arguing that the most important part of schooling was the *pre-school* period.

Weston, 1998: 1

Froebel presented 'gifts' to children to match their stage of development – something we may call 'developmentally appropriate resources' nowadays. Although his gifts look like mathematical shapes, they were intended to be much more than this. He thought that his first set of gifts (a set of rainbow-coloured soft balls) promoted a sense of self, a self-awareness or unity and difference.

The second set of gifts was a hard ball, a cube and a cylinder. The ball is constantly moving, so has links with movement and the cube doesn't roll, but has lots of mathematical language associated with it (edges, corners, sides, number of faces, etc.). The cylinder looks like a circle from the end and a rectangle from the side, showing how 3D shapes consist of 2D shapes (Weston, 1998).

How could you use these simple 3D shapes to develop children's mathematical language?

Quick Summary

Integration of mathematics

Using mathematical language while doing everyday things around the setting helps young children to both learn a wider range of vocabulary and also to understand the specific, meaningful mathematical terms heard in the correct context (Hutchin, 2012). For example, including 'I wonder how much this jug will hold – what is its capacity?' or the 'symmetry' of a pattern or the 'orientation' of a shape. After all, if they know there is a dinosaur called 'Tyrannosaurus Rex', the 'capacity' of a jug is pretty tame!

Holistic links between areas of learning and development

* *Mathematics and language are closely intertwined*
* *Mathematics and physical development*
* *Mathematics is closely linked to children's cultural and social heritages*
* *Mathematics and mark-making*
* *Mathematics is about repeat patterns.*

Mathematics and language are closely intertwined

Children's mathematical development is grounded in the language that they hear and the language that they use. Many of the indicators of progress refer to talking about mathematics, responding to questions (for example, please could you give me two pencils?) and talking about mathematics (such as counting out cups) during play. Therefore, it is important that children hear mathematical language used confidently and correctly by practitioners, including specific and meaningful words, not just 'big and small' (Hutchin, 2012: 184). For example, even when talking to babies, using language such as 'half-full' or comparative language such as 'tall, taller, tallest' is very useful for embedding the language in their vocabulary. Another example of this is the concept of 'more', because 'more milk' (which could be a whole cup full or one drop) looks different to one more apple (which is a discrete amount). Practitioners can increase children's mathematical language by thoughtful use of their own language. In our example here, instead of asking whether children would like 'more milk', you could ask whether children would like 'more milk to fill the cup' or, for older children, ask 'how much more milk would you like?' As children get older, more mathematically specific words should be introduced and used correctly – for example capacity, volume and sphere. Remember to include the subtraction concepts, as well as addition – for example, fewer, less and counting backwards as well as forwards. Using mathematical language gives children a way to express their ideas and gives confidence in understanding mathematics.

By three years old, children begin to know that a number word will correspond to an exact number, even if they don't know what the quantity is or what it would look like. Interestingly, knowledge about number facts (such as 2 + 2 = 4) is stored not in the spatial awareness part of the brain, but in the language area (Goswami, 2015: 21). Sequencing and the order of numbers is core to mathematical development. This is reflected in sequencing during narrative and story-telling activities. Highlighting sequencing in familiar stories – for example, traditional and fairy tales, gives young children a recognisable way to understand sequencing when it is discussed in mathematical terms. For example, the first goat over the bridge was baby goat, then middle-sized goat and finally big billy goat. If this were any other order, the story would not work. Discussing this with the children helps them to see the importance of sequencing.

Activities

Mathematics is in almost every activity, from balancing blocks to pouring water and crawling through a tunnel. They all need a form of understanding of mathematical concepts, whether that is spatial awareness, capacity or centre of gravity.

The activities are not unusual, but have been specifically linked to other areas of learning and development, to help identify the mathematical element of every activity with babies and young children.

Number

Counting out loud during everyday activities, while indicating objects – for example, counting toes before putting on socks, counting fingers when putting on gloves, counting steps and counting toys. This gives babies the number order; even though they may not know the 'two-ness' of two, they will get used to the number sequence.

As children get older, counting for a purpose is more likely to engage children – for example, asking them to count out the right number of spoons for the group. This helps children work together and have good social interactions.

Counting backwards, such as rockets taking off: 'Five, four, three, two, one . . .'

Noticing and indicating to children where there are numbers in the environment – for example, on the house doors, telephone buttons, clocks and packaging. This can be a good link to under-standing the world, as children may notice the similarities or differences between their own significant numbers.

Space

Everything has a shape and geometry. Spotting shapes in the environment (round window, round bowl, round bangle) helps babies to make connections between the shapes and to make sense of the word *round*.

As toddlers become more proficient in recognising and sorting the same shapes, even if they can't remember the names, start to introduce 3D shapes, such as balls, cubes and pyramids, and notice the shapes in them, such as circle and square. Children will remember these shapes by having 3D shapes to handle, stack, roll and build with.

As children's mathematical knowledge develops, and their drawings and modelling becomes more developed, start to interpret the spatial relations and give children the language to describe the shapes they have drawn or made.

Balance, as a mathematical concept, occurs in the EYFS across both Expressive Arts and Design (balance during construction and block play) and Physical Development (fine motor skills for balancing blocks). This is an interesting area to explore with toddlers and young children and

easily done using everyday resources – for example, using wooden blocks to balance into a giant tower or balancing blocks onto a ball.

Hook a coat hanger onto a peg, so it is clear of the wall. Hook or Velcro toys first to one side and then the other – where is the balance point?

Shape

Although young children will only learn all the names of the most common shapes over time, it is useful to use the names regularly, easily and during play so they become accustomed to them.

Measure

Measure starts with size and then making comparisons with size – for example, a *long* piece of string, a *shorter* piece of ribbon, the *shortest* pencil. As children become more proficient, introduce more specific language, such as *centimetre* and *metre*, *grams* and *kilograms*.

Include words such as *half* or *quarter* into games or during snack time (making sure they are halves and quarters). Even though fractions are a more sophisticated mathematical concept, it is helpful for children to have heard the language first and have some concrete examples that they can refer back to when they encounter fractions.

 Review Your Practice

How often do you use correct mathematical terms with the younger children? (Think of sphere, cube, cylinder.)

How could you stretch and challenge children's mathematical knowledge? (Think of small, but very heavy objects and large, but very light objects to expand their experiences.)

Case Study

The same!

Harri (aged 2 years, 6 months) was staring at his fingers on his left hand, then his right hand. After a moment's thought, he put his two hands together, fingertips touching, left and right corresponding.

'Look! The same!'

How could you extend Harri's mathematical understanding, using this as a starting point? (Think of doubles, twos, matching.)

What other activities could you provide to build on this interest in equivalence?

What language would you use?

Mathematics and physical development

Learning about space and shape requires physical manipulation of objects, especially 3D shapes, which need to be felt and manipulated to be understood. Babies explore visually and then 'through hands, mouth and feet' (Hutchin, 2012: 186), which is the basis for shape, space and measure. Their physical development will underpin their mathematical development as they explore more and different shapes and spaces. Motor skills and mathematical skills have been linked in children as young as two years old, demonstrating that 'children with weak, middle and strong motor life skills also exhibited low, medium or high levels of skills in mathematics' (Reikerås *et al.*, 2017: 72).

Physicality and movement helps children to visualise and embed the learning, so including mathematics in games or physical situations will help them to remember – for example, walking up the stairs 'that's four, let's do one more step – how many is that now?' Similarly, spatial awareness (where things are in space) can be developed by using positional language combined with the physical movement.

Physical games and maths

For babies, shape-sorter toys (where different 3D shapes are inserted through the corresponding hole) are essential items. These toys help babies to identify shapes by their feel, having concrete experiences and demonstrating a correspondence between the 2D 'flat' shape of the hole and the 3D shape. In addition, they are ideal for physical development, especially hand–eye coordination, stretching and fine motor skills.

Block play is particularly good for explanation of shape (Hutchin, 2012), spatial awareness and weight awareness. The combination of lifting, handling and manipulating blocks makes the links between physical shape, size and weight.

Music and movement, especially full body movement, increases spatial awareness and embodiment of mathematical development.

Review Your Practice

Which three outdoor games, with physical movement do the children enjoy best? How could you link those to mathematical development? (Think of numbers in groups, spatial awareness, sequencings, measuring distance, weight.)

If you have trikes in your setting, how could you support mathematical development using them? (Think of shape, size, relative size, weight, length, sorting by colour, type.)

Case Study

Baby Ruby reaches for a toy

Watch the video of Ruby reaching for a toy on YouTube: www.youtube.com/watch?v= 5Q2cL-WteZk

See how she stretches and reaches. This is giving her a sense of perspective and distance.

What physical movement can you see?

What else is she learning?

How often do you allow babies to stretch and reach, rather than just passing them the toy?

Mathematics is closely linked to children's cultural and social heritages

'Children's mathematical graphics is a socio-cultural approach' (Worthington, 2008: 1), which means that the development of mathematics will depend on children's unique and individual experiences, personal interpretation of those experiences and the cultural context in which they occur. By implication this means that being able to give young children rich and enduring mathematical experiences will help to support mathematics. However, the mathematics culture is of some concern in a lot of settings, where practitioners are happy to state they are not confident with maths or don't enjoy it. Often there are fewer observations of mathematics and they tend to be weak, demonstrating a lack of understanding of children's mathematical development. This may impact on children's view of mathematics if they think that culturally it is acceptable to just give up on mathematics. One method to tackle this is approaching mathematics through social interactions, which practitioners tend to be more confident about – for example, using simple mathematics, 'one for you, one for me' (Hutchin, 2012: 184) during play or snack time.

There is a similar argument for young children's early mathematical graphics (the writing that represents mathematical thinking by the children) to be learned through social context in Carruthers and Worthington's (2011: 6) research. This shows that 'above all it is the *social* and *cultural* conditions that teachers and practitioners create that nurture the extent to which children will choose to represent and communicate their personal mathematical meanings'. Consequently, if mathematics and early graphics associated with mathematics are not valued by practitioners, then children will not persevere with their mathematical graphics (which includes sketches, plans, maps and, later on, tables and graphs). Furthermore, Worthington and van Oers' research (2016: 63) shows that 'evidence of mathematics was found within all the children's play' and that 'their cultural knowledge influenced their mathematical thinking by providing coherent contextual and mathematical meanings within their chosen play narratives'.

Finally, mathematics is representational thought, i.e. making one thing stand for another – for example, '4' represents |||| (Geist, 2009: 146), so when children are practising their pretend play, using a block as a telephone, they are laying the foundations for representing quantities using other objects – for example, holding up three fingers to indicate they are three years old.

Activities

- Read babies and young children stories where number is overt ('Goldilocks and the Three Bears'), but also where you can count from the illustrations (How many children went on a bear hunt?).
- Match and sorting games using toys that interest the children.
- Lay a table with a set of cutlery and crockery (note that this may not be a shared experience for some children, so they may need to have this modelled first).

Review Your Practice

Check your setting for links to mathematics – intended or hidden. Make a note of the intended mathematics – for example, cars with numbers on them or numbers on displays. Are these the only types of mathematics in the setting? Compare this with the number of hidden possibilities, for example problem solving, matching toys or socks or shoes, different-sized jugs. Does your setting have a 'mathematical culture' or are the mathematical possibilities hidden from the children?

Case Study

'I'm no good at maths'

A major part of my early consultancy work was working with settings on their observation, assessment and planning cycle. Part of this was to look together at the types and number of observations made, which was often done under each of the areas of learning and development for the EYFS – including Problem Solving, Reasoning and Numeracy (as mathematics was at that time).

Almost always the Problem Solving, Reasoning and Numeracy was the smallest and least creative section in all the observations.

Whenever I would enquire about this (very noticeable) disparity, I would often get told, 'I'm no good at maths' or 'I don't enjoy maths'.

However, when I observed their practice there were often some beautifully creative, stimulating and interesting maths activities, from gluing repeat patterns of beads on a box to shape sorting to measuring out for baking activities. Similarly, the practitioners were doing complex mental arithmetic, spatial awareness and other maths actions (ratios, snack quantities to meet nutritional requirements, how many waterproof sets in what sizes, how to arrange the room to get the best seating for lunch for everyone and how to get all the bikes in the shed neatly) without even thinking about it.

Part of the reason for practitioners saying they are 'no good at maths' is because they haven't been made aware of how good they actually are and how much they use maths every day. It is also partly cultural, because it is culturally acceptable to say that you are no good at maths.

Make a list of all the maths you do as a practitioner during the day. (Think about time/ timings, spatial awareness, weight and measure, money.)

Would it feel different if someone said 'I'm no good at reading'?

Mathematics and mark-making

Practical mathematics gives experiences of concepts, but does not necessarily aid children's understanding of written maths (Worthington, 2008). Interestingly, Worthington (2006: 9) posits that 'most schemas are mathematical', i.e. the patterns of behaviour that are typical of schematic play supports mathematical thinking. Allowing very young children the freedom to make their own marks, rather than copying or reproducing numbers, encourages creativity of thinking and the process of 'playing' with maths, rather than the rote repetition of correct copying. The depth of thinking can be achieved by recording the children's thinking about their mathematical

reasoning: simply copying numbers is very low level and only need minimal – or no – understanding of the maths behind the marks.

The National Strategies (2009: 5) document, *Children Thinking Mathematically*, suggests that 'effective Early Years Pedagogy should value and support children's own mathematical graphics because it helps the written language of mathematics'. Practitioners are quick to praise the first formation of the letters of a child's name, but mathematical marks appear to be less valued or encouraged. However, these are as important as first attempts at letter formations. French (2013: 43) observes that children must 'first recognise that there is a connection between the mark they make and what it stands for', and this can be achieved through many other types of creativity – for example, play dough and paint. Practitioners can support children's mark-making to represent mathematical concepts and then extend the learning through discussions and sustained shared thinking. This should be a regular and common occurrence throughout the day

 Quick Summary

Pedagogy

Pedagogy is the combination of the methods of teaching, the ethos, the interactions between baby or child and practitioner, the learning environment and the curriculum. It is the *way* teaching is conducted, considered as a whole with the content. It could be considered to be the holistic methods by which teaching and learning occur.

for all ages of children, and not a 'special' activity, so that children become used to mathematical writing, just as they would use opportunities to write 'words' elsewhere in the setting. Worthington (2012a: 53) goes on to say that we need to embed a 'sense of ownership' around young children's mathematics and that 'all children can be curious, competent and confident learners of mathematics'.

Activities

When children want to mark make and write for a purpose, remember to include numbers as well – for example, write your name and age on a painting.

Create provocations for writing numbers as well as letters throughout the setting – for example, measuring using a tape measure with large numerals that children can copy down; jugs with clear numbers for filling and emptying.

Review Your Practice

In his seminal review of mathematics teaching in Early Years settings and primary schools (Williams, 2008, or the Williams Review), Sir Peter Williams states that, although emergent writing is a recognised term, there is not an equivalent 'emergent mathematical mark-making', missing a valuable opportunity in the cognitive development of children. He refers to a chart on page 33 which first appeared in Carruthers and Worthington (2006), which is entitled 'Taxonomy: Tracing the development of children's mathematical graphics from birth to 8 years'. This gives a very interesting and detailed explanation of how children learn mathematics, from gesture, movement and speech right through to standard written mathematics, eight years and beyond. It is well worth investigating this taxonomy to understand how children's mathematical development progresses from birth to age eight.

Mathematics is about repeat patterns

Mathematics contains a lot of repeat patterns – for example, times tables. Similarly, music contains rhythm and harmonies, which could be regarded as 'aural patterns' (Trinick *et al.* 2016). Recognising there is a repeat beat or pattern in music can be translated into mathematical knowledge.

Mathematics is also patterns and shapes. One of the first 'patterns' that babies search for is the two dots for eyes and curve for mouth that is representative of a face. It has even been shown that babies when still a foetus prefer this pattern to an inverted triangle pattern of three dots (Reid *et al.*, 2017).

Singing and nursery rhymes reinforce the rhythm and movement of repeat patterns

- Sing songs that have repetitive patterns, such as 'Old MacDonald had a farm', 'Wheels on the Bus'.
- Try rhymes with movement patterns like 'Incy-Wincy Spider' or 'Wind the Bobbin Up'.
- Share stories with patterns:' 'We're Going on a Bear Hunt' or 'Brown Bear, Brown Bear', 'What Do You See?'
- Clapping songs, such as 'Pat-a-cake'.
- Look for patterns outside in nature (petals of a flower), built environment (bricks, flags, steps), clothes and other fabrics such as curtains and wallpaper.

Review Your Practice

How do you encourage or reinforce patterns? Is it just stripes or do you look at repeat patterns such as those on wallpaper and wrapping paper? (Think of all the patterns you see everyday and how you can incorporate those into the children's play.)

Challenges

Dyscalculia

Developmental dyscalculia is when children have difficulties in learning arithmetic facts and performing calculations. It is a specific learning disorder, and is differentiated from global delay or simple lack of exposure to mathematics. It is estimated that around 5 per cent of children have a diagnosis of dyscalculia (as opposed to mathematical learning difficulties, which is around 25 per cent). The types of difficulties that children with dyscalculia may have include:

- counting backwards
- poor estimation ability
- struggling to remember basic facts.

For more information go to: www.bdadyslexia.org.uk/dyslexic/dyscalculia or see Steve Chinn's book, *Maths Learning Difficulties, Dyslexia and Dyscalculia* (2012), published by the British Dyslexia Association.

Foetal alcohol syndrome disorder

As a baby grows in the womb, he or she is affected by the mother's food and drink intake, including alcohol. The brain development, specifically the parietal cortex, can be affected by excessive alcohol, causing foetal alcohol spectrum disorder (FASD) (Goswami, 2015). Children with FASD have a number of cognitive deficits, but mathematical ability seems to be significantly affected, particularly abstract concepts. A new study supports the importance of the left parietal area for mathematical abilities in children with FASD (Lebel *et al.*, 2010). This is becoming a societal problem in the UK, resulting in FASD being raised in a debate in the House Commons in 2014, where it was noted that FASD can cause 'attention deficits; memory deficits; hyperactivity; difficulty with abstract concepts, including maths, time and money; poor problem-solving skills; difficulty learning from consequences; and confused social skills' (Esterson, 2014). Blackburn, Carpenter and Egerton (2009) suggest that children with FASD should be taught maths skills using concrete items, such as real coins.

 Quick Summary

Why incorporate 'neuroscience' into Early Years practice?

Neuroscientists affirm that 'billions of synaptic connections are made within the first five years of life' (Conkbayir, 2017: 22) and that practitioners are part of this process, through planning environments, developmentally appropriate activities and sensory experiences.

The process of incorporating neuroscience into Early Years settings with practitioners may have challenges (including a proliferation of 'neuromyths'), but is worthwhile because it vindicates good practice based on science (causation not correlation) and adds another layer of knowledge to understanding about how young children think, learn and develop.

Opportunities

Practitioners can cue into the mathematical opportunities that babies and children naturally present, from enjoying playing with number words to building blocks and filling jugs. There are also opportunities for practitioners to realise that they can 'do maths' and that it is part of their everyday accomplishments.

Most practitioners are keen to support babies' and young children's language development, and doing this through mathematical learning adds a novel and interesting perspective.

Conclusions

Mathematics is all around, all of the time. It needs to be recognised, understood and appreciated. Babies are demonstrating in all types of research that they have sophisticated mathematical abilities, waiting to be nurtured and extended. Practitioners are doing sophisticated maths during their working day, even if they are unaware of the fact.

There are two parts to mathematical development: first the experiential elements, such as weight, measure and spatial awareness, and second the graphical representations of writing numbers or numerical representations (tallies or pictograms). Babies are constantly experimenting and exploring experiential mathematics, from shape-sorter games to dropping a spoon from the high chair. Young children then start to be aware of how mathematical quantities can be represented, sometimes devising their own unique systems to do this. They also begin to see patterns and associate shapes, essential knowledge for later development. Practitioners may need to teach certain aspects, such as the names of shapes, or number formation, but generally their role will be to encourage and make explicit the mathematical learning that is occurring naturally through play.

Further Reading and Research

In the chapter by Maulfry Worthington, entitled From astronaut to problem solving: Tracing children's symbolic meanings (Worthington, 2011), there are a series of cameos that illustrate how children's 'marks, symbols and other graphical representations can mean or "signify" something' during their symbolic play. This chapter is interesting because it extends beyond the EYFS into Key Stage 1, and even considers the implications for Key Stage 2 written mathematics, demonstrating how important it is to get a firm grounding in mathematics during the Early Years.

In Daniel Tammet's fascinating book: *Thinking in Numbers: On Life, Love, Meaning, and Math* (2012), he explains in chapter 3 how, in Iceland, if asked 'what comes after three' the answer would be 'three what?' because they have different words for 'four' depending on what you are counting. He goes on to describe how, in Chinese, it is even more complicated, with the number used depending on the shape or use of the object.

It is a thought-provoking chapter, which highlights how much is taken for granted when counting and how number is viewed through a cultural lens.

References

Blackburn, C., Carpenter, B. and Egerton, J. (2009) *Students with Foetal Alcohol Spectrum Disorders: Literature Review.* London: National Organisation on Fetal Alcohol Syndrome UK.

Carruthers, E. and Worthington, M. (2006) (2nd edn) *Children's Mathematics: Making Marks, Making Meaning.* London: SAGE.

Carruthers, E. and Worthington, M. (2011) *Understanding Children's Mathematical Graphics: Beginnings in Play.* Maidenhead: Open University Press.

Chinn, S. (2012) *Maths Learning Difficulties, Dyslexia and Dyscalculia.* Bracknell: British Dyslexia Association.

Conkbayir, M. (2017) *Early Childhood and Neuroscience: Theory, Research and Implications for Practice.* London: Bloomsbury.

David, T., Goouch, K., Powell, S. and Abbott, L. (2003) *Birth to Three Matters: A Review of the Literature Compiled to Inform The Framework to Support Children in their Earliest Years.* London: DfES.

Denison, S., Reed, C. and Xu, F. (2013) The emergence of probabilistic reasoning in very young infants: Evidence from 4.5- and 6-month-olds. *Developmental Psychology* Vol. 49 Iss. 2, pp. 243-9.

Denison, S. and Xu, F. (2014) The origins of probabilistic inference in human infants. *Cognition* Vol. 130 Iss. 3, pp. 335-47.

Early Education (2012) *Development Matters in the Early Years Foundation Stage (EYFS)*. London: DfE.

Edwards, L., Ferrara, F. and Moore-Russo, D. (2014) (eds) *Emerging Perspectives on Gesture and Embodiment in Mathematics*. Charlotte, NC: Information Age.

Esterson, B. (2014) House of Commons Debate: Foetal Alcohol Syndrome [Mr Andrew Turner in the Chair]. Available from: www.publications.parliament.uk/pa/cm201415/cmhansrd/cm141014/halltext/141014h0001. htm. Accessed 14 May 2017.

Evangelou, M., Sylva, K., Kyriacou, M., Wild, M. and Glenny, G. (2009) *Early Years Learning and Development. Literature Review*. Oxford: DCSF.

EYFS (2017) *Statutory Framework for the Early Years Foundation Stage Setting the Standards for Learning, Development and Care for Children from Birth to Five*. London: DfE.

French, G. (2013) Early literacy and numeracy matters. *Journal of Early Childhood Studies* Vol. 7.

Geist, E. (2009) *Children are Born Mathematicians: Supporting Mathematical Development, Birth to Age Eight*. Cambridge: Pearson.

Gifford, S. (2004) A new mathematics pedagogy for the early years: In search of principles for practice. *International Journal of Early Years Education* Vol. 12 Iss. 2, pp. 99-115.

Goswami, U. (2015) *Children's Cognitive Development and Learning*. York: Cambridge Primary Review Trust.

Hutchin, V. (2012) *The EYFS: A Practical Guide for Students and Professionals*. Abingdon: Hodder Education.

Izard, V., Sann, C., Spelke, E.S., and Streri, A. (2009) Newborn infants perceive abstract numbers. *Proceedings of the National Academy of Sciences of the United States of America* Vol. 106 Iss. 25, pp. 10382-5.

Lebel, C., Rasmussen, C., Wyper, K. Andrew, G. and Beaulieu, C. (2010) Brain microstructure is related to math ability in children with fetal alcohol spectrum disorder. *Alcoholism: Clinical and Experimental Research* Vol. 34 Iss. 2.

Marmasse, N., Bletsas, A. and Marti, S. (2000) *Numerical Mechanisms and Children's Concept of Numbers*. Cambridge, MA: MIT.

National Strategies (2009) *Children Thinking Mathematically: PSRN Essential Knowledge for Early Years Practitioners*. Nottingham: DCSF.

Ojose, B. (2008) Applying Piaget's Theory of Cognitive Development to mathematics instruction. *The Mathematics Educator* Vol. 18, Iss. 1, pp. 26-30.

Pound, L. (2005) *How Children Learn*. London: Step Forward.

Reid, V., Dunn, K., Young, R.J., Amu, J., Donovan, T. and Reissland, N. (2017) The human fetus preferentially engages with face-like visual stimuli. *Current Biology* Iss. 27, pp. 1825-8.

Reikerås, E., Moser, T. and Tønnessen, F. (2017) Mathematical skills and motor life skills in toddlers: Do differences in mathematical skills reflect differences in motor skills? *European Early Childhood Education Research Journal* Vol. 25 Iss. 1, pp. 72-88.

Siegler, R.S. (2016). Magnitude knowledge: The common core of numerical development. *Developmental Science* Vol. 19, pp. 341-61.

Starr, A., Libertus, M. and Brannon, E. (2013) Number sense in infancy predicts mathematical abilities in childhood. *Social Sciences – Psychological and Cognitive Sciences* Vol. 45 Iss. 110, pp. 18116-20.

Tammet, D. (2012) *Thinking in Numbers: On Life, Love, Meaning, and Math*. London: Hodder and Stoughton.

Trinick, R., Major, K., Ledger, G. and Perger, P. (2016) More than counting beats: Connecting music and mathematics in the primary classroom. *International Journal for Mathematics Teaching and Learning* Vol. 17 Iss. 3.

Wall, S. Litjens, I. and Taguma, M. (2015) *Pedagogy in Early Childhood Education and Care (ECEC): An International Comparative Study of Approaches and Policies*. London: DfE.

Weston, P. (1998) *Friedrich Froebel: His Life, Times and Significance*. London: Roehampton University.

Williams, P. (2008) *Independent Review of Mathematics Teaching in Early Years Settings and Primary Schools. Final Report*. Nottingham: DCSF.

Worthington, M. (2006) Creativity meets maths. *Practical Pre-school* Iss. 66.

Worthington, M. (2008) *Children's Mathematical Graphics Overview*. Available from: www.childrens-mathematics.net/. Accessed 3 November 2016.

Worthington, M. (2011) From astronaut to problem solving: tracing children's symbolic meanings, in J. Moyles., J. Georgeson and J. Payler (eds) *Beginning Teaching, Beginning Learning in Early Years and Primary Education* (4th edn). Maidenhead: Open University, pp. 139-51.

Worthington, M. (2012a) Children becoming expert symbol users, in McAteer, M. (ed.) *Improving Primary Mathematics Teaching and Learning*. Maidenhead: Open University.

Worthington, M. (2012b) *Pretend Play and Mathematics - Informing the 'School Readiness' Debate*. Available from: http://tactyc.org.uk/. Accessed 4 November 2016.

Worthington, M. and van Oers, B. (2016) Pretend play and the cultural foundations of mathematics. *European Early Childhood Education Research Journal* Vol. 24 Iss. 1, pp. 51-66.

7 Cognitive development

Language and thought are developmentally linked - each depends on and also promotes the development of the other.

David *et al.*, 2003: 9

Introduction

Cognitive development is the development of intelligence or of mental abilities, such as thought processes, problem solving, reasoning, knowledge acquisition, memory and perception. By this definition, it is evident that cognitive development is holistic by its nature, drawing on all areas of learning and development to make sense and construct knowledge from these experiences. Cognitive abilities cannot be seen directly, they can only be deduced from children's actions, behaviours or words. Therefore, this chapter considers some particular attributes or dispositions that help these processes and enable babies and young children to construct understanding. Prior to having language to communicate with, cognitive development is much harder to assess. We can only guess at a baby's motivation or thought processes. However, using the correct observational frameworks for the birth to three age group can help to reveal some of cognition that is happening. Therefore, observation of babies using the Characteristics of Effective Learning and the Leuven Scales is considered later on in this chapter.

Cognition

Cognition can be defined, but for our youngest children this is difficult to discern - how can you tell what a baby is actually thinking (even the neuroscience is a 'best guess' at what is happening inside the brain)? Thinking and learning are closely related, especially under the consideration of holistic development. There is a natural progression:

Sense reception (sees a toy) >> thinking (that looks interesting) >> action (reaches for the toy) >> learning (this toy rattles, is cold, is light)

Evidently this does not happen in a vacuum, but is dependent on the experiences to which children are exposed, their perceptions and actions as a result, which leads to the actual learning taking place. This is précised well by David *et al.* (2003: 22):

Quick Summary

Learning theories

There are many theories about how babies and children learn, some based on behaviours, some on social context and some on environment. A few of the major theorists are listed here.

Bandura proposed a Social Learning Theory. Bandura showed that children learn by imitating what they see other people doing in their own environment. The actions of others become the model that children will copy.

Vygotsky hypothesised that children's learning is within a social context, that the two cannot be separated and that language (and use of language) is central to cognitive development.

Piaget believed that children 'interiorised' (David *et al.*, 2003) actions, so their cognitive ability was a series of assimilations and accommodations to build up their knowledge and beliefs.

Skinner theorised that children repeated actions that were positively reinforced (e.g. praised or got a reward) and undesirable behaviour could be ameliorated by punishment.

For much more detailed information and links to the EYFS (as well as to other curricula in the UK), see Featherstone, S. (2016) *An Anthology of Educational Thinkers* London: Featherstone Education.

- Children learn best when they are given appropriate responsibility, allowed to make errors, decisions and choices, and respected as autonomous and competent learners.
- Children learn most effectively when, with the support of a knowledgeable and trusted adult, they are actively involved and interested.
- Children learn best by doing rather than by being told.
- Children are competent learners from birth.

The sensory input (whether this is a smile from a mum or feeling jelly with your feet) may trigger a thought, resulting in an action (or possibly an involuntary reflex). From this sequence, the children learn about the experience, which is why a richness of sensory experiences is so important. A realistic picture of an apple can only give you visual input, which limits the sensory experience and therefore the thinking process, action, learning process. However, taking a bite from a juicy apple provides an number of sensory experiences to think about - taste, smell, physical feel, size, temperature etc., which may result in a number of actions and therefore more learning pathways.

Thinking

It is important to note at this point that babies and children are not vessels to be 'filled' with information, but a better analogy would be 'a fire to be lit', i.e. their early experiences of learning and thought processes should be encouraging and enjoyable. Page, Clare and Nutbrown (2013: 25) note that babies' and young children's 'learning is about self and place and space and relationships' – it is part of being a baby, as Dowling (2014: 78) explains perfectly: 'we do not have to teach babies to think'. Corsaro (1997) noted that developmental psychologists have long stressed the importance of conflict and challenges for creating new cognitive structures and skills (French, 2007).

Neuroscience

There are more and more neuroscience studies, using new techniques such as fMRI scans, electroencephalography (EEG), diffusion tensor imaging (DTI) and tractography (Finnegan, 2016) that are helping to shed light on brain activity in very young children and even babies. This helps us to understand how (or if) the child's brain is affected by experiences, or whether different brain biology is affecting children's development. Although it is incredibly difficult to separate cause and effect, being able to see the brain's activities does give us clues as to the areas that are being affected – for example, whether it is short- or long-term memory.

Hanson *et al.* (2013) conducted a longitudinal study of the effects of poverty on babies and children aged between 5 months and 4 years. The children underwent MRI scanning, completing between 1 and 7 scans over time. By age 36 months, those children from higher socio-economic status (SES) were showing considerably more grey matter (sensory and other information processing areas) in the brain than those children from low SES. This has implications for the nature/nurture debate, as well as wider social debate on the effects of poverty on children's holistic growth and development. This type of research gives physical evidence of differences in growth and development, which could only be guessed at in the past.

Brain activity can be measured using an electroencephalogram (EEG), where sensors are attached to the child's head. These detect any electrical activity in the brain, showing where there are connections being made. Kurth *et al.* (2013) found that during sleep the brains of two-, three- and five-year-olds in their study made 20 per cent more inter-hemispheric connections overnight. They conclude that sleep does alter the brain connectivity in early childhood. This is probably something that you've always 'known', but this advance in neuroscience and actually being able to measure the difference gives much stronger proof of the importance of sleep for very young children.

In their fMRI scans, Gaffrey *et al.* (2013) found that disrupted functioning in an area of the brain called the amygdala when depressed pre-schoolers watched different facial expressions. This would suggest that there is a biomarker that is related to depression, although whether this is causality or consequence is unclear. Analysis of brain systems is increasing our understanding of exactly how early life experiences affect our happiness, our health and our behaviour (Sukel, 2015), thus determining the types of positive experiences that we should be giving children.

The research in neuroscience is constantly developing, and currently confirms some of the good practice that has been developed over the years – for example that during the first five years of a child's life, 'well-being, good nutrition, health and exercise are critical to brain development and learning' (Winter, 2010). Kurth *et al.* (2013: 1456) investigated whether sleep and sleep disturbances affected brain development, by tracking coherent electroencephalogram (EEG) activity in the brains of young children. They concluded that during 'sensitive windows' when there is brain maturation (i.e. skills development in the brain), children may be 'particularly vulnerable to sleep disturbances'. This information could only be guessed at before having it confirmed by monitoring the brain's activity.

The exponential growth of neuroscience research and increasingly more sophisticated methods for 'seeing' what is happening in babies' and young children's brains means that we are able to make links between learning and experiences with much greater confidence. For example, when an experience 'lights up' the area of the brain associated with language, we can quite confidently predict that this experience is good for language development. This is especially relevant when working with babies and very young children because they have limited ways of demonstrating their growing knowledge. Neuroscience may help to pinpoint the critical or sensitive periods for learning, and also the critical periods of vulnerability, when children may need extra care and attention, so early intervention may be most effective.

Quick Summary

Why incorporate 'neuroscience' into Early Years practice?

Neuroscientists affirm that 'billions of synaptic connections are made within the first five years of life' (Conkbayir, 2017: 22) and that practitioners are part of this process, through planning environments, developmentally appropriate activities and sensory experiences.

The process of incorporating neuroscience into Early Years settings with practitioners may have challenges (including a proliferation of 'neuromyths'), but is worthwhile because it vindicates good practice based on science (causation not correlation) and adds another layer of knowledge to our understanding of how young children think, learn and develop.

There are many aspects of brain development that are being investigated, but there is still much uncertainty about how unique experiences affect the brain, and thus the learning and development, of unique children. For example, Goswami (2015: 22) explains how neuroconstructivism, a theoretical framework for cognitive development, draws together the biological action of genes and how 'genetic activity is modified by neural, behavioural and external environmental events' to effect cognitive development. For example, the sounds we hear are restricted by the ability of the human ear to hear within certain frequencies. Therefore, we must rely on close and accurate observations of children to surmise how their experiences are affecting their learning and development. However, it is very sensible to frequently review and reflect on new research to inform your practice.

'Critical' and sensitive periods

There is research, as well as a rich history of theorists, who believe that there is a critical period for certain types of development. This can be defined as the optimal combination of physical and cognitive conditions that lend themselves to children learning with ease.

Montessori (2009) detailed 'sensitive periods' when children are particularly engaged or open to learning in one area. For example, according to Montessori, children have a sensitive period for movement from birth to four years old, so they learn about their environment through movement while gross and fine motor skills and coordination are being developed. However, children's sensitive period for order, where they learn about routines, the order in their physical environment and the world about them, starts when they are about 18 months old.

Imprinting is a phenomenon that Lorenz (2011) studied in birds, particularly ducks and geese. This is a behavioural response that results in the bird coming to recognise the first thing with which it interacts as its 'parent'. Obviously in nature this is almost always one of the bird's actual parents, but Lorenz separated a batch of eggs into two lots. The mother goose hatched one half, while the male cared for the other half. Most importantly, the male was the first thing that they saw and interacted with – he became their 'parent'. Lorenz analysed the bird's responses to visual and auditory stimuli as soon as the birds hatched. He found that there was a critical time, 12–17 hours, during which time there was the strongest response to imprinting, whereas after 32 hours there was little or no imprinting.

Although babies don't imprint onto their parents in the same ways as birds do, imprinting does demonstrate that there are some biological factors associated with critical or sensitive periods of development. The 1,001 critical days cross-party manifesto aims to 'highlight the importance of intervening early in the 1001 critical days between conception to age 2 to enhance the outcomes for children' (Best Beginnings, 2016). Among those who are backing the campaign are midwives, children's charities, the NSPCC, the Parent–Infant Partnership, health visitors, psychiatrists, psychotherapists and Members of Parliament, illustrating its holistic nature. The goal is for 'every baby to receive sensitive and responsive care from their main caregivers in the first years of life' (Leadsom *et al.*, 2013). The holistic approach is emphasised during the first 1,001 days, so that conception, antenatal and postnatal services all work together to provide parents with support and access to their services. This is based on evidence that shows that by the 1,001st day a child's brain is 80 per cent of its adult weight, and thus the critical importance of providing the 'optimum development and nurturing during this peak period of growth' (Leadsom *et al.*, 2013: 5). It has been clearly demonstrated that experience will shape a baby's mental, emotional and physical health. As just one example, a baby's exposure to 'corrosive' cortisol before birth and during the first few months of life can negatively affect his or her response to stress (Gerhardt, 2004).

Balbernie (2011) calls these 'windows of opportunity' and discusses how these change as babies grow:

- For the first six months, the first critical window is 'vision, vocabulary and emotional development'.
- From six to twelve months, speech and emotional development (especially governing emotions) are critical.
- Twelve to eighteen months is critical for most of the 'windows', laying down neural pathways for a 'lifetime of skill and potential'.

- Eighteen to twenty-four months has a critical window for motor skills, empathy and sharing, and maths starts to be more apparent.
- Up to age three, 'much of a child's brain growth and density is complete'. Vocabulary building is important.

Note that the corollary of this should be that if the critical period is missed, then there may be lasting and detrimental effects and that children may never learn that particular skill. However, more and more research is showing that the plasticity of the brain is much more sophisticated than originally thought, and that children are able to learn even in circumstances that could be considered less than ideal. Therefore, although there may be periods in a child's life that are the preferred time to learn, the presentation of other opportunities may ameliorate the effects of missing these times (Bruer, 2010).

Developmentally appropriate practice

It is vital that practitioners are aware of the importance of early development and how this lays a foundation for all other development, as suggested by many theorists and shown by many researchers. Developmentally appropriate practice means that practitioners are cognisant of babies' and young children's current level of development, how to support and nurture this, while also using opportunities to stretch and challenge babies and young children.

Blaustein (2005: 2) explains how one programme, which attempts to improve reading competency for three-year-olds and older, 'ignores the fact that developmentally children are ready to read at different ages' and that formal instructional methods used later on in schools is not effective. To be prepared for later years, and particularly statutory schooling, children 'need time to refine physical movements, learn how the emotional and social world works, and develop practical hands-on knowledge' (Blaustein 2005: 4).

Children's early cognitive experiences should be built on appropriate activities that integrate social, emotional, physical and cognitive experiences through:

- Interactions that are sustained, meaningful, social and multiple
- Imaginative worlds with both real and abstract concepts, in all areas of the curriculum
- Integration of play experiences, learning experiences, sensory experiences, physical actions and social experiences.

adapted from Blaustein, 2005: 8

In particular, the first 1,001 days are critical, punctuated with sensitive periods within them. Therefore, children under the age of three must be seen as constantly learning, even if they are unable to tell you. Hopefully you won't encounter anyone who thinks that 'babies don't do anything'!

Myths of cognitive development

There is always the risk that any new science is misused, either deliberately or by people being over-ambitious about generalising results. For example, the 'Mozart effect' was a phenomenon first published in 1993 in the journal *Science* by Rauscher, Shaw and Ky. The claim was that students who listened to Mozart's music performed better in reasoning tests than those who listened

to something else or those who had listened to nothing. Note that this was with adults, in spatial reasoning only and the effect seemed to last only 10-15 minutes. There was no research on the Mozart effect on babies and there was no suggestion that this may ever have been the case. Nonetheless, an enterprising company – later bought out by the Walt Disney Company – produced a range of products based on the research, claiming to turn your baby into a 'baby Einstein' using the Mozart effect. This claim was challenged in court, and Disney had to refund or replace the merchandise (Lewin, 2009). Note, however that by this stage there was an annual $200 million market for the products, which is testament to their popularity and the willingness of the buying public to believe the 'research'.

Occasionally there are still some practitioners who believe that cognitive development – for example, the purposeful learning of knowledge and understanding thinking processes – only starts when children start school at around five or six years of age. Although there is a greater emphasis on 'academic' subjects at school, such as joined-up handwriting and arithmetic, babies and young children are developing cognitively from birth. The challenge is to demonstrate to practitioners that babies are developing cognitively and this has to be supported, as with any other area of learning and development.

John Bruer, author of the book *The Myth of the First Three Years*, challenged three main myths in 2011:

1   It is only in early childhood (up to the age of three) where there are periods of rapid developmental synaptogenesis (creating of synapses) followed by synaptic pruning (reducing synapses) at puberty. However, it is known that synaptogenesis in some parts of the brain goes on well into puberty (for example, synaptic elimination is completed by 12 years of age, but continued in the frontal cortex until mid-adolescence).

2   There are critical (or sensitive) periods in development up to the age of three, where normal experience is required for normal development and outside of these the 'windows of opportunity' for development are firmly closed. However, it is known that the brain is much more

plastic and adaptable than that, and that 'critical' learning occurs well beyond three-years old. This can be showed by cultural difference in childcare. In Western cultures, 'motherese' is spoken to children, in other cultures it is not, and yet children still develop language satisfactorily.

3   Rearing animals in complex environments has demonstrable effects on brain structure, but this research was with rats (can this be generalised to babies?) and compared a completely bare environment (an empty box) to an enriched environment. Also, the effects were over the whole lifetime of the rat, not just its early years.

adapted from Bruer, 2011

However, any new research is an exciting opportunity to expand knowledge, to reflect on practice and to analyse reasons for doing things. It is also a good opportunity to think critically and read around the subject to ensure that the research has not been misrepresented.

Observing babies

Characteristics of Effective Learning

Using the Characteristics of Effective Learning (CoEL) gives a truly holistic perspective of babies' and children's development. For some of the descriptors for the birth to 20 months age ranges in *Development Matters* (the guidance document that can be used alongside the Early Years Foundation Stage (EYFS)), there is only reference to the CoEL. For example, Understanding the World: Technology, the guidance given is:

The beginnings of understanding technology lie in babies exploring and making sense of objects and how they behave. See Characteristics of Effective Learning – Playing and Exploring and Creating and Thinking Critically.

Early Education, 2012: 41

Quick Summary

Characteristics of Effective Learning (CoEL)

The Characteristics of Effective Learning are divided into three broad areas:

Playing and exploring: engagement (skill)

- Finding out and exploring
- Playing with what they know
- Being willing to 'have a go'.

Active learning: motivation (will)

- Being involved and concentrating
- Keeping trying
- Enjoying achieving what they set out to do.

Creating and thinking critically: thinking (thrill)

- Having their own ideas
- Making links
- Choosing ways to do things.

Although these areas are not strictly hierarchical, there is a certain logic to them working from 1 through to 3, i.e. it is unlikely that a child will be curious and have creative thinking if they are unwilling to get involved with play or exploration.

Early Education, 2012: 5

Note that these are sometimes referred to as the Characteristics of Effective Teaching and Learning, CoETL, to reflect that a part of practitioners' role is to teach children as well as to enable learning. Moylett (2013: 1) refers to this as 'being a partner with children', enjoying with them the power of their curiosity and the 'skill, will and thrill' of finding out what they can do.

The CoEL move through all areas of learning, and are not bound by individual areas of learning and development. In fact, on almost every page of *Development Matters*, there is a reminder that 'Playing and Exploring, Active Learning, and Creating and Thinking Critically support children's learning across all areas' (Early Education, 2012). Therefore, using the CoEL descriptors as an observation tool for babies is more meaningful than trying to observe 'literacy' or early mark-making.

Leuven Scales of well-being and involvement

Another pair of useful observation frameworks is the Leuven Scales. These should be used as a tool when you want to investigate an aspect of a child's learning and development, but they are not to be used all the time because they lose their efficacy (Allingham, 2017). They can be used if practitioners notice a difference in well-being or involvement from the children, to help to identify and quantify this. In this respect they form part of the ongoing, formative assessment of children, used to support their holistic learning and development.

There are two sets of scales that go from 1 to 5, where number 1 is the lowest evaluation and number 5 is the highest. The first set of scales is the well-being scales and the second set is the involvement scales.

For example, on the well-being scales, extremely low well-being (Level 1) is characterised by:

> The child clearly shows signs of discomfort such as crying or screaming. They may look dejected, sad, frightened or angry. The child does not respond to the environment, avoids contact and is withdrawn. The child may behave aggressively, hurting him/herself or others.

Whereas an extremely high well-being (Level 5) is characterised by:

> The child looks happy and cheerful, smiles, cries out with pleasure. They may be lively and full of energy. Actions can be spontaneous and expressive. The child may talk to him/herself, play with sounds, hum, sing. The child appears relaxed and does not show any signs of stress or tension. He/she is open and accessible to the environment. The child expresses self-confidence and self-assurance.

Allingham (2017) recommends always using the well-being scales first, because levels of involvement are likely to rest on the well-being of the children. If children are anxious or frightened (as reflected on the well-being scales), then it is extremely unlikely that they will be highly involved in activities or have high levels of engagement. However, settings have to be mindful of both scales, as they are complementary. Both scales can be used with babies and young children, as well as older children. As Laevers (2015: 2) describes, 'the baby in the cradle playing with his or her voice' is showing high levels of involvement.

Further Reading and Research

Leuven Scales

The full information about the Leuven Scales can be found here: Laevers, F. (1994) *The Leuven Involvement Scale for Young Children.* Manual and video. Experiential Education Series, No 1. Leuven: Centre for Experiential Education.

It is strongly advised that practitioners attend training on using the Leuven Scales, so they are used to their best effect. An Internet search will give trainers who are able to do this.

Observing babies

Understanding and being able to apply child development knowledge is important whenever observing children of any age. However, with babies this becomes vital, because babies communicate through the subtlest of movements, eye gaze and a range of vocalisations, prior to being able to talk. This means that practitioners have to interpret all these signals in order to assess development and progress.

Examples include:

- Holding proto-conversations, where the adult and the baby take it in turns to 'say' something (vocalising or making sounds), indicates that the baby is beginning to understand the basics of a language exchange.
- Getting excited when they hear a sound that they recognise, such as the doorbell, suggesting that the baby knows that a parent is about to arrive.
- Being fascinated by their own toes and fingers, grasping their toes and getting excited when bells are strapped to their wrists, all suggest that the baby is beginning to understand they are a separate, physical person who can move independently and at will.
- Gurgling and 'chatting' to themselves in the cot or during quiet times suggests high levels of well-being and contentment.

Under research conditions, there are a number of techniques used to try to identify what the baby may be thinking. For example:

- Looking/time measure. A baby is shown an activity again and again. Then the researcher changes it. What does the baby look at? What catches their attention?
- Anticipatory looking measures. A baby is shown something happening (for example, a ball rolling). Where does he or she look? What does the baby anticipate is going to happen?
- Neuroscience and brain imaging. A baby has a cap with electrodes fitted and the brain is scanned to see which parts of the brain 'light up' when the baby sees an action or hears language. By knowing which areas of the brain correspond to which areas of knowledge (for example, language), researchers can predict how babies make sense of the world around them.

 Quick Summary

Stages of language development

- Birth to six months: Babies will turn towards sounds, watch faces and start to make a range of noises.
- Six to 12 months: Babies will babble and hold proto-conversations.
- 12 to 18 months: Understand words, simple instructions, gesture and use a few words themselves.
- 18 to 24 months: Children will understand 200 words or more and be using 50 or more words of their own.
- Two to three years: Use around 300 words and create sentences.

Different cognitive development is valued in different cultures

Cognitive development is 'encultured' (Evangelou *et al.*, 2009: 81), with babies and young children learning what is valued cognitively and their own social norms within the environments and culture in which they find themselves, whether that is an Early Years setting, or home or with their extended family. It would be impossible to separate cognition from culture because they affect each other so much. This includes how (or if) emotions are displayed, the form of language used and types of acceptable behaviours. For example, Nisbett *et al.* (2001: 291) found 'East Asians to be holistic . . . whereas Westerners are more analytic'. Later research from Koopmann-Holm and Tsai (2014) has found that, when expressing sympathy that there are cultural differences between Germans and Americans, with the Americans focusing on the negative emotional states less than their German counterparts.

An example in the UK culture is map reading. As satellite navigation (satnav) and maps on smart phones become more and more prevalent, it is unlikely that children will ever have to refer to a paper map or A to Z maps. Being able to read a map will go from being an essential cognitive ability to being obsolete (unless you want to play pirates with the children and you need a treasure map!).

Reflective Questions

Cultural considerations

Consider your own culture (and this can be within your own family group) and how you may value different types of knowledge or cognition. For example, is it important in your social group to read books? Or follow the story lines of the same TV programmes?

What type of cultural 'norms' do you teach the children? (Think of manners, how you address adults, especially new adults, answer the phone, wave hello or goodbye.)

Holistic links in this chapter

* *Self-regulation and metacognition*
* *Executive functioning*
* *Physical development and cognition*
* *Active and observational experiences.*

Self-regulation and metacognition

In Moylett's book (2013) it is stated that 'metacognitive and self-regulatory abilities are the single most powerful determinants of children's academic success' (Whitebread 2013: 26), based on longitudinal studies, cognitive studies and meta-analyses of educational interventions. Self-regulation can be described as a child's ability to adjust their emotional state and behaviour in a socially acceptable manner. This will start at around one year old, when young children are learning about appropriate social interactions, and by around two years old children can self-control (so they don't have to keep being reminded about the 'rules'). By around three years old, children will be able to self-regulate holistically across sensory (i.e. able to control their sensory reactions appropriately to the environment), emotional, social and cognitive areas of development. Dowling (in Brodie, 2017: 5) explains not having self-regulation as being 'hostage to our impulses and emotions, it makes it much more difficult for us to persevere and concentrate on things'. These are skills that need to be learned and practised, just as other skills. Generally, babies and young children will have very immediate emotions, and it will be obvious as to whether they are happy or sad. By the time children are able to control their emotions and have better understanding of social interactions, they will start to understand the benefits of self-regulation and may hold back the emotions when upset (Lindon and Brodie, 2016: 104). When it is considered how many and how wide a range of different sensory inputs babies and children are receiving, and for the first time, to be able to analyse, evaluate and then self-regulate all of these will take time, practice and support. It is self-evident as to why Evangelou *et al.* (2009: 5), call this 'the development of effortful control'. It has been found that children who are still learning to self-regulate anxiety tend not to engage with more challenging activities, but children who can self-regulate can 'relax and focus on learning cognitive skills' (Florez, 2011: 47). This would seem to reflect adult experiences. If an adult feels in control, not prone to anxiety and able to 'cope', then he or she is more likely to be able to study or work more effectively.

Metacognition

Metacognition is thinking about our own thinking processes and how we problem solve, make decisions, choose - anything to do with thinking. For example, if you had to add 15 and 39 in your head, how would you do this? Just take a minute to think of your method.

Here are three different methods for doing this simple sum:

Some people may add the 5 and 9, carry the ten, add the 1 and 3 and carry one, making a total of 54.

For other people that method doesn't make any sense. They may say 39 is 2 lots of 15, plus a 9 so we have 3 lots of 15 = 45 plus a 9, equals 54.

Then again, you may 'borrow' one from the 15, making that 14, to add to the 39, making that 40. Now you have 40 + 14 = 54.

Which method did you use?

The thinking of the method (rather than the maths) is an example of simple metacognition. Young children do not have the language or thought processes to explain *how* they came to a solution or decision, so we have to make informed guesses, from observations, as to how they came to their own solution. However, it is good practice to start to model metacognition for children, especially as they reach the age of three years old, because it has been shown to be an important component of cognitive development, although it could be 'a consequence, not a cause of competent cognitive behaviour' (Bjorklund and Causey, 2017: 282).

Self-regulation activities

These activities all have an element of young children having to think consciously about their actions. They also have a significant physical development link, because up to the age of three, many activities are still very physical, full body activities.

Examples of games to play:

- Simon Says (all follow the instructions 'Simon Says . . .', but if the instruction is NOT preceded by 'Simon Says . . .' the children don't do the action).
- Musical chairs, musical bumps, musical statutes (when the music stops, the children must find a chair, sit down or stand very still, respectively).
- Games where children have to wait – for example, races where they have to wait for the Go in 'Ready, Steady . . . Go!' or 'What's the time, Mr Wolf', where they have to stand still when the 'wolf' turns round (this also has good mathematical links).

Metacognition activities

Practitioners should give children choices and allow them to think through the options. Modelling this first for children can be helpful – for example, 'I think I'll have an apple today, because it looks juicy'.

Co-construct strategies – for example, doing jigsaw puzzles in a certain order or making gloop (cornflour and water) by adding the water a bit at a time, and discussing these with the children, will help them think through the strategy.

Encourage children to think about how they make connections. This is particularly if they have schematic play, so you can encourage them to find the connection between their fascination with a spinning bike wheel and the spinning washing machine, for example.

 Review Your Practice

How often are the toddlers asked to wait for something? Consider each individual child's reaction. Do some of your three-year-olds still find this a challenge?

Reflect on *when* certain children are unable to self-regulate their emotions. Is this in certain social situations? Or maybe there was a lot of sensory stimulation, such as being noisy? Targeted activities can be designed by identifying a specific area of need.

Case Study

Dr Allan Schore

Watch the YouTube video by Dr Allan Schore about self-regulation and the processing of emotions in the first few years of a young child's life: www.youtube.com/watch?v=cbfuBex-3jE

What does he believe the care-giver's role is?

How does he explain the critical nature of self-regulation?

On a more general, philosophical level, watch Dr Sara Goering talk at TEDxOverlake about Philosophy for Kids: Sparking a Love of Learning. She explains how children are natural philosophers and how they ask the hard questions ('Who made God?'). Dr Goering explains really well how to start children thinking about their own thoughts, beliefs and understanding, to enhance their cognitive skills, creative thinking and behavioural skills, such as listening and appreciating each other's views: www.youtube.com/watch?v=7DLzXAjscXk

Executive functioning

Executive functioning is how the brain organises, and then acts, on information that it receives. Some of the key skills for executive functioning are working memory, control (both impulse and emotional), organisation and mental flexibility. Babies and young children must practise coordinating these skills and using them in different circumstances. They need to be able to pay attention, listen and get deeply involved, sometimes described as being in a 'state of flow', to achieve deep level learning (Laevers, 2015).

Each type of executive function skill draws on elements of the others.

*   Working memory governs our ability to retain and manipulate distinct pieces of information over short periods of time.
*   Mental flexibility helps us to sustain or shift attention in response to different demands or to apply different rules in different settings.
*   Self-control enables us to set priorities and resist impulsive actions or responses.

Centre on the Developing Child, 2017

Activities to support executive function

Babies and toddlers

Playing peek-a-boo, where you hide behind your hands and then 'peek' out, saying 'Boo'. This supports working memory as babies have to hold in mind who is hiding, especially if there is a delay before 'Boo'.

For toddlers, 'Kim's game' expands the working memory. On a tray, under a cloth, have a few items. These can be small toys such as cars or bricks or any item that the children have an interest in. Let the children look at the items first and then cover the tray with a cloth. Remove an item, unseen, and take off the cloth. What has been removed? The number of items can be increased as the children become more proficient.

Taking turns doing an activity and copying each other – for example, lining the train carriages up in the same order. The children will have to use their working memory to get the order right, and will also need to concentrate and maintain attention for longer periods.

Toddlers and older children

Copying and following simple imitations are still important, but games can be more active, such as 'Simon Says . . .', where the practitioner tells the children what to do by starting with 'Simon Says . . . hop' or 'Simon Says . . . sit down'. If the practitioner doesn't say 'Simon Says . . .' first, then the children must not do it. This means children have to listen, remember what is being said, pay attention and concentrate, using a huge range of executive function skills. At the beginning it is unlikely that the children will get it right all the time, but practice and repetition will help.

Sorting games require memory and selective attention. These can be easily incorporated into every session through activities such as tidy-up time (only put the red Lego in the box. Now just the blue Lego. Now the double blocks) or putting out the paintbrushes (all the big ones this end, then medium, then small). For older children, the games can be extended to be a combination of characteristics (only the blue double blocks, then the red single blocks).

Review Your Practice

When children are really involved in a game or activity (in a state of 'flow'; Csikszentmihalyi, 2002), it is very tempting to go over and join in or ask questions. However, it is sometimes much better to stand back and observe.

Think how often you allow the children to play without interruption.

For more inspiration, read Prof. Julie Fisher's book, *Interacting or Interfering? Improving Interactions in The Early Years.*

Case Study

Dingle dangle scarecrow

When one of my sons and I used to go to a stay and play session, his favourite song was 'Dingle Dangle Scarecrow with the Flippy, Floppy Hat'.

In this song, you have to start curled up on the floor (When all the cows were sleeping . . .) and at the correct moment in the song, pop up to be a scarecrow.

When we started at the sessions this was really difficult for my young son as he just wanted to be the Dingle dangle scarecrow immediately.

However, as the weeks went on and he became more used to the song and the actions, he became an expert at jumping up at just the right moment.

In this song, he really had to stop himself, concentrate, listen and then coordinate his movements. He would look to me initially to take the lead, but then you could see him start to do this for himself.

What other types of action songs do you do with the children where they have to use their executive functioning skills in this way?

Are there games you could create which would improve these skills?

Physical development and cognition

Children learn with their whole bodies and even more so when the activities are child-led, play-based and developmentally appropriate. Providing 'visual aids to support learning and providing an environment with age-appropriate furniture and equipment' (Callanan *et al.*, 2017: 9) is important to ensure that the physical needs of the children are met. Encouraging full body movement, as well as the full range of fine and gross motor skills, helps young children to have deep-level learning through their experiences.

Activities for cognition

Getting both sides of the brain to work together is an important physiological development and is essential for further learning. Good activities for this include:

- Crawling – the brain is having to use both sides in unison as the baby uses left, right, left, right arms and legs
- Obstacle courses, which are good for hard work for muscles and using the body in coordination
- Stabilising toys, e.g. holding a tower with one hand and building with the other
- Threading, holding the card with one hand and threading with the other
- Floor work of all sorts
- Visual AND auditory instructions.

Learn gross motor skills through different methods:

- Chalk board so muscles get feedback
- Different media, such as paint
- Water on a wall, especially a rough wall, which gives resistance.

Stereognosis, or knowing the feeling due to sensory feedback of something that you are touching, is an important skill for babies to master for example, knowing the difference between a piece of Lego and play dough through touch alone, without looking. Babies need things that give sensory feedback, such as bells on their wrists, ankles and hands so they know where their limbs are.

Review Your Practice

Reflect on the types of experiences that you provide for the babies and young children. Are they all of the same type? (For example, play dough, gloop, paint, or do you have a full range that will exercise the whole body?) How will these support learning? (Think of the processes or experiences the children are having rather than the product.)

Active and observational experiences

Cognitive development relies on babies' and young children's working memory, so that they can remember actions that they observe others doing and then convert these into 'cause and effect' theories. For example, if a practitioner reaches forward to pick up a baby laying on a changing table, the baby will start to associate this action with being picked up and will lie still in expectation. As the baby gets older, he or she may hold up his or her hands, ready to be picked up, having remembered this action. Thus there is an understanding about being picked up, from watching the practitioner's behaviour to 'understanding others' minds' (Hunnius and Bekkering, 2014). Repeated experiences will embed actions into the memory more firmly. Similarly, as children's cognitive development increases and they begin to gain increasing control, they will start to use short cuts to quickly get to solutions, sometimes referred to as 'strategies', which can be defined as 'deliberate, goal-directed mental operations aimed at solving a problem' (Bjorklund and Causey, 2017: 20).

Activities

Repetition and regular routines help young children to remember what is coming next and what is expected of them. Although there may be variations sometimes, it is very useful to have a visual timetable.

Quick Summary

Top three thoughts on good practice

1   Consider all the senses during sensory play. Do you always include a sense of smell? Do you present prickly or scratchy items?

2 Visual timelines support all children. How do children know what will be happening next? How can they judge how long until home time?

3 Regularly review your environment from the children's perspective. Is it cluttered? How would a child with a hearing or visual impairment experience the environment?

Review Your Practice

Reflect on the types of experiences that you provide for the babies and young children. Are they all of the same type? (For example, play dough, gloop, paint, or do you have a full range that will exercise the whole body?) When you alter the baby room, do you allow time for the babies to explore, survey and assimilate these changes? (Think how you would feel if your favourite room was redecorated in your absence.)

When there are going to be changes in the room layout or changes in routines, do you discuss this with the children first?

How can you include them in any changes?

How often do you repeat or return to the same home corner (for example) so children can repeat their experiences and embed learning? How will these support learning? (Think of the processes or experiences the children are having rather than the product.)

Challenges

Poverty is still a factor in cognitive development. The Field Review in 2010 found that:

> Poorer children systematically do worse on both cognitive and behavioural outcomes at both age three and age five. By age five, children from better off families who had low cognitive ability at age two have almost caught up with high ability children from poorer families. This means that poorer children tend to be less ready for school and less ready to take advantage of the resources invested in the universal education system.
>
> Field, 2010: 38

Similarly, Hobcraft and Kiernan (2010: 25) found that at aged five 'one in five of the children in persistently poor households is exhibiting what could be regarded as cognitive delay'. More recently Marmot (2016: 123) stated that, while recognising that poverty is relative depending on the context, 'reduce poverty and you reduce inequalities in early child development. Poverty is important'. Obviously this is much easier said than done; however, Marmot, with an optimist perspective, goes on to say 'poverty is not destiny' (2016: 124) and that some local authorities were successfully alleviating the negative effects of poverty on child development.

Opportunities

It was generally considered for a long time that 'intelligence' was both fixed and could be measured on a simple scale. However, more and more research in different disciplines is showing that cognitive abilities can, and do, change over time, that 'human intelligence can be substantially modified under certain circumstances' (Bjorklund and Causey, 2017: 20). This gives practitioners exciting opportunities to lay the foundations for young children's cognitive abilities and growth.

Conclusions

Babies' and young children's cognitive abilities depend on concrete experiences, repeated and novel experiences and the support of parents, practitioners and other adults. Goswami (2015: 25) gives the example of a concept in science needing 'neurons being simultaneously active in visual, spatial, memory, deductive and kinaesthetic regions, in both brain hemispheres'. As children start building cognitive abilities it is important to ensure that activities are developmentally appropriate. Reading and re-reading the same book again and again may not be fun for the practitioner, but the repetition is important for young children. Integration of learning and helping children to make links between learning supports young children's metacognition skills – for example, noticing with the children that the icy puddle outside is the same ice as the ice cubes in the water tray.

Further Reading and Research

Sam Wass has published a very interesting journal article, examining a range of studies from both typical and atypically developing children. Wass (2015: 160) suggests that 'individual differences in attentional control and working memory may play a role in mediating later-emerging differences in learning in academic and other settings'. Furthermore, there may be some interventions that can be effective, even if they are only a few hours, for babies and young children.

If you want to know more about working memory and training atypical development, see: Wass, S. (2015) Applying cognitive training to target executive functions during early development. *Child Neuropsychology* Vol 21 Iss.2, pp. 150–66.

An interesting journal article on sleep and how this affects higher-order cognition: Bernier, A., Beauchamp, M., Bouvette-Turcot, A., Carlson, S. and Carrier, J. (2013) Sleep and cognition in preschool years: Specific links to executive functioning. *Child Development* Vol. 84 Iss. 5, pp. 1542–53.

Goldhaber, D. (2012) *The Nature-Nurture Debates: Bridging the Gap.* New York: Cambridge University Press.

Hear some of the experiments that Alison Gopnik has done with babies and young children: 'Babies and young children are like the R&D division of the human species'. Her research explores the sophisticated intelligence-gathering and decision making that babies are really doing when they play: www.ted.com/talks/alison_gopnik_what_do_babies_think

References

Allingham, S. (2017) Using the Leuven Scales to improve our practice, in Brodie, K. (ed.) *Early Years Summit: Personal, Social and Emotional Well-being in Young Children*. Wilmslow: Rainmaker Academy.

Anderson Moore, K., Bethell, C., Murphey, D., Carver Martin, M., Beltz, M. (2017) *Flourishing From the Start: What Is It and How Can It Be Measured?* Child Trends. Available from: www.childtrends.org. Accessed 28 March 2017.

Archer, C. and Siraj, I. (2015) Measuring the quality of movement-play in Early Childhood Education settings: Linking movement-play and neuroscience. *European Early Childhood Education Research Journal* Vol. 23 Iss. 1, pp. 21-42.

Balbernie, R. (2011) *The Consequences of Early Relationships: A View from Interpersonal Neurobiology*. UNICEF UK Baby Friendly Initiative.

Best Beginnings (2016) *The 1,001 Critical Days*. Available from: www.1001criticaldays.co.uk. Accessed 11 June 2016.

Bjorklund, D. and Causey, K. (2017) (6th edn) *Children's Thinking: Cognitive Development and Individual Differences*. London: SAGE.

Blaustein, M. (2005) See Hear Touch: The basics of learning readiness. *Beyond the Journal: Young Children on the Web*. Available from: www.naeyc.org/files/yc/file/200507/01Blaustein.pdf. Accessed 8 June 2017.

Brodie, K. (2017) *Personal, Social and Emotional Well-being in Young Children*. Wilmslow: Rainmaker Academy.

Bruce, T. (2004) *Cultivating Creativity in Babies, Toddlers and Young Children*. Abingdon: Hodder Education.

Bruer, J. (2010) *The Myth of the First Three Years*. New York: The Free Press.

Bruer, J. (2011) *Revisiting 'The Myth of the First Three Years'*. Centre for Parenting Studies.

Callanan, M., Anderson, M., Haywood, S., Hudson, R. and Speight, S. (2017) *Study of Early Education and Development: Good Practice in Early Education*. Research report London: DfE. Available from: www.gov.uk/government/publications

Centre on the Developing Child (2017) *Executive Function & Self-Regulation*. Available from: http://developingchild.harvard.edu/science/key-concepts/executive-function/. Accessed 31 May 2017.

Conkbayir, M. (2017) *Early Childhood and Neuroscience: Theory, Research and Implications for Practice*. London: Bloomsbury.

Corsaro, W. (1997) *The Sociology of Childhood*. Thousand Oaks, CA: Pine Forge.

Csikszentmihalyi, M. (2002) *Flow: The Psychology of Happiness: The Classic Work on How to Achieve Happiness*. London: Rider.

David, T., Goouch, K., Powell, S. and Abbott, L. (2003) *Birth to Three Matters: A Review of the Literature Compiled to Inform The Framework to Support Children in Their Earliest Years*. London: DfES.

Dowling, M. (2014) (4th edn) *Young Children's Personal, Social and Emotional Development*. London: SAGE.

Early Education (2012) *Development Matters*. London: DfE.

Evangelou, M., Sylva, K., Kyriacou, M., Wild, M. and Glenny, G. (2009) *Early Years Learning and Development. Literature Review*. Oxford: DCSF.

Field, F. (2010) *The Foundation Years: Preventing Poor Children Becoming Poor Adults. The Report of the Independent Review on Poverty and Life Chances*. London: Cabinet Office.

Finnegan, J. (2016) *Lighting up Young Brains*. London: Save the Children.

Fisher, J. (2016) *Interacting or Interfering? Improving Interactions in The Early Years*. Maidenhead: Open University Press.

Florez, I. (2011) Developing young children's self-regulation through everyday experiences. *Young Children*. Available at: www.naeyc.org, pp. 46-51.

French, G. (2007) *Children's Early Learning and Development: A Research Paper*. Dublin: National Council for Curriculum and Assessment (NCCA).

Gaffrey, M., Barch, D., Singer, J., Shenoy, R. and Luby, J. (2013) Disrupted amygdala reactivity in depressed 4- to 6-year-old children. *Journal of the American Academy of Child & Adolescent Psychiatry*, pp. 737-46.

Gerhardt, S. (2004) *Why Love Matters*. Hove: Routledge.

Gopnik, A., Meltzoff, A. and Kuhl, P.K. (2007) *The Scientist in the Crib: What Early Learning Tells Us About The Mind*. New York: William Morrow.

Goswami, U. (2015) *Children's Cognitive Development and Learning*. York: Cambridge Primary Review Trust.

Hanson, J.L., Hair, N., Shen, D.G., Shi, F., Gilmore, J.H., Wolfe, B.L. and Pollak S.D. (2013) Family poverty affects the rate of human infant brain growth. *PLoS ONE* Vol. 8 Iss. 12, e80954. Available from: doi: 10.1371/journal.pone.0080954

Hobcraft, J. and Kiernan, K. (2010) *Predictive Factors from Age 3 and Infancy for Poor Child Outcomes at Age 5 Relating to Children's Development, Behaviour and Health: Evidence from the Millennium Cohort Study*. York: University of York.

Hunnius, S. and Bekkering, H. (2014) What are you doing? How active and observational experience shape infants' action understanding. *Philosophical Transactions of the Royal Society B* Vol. 369. Available from: http://dx.doi.org/10.1098/rstb.2013.0490. Accessed 31 May 2017.

Koopmann-Holm, B. and Tsai, J.L. (2014) Focusing on the negative: Cultural differences in expressions of sympathy. *Journal of Personality and Social Psychology* Vol. 107 Iss. 6, pp. 1092-115.

Kurth, S., Achermann, P., Rusterholz, P. and LeBourgeois, M. (2013) Development of brain EEG connectivity across early childhood: Does sleep play a role? *Brain Science* Vol. 3 Iss. 4, pp. 1445-60.

Laevers, F. (1994) *The Leuven Involvement Scale for Young Children*. Manual and video. Experiential Education Series, No 1. Leuven: Centre for Experiential Education.

Laevers, F. (2015) *Making Care and Education More Effective through Wellbeing and Involvement. An Introduction to Experiential Education*. Leuven: Centre for Experiential Education.

Leadsom, A., Field, F., Burstow, P. and Lucas, C. (2013) *The 1001 Critical Days*. London: Wave Trust and NSPCC.

Lewin, T. (2009) *No Einstein in your crib? Get a refund. New York Times*. Available from: www.nytimes.com/2009/10/24/education/24baby.html. Accessed 30 May 2017.

Lindon, J. and Brodie, K. (2016) *Understanding Child Development 0-8 Years* (4th edn). London: Hodder Education.

Lorenz, K. (2011) *Comparative Studies on the Behaviour of Anatinae*. London: Read Books.

Marmot, M. (2016) *The Health Gap: The Challenge of an Unequal World*. London: Bloomsbury.

Montessori, M. (2009) *The Absorbent Mind*. Radford: Wilder.

Moylett, H. (ed.) (2013) *Characteristics of Effective Early Learning*. Maidenhead: Open University.

Nisbett, R.E., Peng, K., Choi, I. and Norenzayan, A. (2001) Culture and systems of thought: Holistic versus analytic cognition. *Psychological Review* Vol. 108 Iss. 2, pp. 291-310.

Page, J., Clare, A. and Nutbrown, C. (2013) (2nd edn) *Working with Babies & Children from Birth to Three*. London: SAGE.

Piaget, J. and Inhelder, B. (1969) *The Psychology of the Child*. New York: Basic Books.

Rauscher, F.H., Shaw, G.L. and Ky, C.N. (1993) Music and spatial task performance. *Nature* Vol. 365 Iss. 611.

Robson, S. (2006) *Developing Thinking and Understanding in Young Children*. Abingdon: Routledge.

Sukel, K. (2015) *Early Life Experience, Critical Periods, and Brain Development*. Available from: www.dana.org/News/Early_Life_Experience,_Critical_Periods,_and_Brain_Development/. Accessed 15 June 2016.

Wass, S. (2015) Applying cognitive training to target executive functions during early development. *Child Neuropsychology* Vol. 21 Iss.2, pp. 150-66.

Whitebread, D. (2013) The importance of self-regulation from birth, in H. Moylett, *Characteristics of Effective Early Learning*. Maidenhead: Open University.

Winter, P. (2010) *Neuroscience and Early Childhood Development*. Department of Education and Children's Services, South Australia.

8 Special Educational Needs

A Rainbow of Differences

Myers, 2016

Introduction

For some children, they will come to the setting from birth with a diagnosed additional or SEN. However, there are some children who are diagnosed with an SEN during the birth to three age range. This means that practitioners may be caring for children with an undiagnosed additional need, which may remain undiagnosed for some time. Therefore, this chapter investigates how good practice ideas supporting all children could especially benefit children with SEN, even if they are not yet formally diagnosed.

Special Educational Needs are defined as:

> For children aged two or more, special educational provision is educational or training provision that is additional to or different from that made generally for other children or young people of the same age by mainstream schools, maintained nursery schools, mainstream post-16 institutions or by relevant early years providers.

> For a child under two years of age, special educational provision means educational provision of any kind. A child or young person has SEN if they have a learning difficulty or disability, which calls for special educational provision to be made for him or her.
>
> DfE, 2015: 15

Integrated working

The Early Years Foundation Stage (EYFS) in England has a statutory requirement for a progress check on all children aged between two and three years old. This necessitates closer working between parents, health professionals and educational professionals, whether you are a childminder, nanny, Early Years teacher or qualified practitioner. Similarly, the Special Educational Needs and Disability (SEND) legislation (DfE, 2015) demands closer working relationships and early intervention as a priority. This will result in practitioners needing the skills and knowledge to flag possible SEN even earlier in a child's life.

Young children's development from birth to three has a particularly 'spiky' profile, i.e. rates of development in different areas can have significant variation, and progress will also vary substantially over time. For example, some children will concentrate on talking before walking. This makes identifying SEN very difficult because traditionally practitioners would look for an unusual form of profile to help identify suspected SEN. Therefore, targeted and careful observations are necessary to make this process more reliable and give practitioners more confidence to talk to families and/or contact outside agencies.

Types of observations

Observations are more than just watching the babies or children playing. An effective observation includes the things that practitioners hear, such as the babbling of a baby or a new word from a toddler and the dispositions that the children display, such as tenacity and resilience. In addition, observations must be clear, factual and accurate so they are a true account of the occurrence. Of course, observations need to be acted on if they are to have any value. Therefore, practitioners must reflect on their observations, including *why* it was significant to that baby or child at that time in those circumstances and then incorporate any actions into their plans to support children.

In the following types of observations, some can be used for all ages, such as photographs and videos, magic moments, learning journeys and narrative. The other observational techniques, namely sociogram, time sample and tracking, are suitable for mobile toddlers and young children.

Photographs and video

It is now common practice to have practitioners photographing and videoing children in all types of settings. More and more often these are now integrated into an electronic system that links the observation with the children's full profile, so that trends can be spotted easily – for example, whether physical development is progressing at the expected rate. Because there is so much

growth and development in the birth to three age range, these become delightful to look back on and be amazed at how much has changed in such a short time.

Having photo albums available for children to look through, or having photos and videos on the computer, is a good way to remind them how they were as babies. Children will often be fascinated by the fact that they were once tiny babies and how much they can now do compared to their younger selves. This can be a great boost in self-confidence for some children who may feel that their peers are more able.

Sharing photos and videos with parents has never been easier, and this can strengthen parent partnerships by demonstrating the activities that are happening in the setting, but also so they can see that their child is happy and enjoying themselves. This can be especially important for parents of babies or pre-verbal children who are unable to explain the day's activities.

Magic moments

These are those special 'firsts' and interesting things that babies and children achieve. In the birth to three age range there are a multitude of 'firsts', from first smile, first word, first step and first friendship. It is always a pleasure to record and document such special moments, but these are also vital for future reference if there are additional needs in the future. For example, if a toddler starts to talk and interact typically, but then their speech starts to plateau or deteriorate, this may be a sign of a social and communication disorder.

With babies, the magic moments may be very subtle and fleeting - for example, when they notice their toes and pull them towards their mouth or when he or she turns intentionally towards his or her name being called. These can be recorded briefly, either electronically on an iPad, via photos and videos or simply written down.

Learning journeys

Learning journeys are, as the name suggests, a record of the baby's or child's journey to achievement. In the birth to three age range there are some very significant learning journeys - for example, from crawling to cruising around the furniture to first steps. These can be important from an SEN perspective, because any stages that are missed may incur problems later on. For example, a baby who doesn't have 'tummy time' may not have the core strength to sit up or crawl. Similarly, babies who are discouraged from crawling once they can walk are missing out on hand-eye coordination, cross-body movements and upper body strength.

Narrative

A narrative observation is a 'long' observation of all the events that occur over a period of time, usually around 10 minutes for this age group. This captures every social interaction, levels of involvement and dispositions, as well as words and actions. These can be useful for SEN if it is felt that the problems are situational - for example, that the toddler only talks when a certain practitioner is in the room or if a baby cries at a certain noise.

This type of observation is good for capturing progress, because it records full situations rather than just the snapshot of a magic moment, and reflection on these observations can demonstrate the set of circumstances that result in the best results. For example, when a treasure basket is presented to a group of babies, practitioners are there to observe, ensure safety and encourage, which can be very counterintuitive for some practitioners. A narrative observation can demonstrate the level of practitioner involvement (or interference).

Quick Summary

Tummy time

Tummy time (putting babies on the carpet on their tummies) is key for neck strength and trunk control (try doing a jigsaw yourself on the floor!). Tummy time builds up core stability in the trunk, which is needed before children can have secure arm and leg movements, as they develop physically from the centre of their bodies outwards. Archer and Siraj (2015) explain how babies using their arms to push up from the floor give the strength and alignment in the spine that will be needed for an upright posture. Interestingly, lots of tummy time stimulates the pelvic area, helping to support toilet training when the time comes. Good core stability is essential for children later on when writing or doing other activities sat at a desk, because they need to be able to support their bodies sufficiently to support their arms, elbows, wrists and finally finger movement. Babies should be on their tummy from ten weeks old until seven months (unless sleeping or being held).

For toddlers a narrative observation is good evidence of embedded knowledge and deep-level learning. For example, a toddler may be using the words 'one, two, three' but the practitioner is unsure whether this is just a string of words that is being repeated. A narrative observation of the toddler counting out plates in the home corner using one-to-one correspondence and then counting out the cups to match demonstrates that the meaning of the words is also understood. From an SEN perspective, this can be particularly useful if echolalia (or just repeating back series of words without any understanding of meaning) is suspected.

Time sample

A time sample is making an observation of the baby or child at regular time intervals, say every five minutes, over a long period or even a whole session. The observation itself may be brief, but the critical aspect of this type of observation is spotting what the babies are interested in. For example, does the baby get involved in messy play for a lot of the day? Or are they more active with one practitioner than another?

For toddlers, time sampling is useful for following the flow of play. There can sometimes be a concern about children 'flitting' (only staying briefly at one activity and then moving on to the next). However, time sampling may show a pattern to this. For example, is the toddler carrying a toy car and trying it out in the water, then the sand and then outdoors?

Time sampling can be used to show the activities during the day that children never get involved in, such as singing. This may be indicative of a possible additional need (such as hearing loss or sensory sensitivity).

Sociogram

Sociograms are an under-used form of observation that can be very revealing about children's social interactions and friendships. This is vitally important in the toddler age range as the children negotiate their first friendships and navigate the social rules in their setting and families. Sociograms are a running record of who children play with, where and when. It could be that there is a regular social group, or that there is a social group that only comes together to play football or that a toddler always gravitates towards the older children in a mixed-age setting or childminders.

Observing social groups can also give some surprises. There are some excellent vignettes in Grieshaber and McArdle's book, *The Trouble with Play*. For example, the girl who was included in the play by a practitioner is forced to play the role of 'the piece of paper in front of the fireplace, collecting the cinders' (Grieshaber and McArdle, 2010: 28).

Tracking

Tracking is making observations of the children as they move around the setting, plotted onto a floor plan. It is similar to time sampling, but takes a bit longer to complete because the child needs to be observed regularly and the practitioner needs to be aware at all times of the child's movements. However, tracking can give plenty of information about the child's interests and motivations – for example, noticing that he or she always goes to the areas where mark-making resources are available. It also gives additional information about how the setting is being used, which areas are popular and even which areas may be more appealing to either boys or girls.

For children who may have additional needs, tracking gives a wealth of information about their abilities and preferences. For example, children who play with activities that need very little, if any, explanation, may not be able to follow instructions due to speech and language difficulties.

Different people making observations

It is generally beneficial to have several different practitioners making observations of babies and children, because different people have different perspectives on children's learning and development.

Children with SEN will develop holistically, but the children's 'spiky' profiles may mean that additional provision is needed to support that. These enhancements will also be good for children with more typical development (and you may not even realise it!).

 Quick Summary

Key person

A key person in a setting is a named person who has special responsibility for their key children, their family and any other agencies involved with the family. This good practice is the practical application of Attachment Theory, which says that a baby's emotional well-being is greatly improved if he or she has at least one adult with whom they can 'attach' or bond.

The key person role includes emotional support, keeping the child in mind, observing (and acting on, where necessary) any changes in mood, health or behaviour, liaising with parents and being a special person for their children.

For children with SEN, this will include liaising with other professionals such as the speech and language therapist, physiotherapist and paediatrician. This could be in meetings and also submitting reports or observations ready for assessments. It may be necessary for the key person to have specialist training to be able to support their key child effectively.

The key person will often be the advocate for their key child in multi-agency or multi-professional meetings.

Often the key person is the first one to notice progress or problems with their key children, in all areas of learning and development.

Children who already have a diagnosis may have a programme from a multi-agency professional, who may be able to support you with identifying changes and improvements for the children.

Quick Summary

Top three thoughts on good practice

1 Consider all the senses during sensory play. Do you always include a sense of smell? Do you present prickly or scratchy items?
2 Visual timelines support all children. How do children know what will be happening next? How can they judge how long until home time?
3 Regularly review your environment from the children's perspective. Is it cluttered? How would a child with a hearing or visual impairment experience the environment?

Holistic links in this chapter

These activities detail the additional support needed. These will benefit all children, so there is no 'down-side' and they may well give children who are at a critical phase of development the support they need, even if they don't yet have an official diagnosis.

- *Visual timelines*
- *Sensory play*
- *Seeing, and hearing, your environment from a different perspective*
- *Declutter your environment*

- *Language development – stop and wait!*
- *All behaviour is communication*
- *Effects of SEN on other areas of unrelated development.*

Visual timelines

A visual timeline can be defined as something that 'uses pictures to break down the steps of a task or a routine throughout the day' (iCan, 2016). In practice, these are strips of pictures (usually displayed horizontally), each representing an activity from arrival at the setting until home time. For example, you would have pictures for arrival, snack time, lunchtime, playing outdoors, playing in the sand and going home time. Once an activity is completed, the picture is taken from the timeline, so the first picture is always the current activity. This gives children a point of reference during their day, so they can always go to check to see what is happening next, or how many activities until lunchtime.

Being able to self-check on progress throughout the day can calm children with anxiety (whether they have SEN or not), encourage understanding of sequencing (as one activity follows another) and help to support those new to the setting or when there is a change in routine.

The timeline should be demonstrated at the beginning of the day (or at change-over times) and referred to throughout the day, to ensure that children understand the meanings of the pictures and the implications of the sequence of events. It has even been suggested that it can 'develop literacy, be motivated, remind and reinforce concepts [children] know and lead to more independence' (iCan, 2016: 2).

Making a visual timeline

There are various ways of making a timeline, but it is generally accepted that pictures should be displayed in chronological order from left to right because this is the way that children in Western societies will learn to read. The next decision is whether to use symbols (e.g. Makaton symbols) or photographs of pertinent objects or objects of reference, which are objects to represent the activity (a cup for snack time, a ball for playing outdoors). The timeline has to be made so that the symbols or objects can be easily removed after the activity has finished, and are interchangeable. This can be done using Velcro or Blu Tack on the back of the pictures and on the timeline.

 Reflective Questions

Visual timelines

How might you have to adapt a visual timeline for children who are used to reading from top to bottom – for example, in Japanese cultures?

Sensory play

Children learn best through experiential play, especially when they use all their senses. Initially, babies have reflexes, such as being startled by a sudden, loud noise or grasping your finger. Gradually these are modulated to be purposeful reactions to their environment, such as being excited when they hear the key in the door, or reaching out to be picked up. The senses need to be integrated to be effective and to develop the full range of skills and knowledge that children will need (Bodison *et al.*, 2008). In typically developing children, the senses will integrate and work together to reinforce the experiences of the world. However, if even one of the senses is not functioning fully, then this can cause problems with other areas of development. For example, if a baby has hearing loss, then he or she won't turn towards sound, so may not see things of interest and may be startled when people and objects suddenly appear in front of him or her. This may lead to less confidence, so he or she may be more hesitant to try new experiences.

Presenting a full range of sensory experiences is beneficial because it allows babies and children to learn from these and integrate them. In addition, it enables practitioners to make beneficial observations, which could help to identify SEN or additional needs. For example, if you have a baby who never enjoys the getting their hands messy and doesn't seem to enjoy having their feet tickled and gets fussy about having a nappy change, it could be that he or she has skin hypersensitivity (obviously a lot more observations and investigation would need to be done before asking a health professional for a diagnosis).

Full sensory activities from birth to three years

There are many, many activities that practitioners do with babies and children to support all their senses. The activities here have been chosen because they involve all the senses and help children to integrate them.

Babies

- Gloop (cornflour and water mixed to a thin paste). Add glitter, colour and scent for additional sensory interest
- Different types of musical instruments that can be easily rattled, but which have different textures - for example, jingle bells, tambourine, rain sticks and maracas
- Clear sealed plastic bottles filled with rice, pasta, water and oil, glitter or small toys, small enough for babies to manipulate and watch themselves.

Toddlers

Toddlers will still enjoy the baby activities, but add these more challenging and stimulating activities too:

- Rubbery gloop (thicker than gloop so the fingers have to work harder) made by adding bicarbonate of soda to the gloop recipe and warming. Allow to cool before use
- Sand, both wet and dry, gives opportunities to feel different textures and discuss how they flow differently, ability to build sandcastles, etc
- Lengths of fabric with different textures and movement, such as silk, corduroy, sequin-covered, plastic, rubber and leather.

Three-year-olds

- Matching the smell. Using small plastic spice tubs, add cotton wool with a few drops of essence (for example, lavender, lemon) or use small drawstring washing bags and add some herbs. Have two of each and see whether the children can match the smells.
- Going on an outdoors walk. Discuss what you can hear, see and smell.
- Crawling through tunnels or dens, with different textures on the floor, such as rubbery mats, fluffy material and foam.

Review Your Practice

How could you include more scent or olfactory (sense of smell) activities in your daily routine? Do you include regular smells, such as herbs and spices, as well as stronger smells, such as wet bark? (Think about other natural scents you could include.)

How often do you let the babies and children use all seven senses?

Case Study

Using sensory experiences to enhance understanding

In a school, with which I am familiar, that specialises in children with profound and multiple difficulties, they have a colour, scent and tune of the day. For example, on Monday it could be orange, with a spray of orange-scented water and orange fabric used to cover the floor at circle time; Tuesday could be lavender, with lavender scent and lavender-coloured fabric, etc.

The coloured fabric and scent is used first thing in the morning and at the beginning of the afternoon session, along with the appropriate welcome song.

The colour and scent is kept consistent for each day of the week, so that the children have a full sensory experience – visual, olfactory and auditory – to cue them into the day's activities.

How do you encourage children to think about the different days of the week and different times of the day?

How do you use the sense of smell with the children in your setting?

Seeing, and hearing, your environment from a different perspective

Children may have varying levels of visual impairment and it may be corrected while they are at your setting, using a patch or glasses, for example. However, even if a visual impairment has yet to be diagnosed, there are a number of considerations for the development of good vision. Babies will focus on objects with a strong contrast – for example, a black shape on a white background, and will gaze longer at a shape of patterns resembling a face. Studies with primates have shown that if they have face-to-face interactions from birth, they are more social later on (Dettmer *et al.* 2016). It is even more important to be aware of this for children who may have a visual impairment. For example, coloured, multi-patterned tablecloths will be too visually confusing; and glossy laminating pouches will produce glare, so the contents are obscured and the quality of both natural and artificial light should be evaluated.

Children with a hearing impairment (some people prefer the term deaf – for example, the National Deaf Children's Society) will experience your setting in a very different way to other children. For example, if you have a 'tidy-up' song to get the attention of the children so they are aware that there is about to be a transition time, how would a child with hearing problems be alerted?

This is especially important with very young children, where hearing loss may not be detected until later in life, although the newborn hearing tests now offered in the UK have improved this (NHS, 2017). In addition, many children will have temporary hearing loss over the winter months, when they may suffer from glue ear (otitis media with effusion, or OME). This may vary from day to day, or even during the day, so should always be considered a possibility.

The most obvious effect of hearing loss on holistic development is language and communication. It is very difficult to replicate speech sounds if you have never heard them; similarly, speaking at an appropriate volume may present difficulties. It may be the case with temporary hearing loss or glue ear that only certain parts of words or specific sounds can be heard, with the rest of the word getting 'lost', so children may not understand what is being said to them. Communication is a two-way exchange, whether that is via spoken language, body language or sign language. In order to start the exchange, you must first get the child's attention, which would typically be done by saying their name. However, with a child who has a hearing loss, you may need to be more inventive and have visual cues, such as turning a light on and off, or gently touching them on the arm before speaking or communicating. Visual clues, such as holding a cup for snack time, and body language, including facial expressions, are very important for reinforcing messages and help with clear understanding.

Less obvious problems include social isolation (ASHA, 2017), especially as young children start to gain their independence and introduce themselves. If another child doesn't hear and doesn't respond, children are likely to just wander off and the opportunity is missed.

Enhancements to your setting

Visual impairment: have chairs and tables with good contrast to the floor – for, example a dark wood floor and a light wood table.

Ensure the environment is laid out clearly, with the doors easy to access.

Evaluate the lighting in your setting. Are there times of the day when the sun is very bright through an uncovered window? Are any of the lights flickering?

For children with hearing loss or children who are deaf: deaden sound as much as possible. Environmental sound within the room - the room's acoustics and reverberation - will affect the noise levels, so think soft and noise absorbing for everything. Consider lining toy boxes with soft fabric to reduce the clatter of toys being put away; soft fabric coverings on table tops to absorb noise; chair leg 'protectors' made from felt on the bottom of chair legs; curtains or voile at the windows to reduce really bright light coming in; wall displays backed with hessian or soft fabric.

Equipment that makes background noise should be reduced - for example, projectors, fans, washing machines, TV, radio and music (especially if the music is on simply for background noise and no other purpose).

Being aware of external noises such as traffic, aircraft or machinery, particularly when the windows are open (or if they are not double glazed), and especially loud, sudden noises such as sirens.

Practitioners should be aware of their own positioning - for example, not directly in front of the window or light (because it casts the face into shadow); to keep the face clearly visible and not covered with a scarf, your hand or untamed beard; ensuring that children sitting at circle or group time or all arranged in front of you (not next to you) so they can clearly see your face.

Consider using quieter rooms for 'listening'-focused activities (NDCS, 2016) if at all possible.

Ensure there are plenty of opportunities to play and interact with other children.

Review Your Practice

How often do you review your setting as if you were a child with a hearing or visual impairment? What improvements could you make?

Case Study

Tidy-up time

I used to care for a girl who was profoundly deaf in a nursery setting. The setting's policy was to jingle some bells five minutes before tidy-up time, to give children enough time to finish their play. However, this clearly was unsuitable for the little girl in my care. Therefore, we turned the lights on and off and also very clearly shook the bells, so she could see that it was coming up to tidy-up time.

What other ways could you solve this problem? Think of ways to visually represent time and draw attention.

Declutter your environment

It is very tempting to have lots of toys, lots of bright, colourful displays and plenty of resources set out for the children to play with. However, children who may have a range of sensory processing challenges, including vision disorders such as depth perception or partial sight, or children with autism, will find this type of environment overpowering and unpleasant to be in. Even for children without any SEN, this type of environment can create confusion and discourage freedom of choice and freedom of movement.

Decluttering, or removing anything that is not essential for the children, can promote more open-ended play by giving larger spaces to play in, give confidence to children with a visual impairment when moving around and reduce noise levels for children who are deaf or who have a hearing impairment.

Maria Montessori, who started out working with children who had SEN (Pound, 2005), believed that the classroom should be uncluttered, calming and places of reflection (American Montessori Society, 2017). Many natural materials are used, but most noticeably in a true Montessori setting is the reduced quantity of resources on the shelves, giving a peaceful and relaxing environment.

Enhancements for your setting

Think about how your baby room is set up. Do they often have their backs to the doors? If so, people arriving and leaving becomes a sudden transition and could be a source of anxiety.

For the toddlers, ideally, move as much out of the room as possible, to start with a 'blank canvas'. This is one of the occasions where 'pack-away' settings (those who share a space with others and have to get all the resources out each day and pack away at the end of the day) have a big advantage over most other settings!

Gradually add back equipment and toys until you feel you have the balance right. Do consider moving chairs and tables if at all possible, as these can become a hazard for children and are not always suited for children under three until they have enough core strength to sit unaided.

 Review Your Practice

Do remember to review every aspect of your provision.

Often we only think about the larger pieces of furniture, but highly beneficial changes can be made with the smallest of changes.

Reflect on the whole room in the baby room. Do you have things hanging from the ceiling? Glittery objects catching the light? Maybe fairy lights? Although these make the room look exciting and inviting for adults, for babies who are trying to understand the physical world around them, these can be unnecessarily distracting and may stop them from watching faces, for example.

Reflect on your table coverings. Do they have 'busy' patterns that may confuse young children who are only still mastering their visual perception? Visual perception is how the brain interprets a visual stimulus to transform this into understanding it is an object – it is 3D, is close or far away, etc. (McLeod, 2007).

Consider the backings on the displays. Do the contrasting colours detract from the display itself?

No chairs, no problem!

A local setting that specialises in provision for two-year-olds has removed all the chairs from the room during free play. This has encouraged children to move around the table to get resources, rather than just play with what is in front of them. It has also increased their physical movement, such as stretching and reaching for resources across the table.

It is now much easier to try different techniques – for example, taping paper under the tables, so children can lie on their backs and draw.

What other advantages could there be if you removed the chairs or rearranged the tables?

 ## Quick Summary

Is the environment suitable?

There are a number of assessment tools available to help to determine the suitability of the environment. For the physical environment there is the American-based ITERS-Infant/Toddler Environment Rating Scale (ITERS-3) (Harms *et al.*, 2017) and the Early Years Quality Improvement Support Programme (EYQISP) (National Strategies, 2008a). In addition, there are the Leuven Scales (Laevers, 1994) and the Sustained Shared Thinking and Emotional Well-being scales (SSTEW)(Siraj *et al.*, 2015) for the emotional environment.

How do you know whether the environment is suitable for babies, toddlers and young children for this area of learning and development?

Is it an enabling, a creative and a learning environment?

Think about how this group of babies or children may have grown and developed since the environment was last reviewed.

Language development – stop and wait!

Learning language is a complex process, which can falter at any number of stages (see the language chain). Well-meaning parents, who constantly talk but don't allow their children to respond,

Quick Summary

Language chain

This is a way of describing the series of processes that the brain has to go through before speech can be attempted.

Receptive language: recognising, understanding and interpreting the language that is being used

Expressive language: choosing the words, syntax, grammar, social norms before talking

Speech: coordinating the facial muscles, tongue and voice box to make speech sounds.

There can be disconnects at any of these stages, which will need different approaches to resolve.

may over-stimulate some children. Alternatively, some children may be linguistically vulnerable – all children are different.

It has been shown that babies who sign from birth go through the same developmental stages when learning sign language as hearing babies who are learning verbal language (Karmiloff and Karmiloff-Smith, 2001) – for example, they will 'fingerbabble' around three to six months old, use 'jargon' and gestures with their hands between six to 12 months, sign their first words around eight months and then go on to develop grammar, syntax, etc. from one year onwards (Andrews, Logan and Phelan, 2008).

If toddlers and children do have speech and language difficulties (diagnosed or not), then it is essential that adults allow enough time for children to understand the language; find their words; compose a response; physically get ready to reply; have confidence to speak and then actually speak. This can take ten seconds. This may not sound like a long time at first, but time ten seconds before answering a question and you will see that it feels like a very long time. Unfortunately the natural response is jump in with another question or some clarification, which effectively resets the clock, so another ten seconds is needed. When any children are learning a language they need that extra time, so stop and wait – don't be afraid of the silence!

For older children, a good rule to remember is the 4 S's:

1   **S**ay less
2   **S**tress key words
3   **S**ilence
4   **S**low down.

Activities for effective communication

In early communication, babies and children need to watch the speaker's facial expressions and mouth shapes as well as listen to the words and the rhythm of the language. Activities that encourage babies to watch the face include:

- Reducing unnecessary background noise, including music or songs
- Holding a toy or something colourful near your face to gain baby's attention before speaking
- Using baby's name at the beginning of the sentence, to gain their attention first.

For older children:

- Get down to child's level so they can see your face clearly (think about lighting too)
- Allow time to your child talk, give them time to think
- Reduce and simplify language
- Don't over-stimulate children by bombarding them with language
- Comment, don't question! For example, 'Look what Pat is doing . . .' rather than 'What is Pat doing?'

Review Your Practice

The way that children learn language is fascinating and, when there are additional needs, you may need to know some further details.

Go to the Elklan website, which is run by speech and language therapists for further information: www.elklan.co.uk/

Case Study

Shhhhh!

If you observe babies and children carefully, you will see that they inform us when they have had enough. Babies, for example, will turn their heads or become fussy when they have had enough.

One practitioner told me a lovely story about how her grandson puts his finger on his lips while thinking of a response. She knows not to interrupt this thinking time, until he takes his finger away. This is an excellent method that her grandson has found to say 'Shhh, I'm thinking!'

What other methods have you seen children use to give themselves time to respond?

How could you support children to do this?

All behaviour is communication

If home life is very different to your setting, whether that is a day nursery, childminder or special provision, then it can be very confusing and a challenge for a young child to learn a whole new set of rules. This can be exacerbated around the two-year-old stage, where emotional control will be difficult anyway. There may be a chaotic lifestyle at home (substance abuse, mental health or simply really busy) that can have serious ongoing effects on the children. Add to that, children who may be only just learning to talk (or who have speech and language difficulties) and it becomes obvious that becoming physical (undesirable behaviour) is an effective way of saying 'I don't know what else to do!'

Distressed children need emotional support. Children may be distressed due to frustrations of not understanding (for example, hearing or cognition problems) or it may be they can't actually do as you are asking (children need to have some physical maturity to 'sit still', for example).

Some strategies for supporting children

Specific praise is the most effective tool. Share this with parents and practitioners. However, you do have to be aware that this can be adult-intensive and will take time to have an effect. You have to be mindful to be consistent with the praise.

Having firm boundaries and discussing these explicitly, frequently and regularly with the children will help them to remember and understand the rules.

Visual prompts can be very powerful – for example, smiley faces, sad faces; kind hands/kind feet; pictures of rules. Visual prompts are more immediate than verbal, but are most effective when reinforced with verbal instruction as well.

Any behaviour strategies HAVE to be setting-wide. All practitioners must know, understand them and implement them consistently. It is helpful if parents can mirror these at home too.

Give time for children to comply and give notice of change, either using a visual timetable or telling the children in advance that there is a change imminent ('Five minutes/until the sand timer runs out until tidy up time').

Give clear, specific and realistic consequences that can be followed through.

Only consider saying 'sorry' after the incidence has calmed. For young children especially, do they need to say sorry?

Adults need to constantly model good behaviour and the use of good language and behavior, such as sharing and turn taking.

Consider that for older children, the behaviour may have been learned over a couple of years and is likely to be embedded into the child's brain, so trying to retrain their neural pathways into more preferable behaviour may take some time.

Review Your Practice

If you work in a day nursery or with a group of staff, how often do you review your strategies for working with the children? How do you ensure they are implemented? (Think about peer observations.)

Case Study

Mind your language

Sandi Phoenix, an Early Years consultant in Queensland, Australia, suggests that instead of using the term 'challenging behaviour' about children, we should talk about the type of behaviour that challenges you (Brodie, 2017). The child is communicating something to you, and it is your response that makes the behaviour challenging. Similarly, Dr Suzanne Zeedyk (Brodie, 2017: 70) uses the language of 'responding to emotional needs', which is a much more positive perspective. She goes on to say, 'I can think of a school that I have worked with in Fife who just changed their language from 'challenging' behaviour to 'distressed' behaviour and they say that it transformed their school'.

How do you describe the children's behaviour, of all types, in your setting?

In what ways could you make your language more positive and supportive when talking with the children?

For more information about Sandi Phoenix and her 'Cups' philosophy, go to: www.phoenix-support.com.au/

For more information about Dr Suzanne Zeedyk and her work, go to: www.suzannezeedyk.com/

Effects of SEN on other areas of unrelated development

Atypical physical development may affect independence and mobility. This can reduce access to the curriculum – for example, reaching the treasure basket or standing at the sand tray. This can affect social interactions and reduce children's self-confidence.

Where children have a full-time support worker, there is a risk of 'learned helplessness' where they stop even attempting to do things, because they know an adult will soon be there to do it for them. This can be a problem for the inclusion worker as well. He or she must support their key child, but not take over or reduce opportunities for development. Very often the inclusion worker doesn't even notice that it is happening, but it may be a colleague or room manager that sees it first.

Sometimes regular activities, such as circle time or story time, can pose a problem for children who are non-verbal or who have hearing or visual impairments. These children could miss out on basic speech and language skills as well as the social interactions. It is essential to be observant and make sure these children are able to access the whole curriculum via other methods.

Activities to support your practice

Ensure observations note where children with SEN do not access and be curious. Is this because they don't enjoy it, or is there a barrier such as being able to reach, unable to see or hear?

Give alternatives so children's voices can still be heard. For example, a recordable speech 'button' (e.g. a BIGmack) onto which a personalised message is saved (and re-recorded) will allow children to join in with stories or circle time.

Review Your Practice

Reflect on all areas of learning and development for the children with SEN. Does the strong focus on their therapy programme (physiotherapy, speech and language, etc.) still allow for development in other areas?

Consider the additional emotional and physical support that an inclusion worker may need.

Challenges

The main challenge with SEN and the birth to three age range is that many of the needs will not yet be identified. It is often down to the combined skill and knowledge of the practitioner and the parents' concerns that SEN is recognised.

There are many different types of SEN, and each of these will also be on a continuum. It would be impossible to discuss them all, but practitioners in settings are sometimes expected to be able to care for children with no training or previous experience. One of the biggest challenges is keeping practitioners up to date on the latest advice, both good practice and medical. In addition, key persons and inclusion workers need to have time to able to prepare for meetings, complete specialist paperwork and implement therapy programmes with their children.

Opportunities

Practitioners have the professional advantage of caring for many different babies and young children, so are often in a good position to notice whether development or progress is atypical or just a bit 'off'. They are then in an ideal situation to liaise between parents and other professionals, while using their expertise to support the children in the setting. Practitioners often become friends and a listening ear for parents as well.

Attending a setting gives the babies and children opportunities to be involved with developmentally appropriate activities suitable to their own needs, including experiences that may not be possible at home, such as messy play and outdoor play.

Conclusions

Sometimes rethinking practice and the environment for children with SEN is a much-needed boost out of the mundane. Activities that support all the senses and all areas of learning and development will be good for all children, regardless of their level of development. Similarly, encouraging practitioners to really consider the setting's environment, routines and making a variety of observations will improve self-reflection and good practice. This will be a benefit for all the children at the setting.

 Further Reading and Research

The Foundation Years website has links to many Special Educational Needs and Disabilities resources, such as case studies, as well as links to the most up-to-date information from the Department for Education (DfE). Find the site here: www.foundationyears.org.uk/?s=SEND

The Special Needs Jungle website has many articles, information and case studies for parents that are also useful for practitioners too. It is an excellent source of information for rare diseases and syndromes. Find the site here: www.specialneedsjungle.com/

Deafness

For further information, refer to: Helping your Deaf Child to Develop Communication and Language (0-2).

The guide includes:
- Information about communication and language development
- Practical ideas to promote communication and language development
- Information about the support you can expect to receive
- A detailed explanation of what we mean when we say communication and language.

It is available from: www.NDCS.org.uk/family_support/education_for_deaf_children/education_in_the_early_years/helping_your_deaf.html

References

American Montessori Society (2017) *Montessori Classrooms*. Available from: https://amshq.org/. Accessed 23 May 2017.

Andrews, J., Logan, R. and Phelan, J. (2008) Milestones of Language Development. *Advance for Speech-Language Pathologists and Audiologists* Vol. 18 Iss. 2, pp. 16–20.

Archer, C. and Siraj, I. (2015) Measuring the quality of movement-play in Early Childhood Education settings: Linking movement-play and neuroscience. *European Early Childhood Education Research Journal* Vol. 23 Iss. 1, pp. 21–42.

ASHA (2017) *Effects of Hearing Loss on Development*. Available from: www.asha.org/public/hearing/Effects-of-Hearing-Loss-on-Development./ Accessed 10 April 2017.

Bodison, S., Watling, R., Miller Kuhaneck, H. and Henry, D. (2008) *Frequently Asked Questions about Ayres Sensory Integration*. Bethesda, MD: American Occupational Therapy Association.

Brodie, K. (2017) *Personal, Social and Emotional Wellbeing of Young Children*. Wilmslow: Rainmaker Academy.

Department for Education (2015) *Special Educational Needs and Disability Code of Practice: 0 to 25 Years*. London: DfE. Available from: www.gov.uk/government/uploads/system/uploads/attachment_data/file/398815/SEND_Code_of_Practice_January_2015.pdf. Accessed 20 June 2017.

Dettmer, A., Kaburu, S., Simpson, D., Paukner, A., Sclafani, V., Byers, K., Murphy, A., Miller, M., Marquez, N., Miller, G., Suomi, S., and Ferrari, P. (2016) Neonatal face-to-face interactions promote later social behaviour in infant rhesus monkeys. *Nature Communications* p. 7 Art. 11940.

DfE (2015) *Special Educational Needs and Disability Code of Practice: 0 to 25 Years Statutory Guidance for Organisations Which Work with and Support Children and Young People who Have Special Educational Needs or Disabilities*. Available from: www.gov.uk/government/uploads/system/uploads/attachment_data/file/398815/SEND_Code_of_Practice_January_2015.pdf. Accessed 10 June 2017.

Grieshaber, S. and McArdle, F. (2010) *The Trouble with Play*. Maidenhead: Open University.

Harms, T., Cryer, D., Clifford, R. and Yazejian, N. (2017) (3rd edn) *Infant/Toddler Environment Rating Scale (ITERS-3)*. New York: Teachers' College Press.

iCan (2016) *Visual Timelines Fact Sheet*. Available from: www.ican.org.uk/help. Accessed 7 April 2017.

Karmiloff, K. and Karmiloff-Smith, A. (2001) *Pathways to Language: From Fetus to Adolescent*. Cambridge, MA: Harvard University Press.

Laevers, F. (ed.) (1994) *Well-being and Involvement in Care Settings. A Process-oriented Self-evaluation Instrument*. Leuven: Leuven University.

McLeod, S.A. (2007) *Visual Perception Theory*. Available from: www.simplypsychology.org/perception-theories.html. Accessed 23 May 2017.

Myers, M. (2016) *A Slice of Autism: What's Normal Anyway?*. London: Createspace.

National Strategies (2008) *Social and Emotional Aspects of Development (SEAD)*. Nottingham: DCSF.

NDCS (2016) *Helping Your Deaf Child to Develop Communication and Language*. North Shields: NDCS.

NHS (2017) *Newborn Hearing Test*. Available from: www.nhs.uk/conditions/pregnancy-and-baby/pages/newborn-hearing-test.aspx. Accessed 10 April 2017.

Pound, L. (2005) *How Children Learn*. London: Step Forward.

Siraj, I., Kingston, D. and Melhuish, E. (2015) *Sustained Shared Thinking and Emotional Well-being (SSTEW) Scale for 2–5 Year Olds Provision*. London: IOE.

9 Suitable physical environments

Children learn and develop well in enabling environments, in which their experiences respond to their individual needs

Early Education, 2012: 2

Introduction

There are significant and important differences between an appropriate physical environment for a baby and a suitable environment for a three-year-old child. For this reason, this chapter will be roughly divided up into non-mobile babies, mobile babies and toddlers (including confident walkers).

Similarly, there are noteworthy differences between the physical environments in different settings. For example, a childminder's home will look very different to a large chain nursery setting. That is not to say that one is superior to the other – each will have its own advantages and challenges, but the environments will still need to be fit for purpose. Therefore, the rationale for the environment is discussed wherever possible. For example, having a comfortable chair or sofa is recommended in the baby room, so you can sit comfortably to give a baby a bottle of milk; having a separate preparation area for milk for hygiene reasons and having an appropriate nappy change area for privacy.

There are two distinct forms of environment that are highlighted – emotional environment and physical environment. This chapter is an exploration of the physical environment, which consists of the building structure, equipment, layout and organisation of the space. Included here is the 'flow' of the space, which is how the space is used. For example, a long, narrow room can be provided with exactly the same equipment, but this is arranged in two ways. First it can be set up with the equipment on either side of a central aisle or second, as clusters or groups throughout the length of the space. The first layout encourages children to run up and down the room, using the empty space. The second layout encourages a more thoughtful engagement with the equipment as children move around the clusters. Although it is exactly the same room, same equipment and the same children, the flow, movement and interaction with the physical environment are very different. The emotional environment is how we feel in the space (whether that is indoors, outdoors or elsewhere) and is discussed in more detail in the chapter on personal, social and emotional development.

A 'quality' environment

As Marion Dowling put it so eloquently: 'Young children deserve more than a comforting and benign environment' (2014: 25). Practitioners and setting managers should be aiming for the highest quality in the baby and toddler rooms, especially as research shows this is not always the case. For example, The Baby Room research by Goouch and Powell (2013: 6) found that the baby room practitioners 'felt they had little control over this aspect of the environment or felt unable to dictate how space should be used in accordance with their understandings and perceptions of the babies' needs'. This can be very problematic because babies will usually only be in the baby room for one year (usually moving up when they can walk), so it is vital that the physical environment can be adapted confidently to the baby's needs. It must also be frustrating for practitioners to be unable to exercise their professional judgement and knowledge due to lack of support. During Dr Ann Clare's working experience, 'the quality of the environment available to a baby or your child was vitally important in its learning, development and wellbeing' (Clare, 2012: 1). Note here that a quality environment, by definition, meets all children's needs and is holistic in nature.

The key when choosing equipment for the environment is quality over quantity. The learning and the value are added to the environment where practitioners play with children, interact sensitively and use the materials to their best advantage. Open-ended resources, such as lengths of fabric, cardboard boxes and cardboard tubes, give the most scope for imaginative play and social play as children co-construct their ideas for games. These do not necessarily cost much (or may even be free) but do allow practitioners to adapt, predict and react to the babies' daily, changing needs.

Continuous provision may look similar for older children, albeit enhanced or differentiated for different abilities and interests. However, for the transition from baby to toddler, the environment has to be substantially different and suited to the vastly different levels of development, being especially mindful of safety – for example, choking hazards and trip hazards.

There are also a myriad of practical considerations for the baby environment that are unique, for example:

- Does your setting require a separate milk kitchen?
- How does the nappy change area work with consumables and hand wash facilities, while still being a warm and pleasant environment for baby and practitioner?
- Is there a suitable sofa or nursery chair?
- Where and how are bottles given to babies?
- Is there a separate area for sleeping where babies won't get disturbed, but which is still inclusive?

These needs change dramatically in a setting as babies grow into toddlers. They don't need milk making up; there is no need to sterilise or use bottles; naps are more likely to be after food time and will need a much less specialised area. It may be that larger furniture, such as armchairs and sofas, is now a potential hazard as children start to use them as climbing frames or trampolines. Therefore, careful and constant review and reflection on the physical environment is essential across the birth to three age group to ensure that it is safe, suitable and engaging.

First, though, are some definitions of different types of environments. Although there are some similarities, you will notice that there is a different emphasis in each. Therefore, when you go into a setting you may see an environment that is more enriched as, say, an enabling environment than a creative one. It is important to be able to evaluate your environment, so you know where improvements can be made, and your areas of strength.

Enabling environment: An environment to make possible or facilitate children's learning. Note that in this definition 'enabling' is an action word (Hutchin, 2012: 31). In addition, furniture and equipment has to be age appropriate (Callanan *et al.*, 2017: 39).

Creative environment: 'where it is possible for children to express their originality through using their imaginations, exploring, taking risks and having fun' (Clare, 2012: 81).

Learning environment: A rich and varied environment supports children's learning and development, which gives children confidence to explore and learn in secure and safe, yet challenging, indoor and outdoor spaces (National Strategies, 2008b: 32).

Assessing and reviewing the environment in the setting can be very difficult – partly due to time constraints, but also because practitioners sometimes get emotionally invested in an area or idea – so being able to change it becomes a challenge.

One way to solve both these issues is to use an audit or review scale that removes the emotional bond to potentially unsuitable areas and also gives you a comparison or scale to work towards improvements.

Quick Summary

Is the environment suitable?

There are a number of assessment tools available to help to determine the suitability of the environment. For the physical environment there is the American-based ITERS – Infant/ Toddler Environment Rating Scale (ITERS-3) (Harms *et al.*, 2017) and the Early Years Quality Improvement Support Programme (EYQISP) (National Strategies, 2008). In addition there are the Leuven Scales (Laevers, 1994) and the Sustained Shared Thinking and Emotional Well-being scales (SSTEW) (Siraj *et al.*, 2015) for the emotional environment.

How do you know whether the environment is suitable for babies, toddlers and young children for this area of learning and development?

Is it an enabling, a creative and a learning environment?

Think about how this group of babies or children may have grown and developed since the environment was last reviewed.

Reflective Questions

The home environment

Impact of the home environment: The children have no garden at home, so they choose to spend all day outdoors, not accessing the writing provision. How would you deal with this? (Think creatively about how every area of learning and development can be represented outdoors.)

'There is growing appreciation of the importance of the natural and built environments in early childhood settings' (ISSA, 2014: 4). How do you evaluate your built environment? And your natural environment? Should they be evaluated in the same way? (Think about how babies and young children use each environment.)

Quick Summary

Pedagogy

Pedagogy is the combination of the methods of teaching, the ethos, the interactions between baby or child and practitioner, the learning environment and the curriculum. It is the *way* teaching is conducted, considered as a whole with the content. It could be considered to be the holistic methods by which teaching and learning occur.

Quick Summary

Playful learning

Playful learning can be child initiated, adult initiated, adult supported or adult led – any type of play where learning occurs through children's play. Typically the play will be exploratory, problem-solving, discovery and experiential.

Holistic links in this chapter

- *Environment and PSED – independence, freedom of movement, self-confidence*
- *The effect of the physical environment on the emotional environment*
- *Environments for talking and listening*
- *Environments for learning and growing – cognition*
- *Environments for inclusion and differentiation*
- *The outdoor environment for babies and young children.*

Environment and PSED – independence, freedom of movement, self-confidence

It is very important that children have as much space as possible in which to move around and explore, and that this is encouraged. For young babies, encourage stretching and movement by placing toys just out of reach so they can see them, but will have to move to get to them. This not only builds on their physical development, but it also encourages good hand-eye coordination, determination and a self-awareness of their own body.

Allowing children to move freely around the room when crawling or bottom shuffling encourages exploration and independence. Very often children will look back to their key person to check they still have that secure emotional base to return to. It may also be the first time that they can choose who to go to and spend time with. In mixed-aged rooms it is common to find the younger children moving towards the older children, observing and learning from them. Independent walking means young children are able to choose toys, activities and areas to play in. From observations, it will be possible to see the types of activities that children are drawn to, or avoid, and to assess play patterns (for example, schematic play) and preferences for which children they play with.

Clare (2012: 60) states that environments for the under-threes are 'possibly the most challenging to organise' due to the number, and often contradictory, requirements.

She notes that rooms must have:

- Quiet reflective spaces to avoid over-stimulation
- Flexibility for children themselves to change them during play

- Meet developmental needs
- Have challenges
- Consider language development, including 'listening spaces' to encourage children to talk.

This becomes even more challenging if you are in a setting with a mixed age group – for example, a childminders or small setting. However, these challenges are offset by the many benefits to having children who are 'more knowledgeable others' to support and guide younger children.

Non-mobile babies

As small babies do not have a regular routine yet, it is critical that the room or space is flexible to be able to accommodate all eventualities – for example, still being able to feed a baby while another is asleep and another is playing with toys.

Consideration needs to be given to seating for adults, so bottle feeds, story time and cuddles can be done in comfort and not rushed.

It is advisable to have a mixture of wipe-clean floor and carpet. This gives the opportunity to have messy play and not worry about the carpet, but also gives a soft surface to lay babies onto their tummies for tummy time.

Nappy change areas should be well organised, with all the consumables, such as nappies, wipes and creams, within easy reach. It is particularly important to have a system in place to identify babies who may be allergic to certain nappies or wipes. The area should be warm and free from draughts or loud noises so that nappy change is a calm and pleasant experience for both practitioner and baby.

It is good practice for the baby's key person to always change nappies or dirty clothing, to help build a relationship of trust and care between them. This will help with attachment and bonding, as well as building professional love between baby and practitioner.

 Reflective Questions

Baby's point of view

A good exercise is to lie on the floor and look at the environment. What can you see at this level? How high are the mobiles or ceiling decorations, bearing in mind that a baby's vision will only be just beyond arm's length?

Mobile babies

The room layout will need to accommodate mobile babies, once they start to crawl or bottom shuffle. This will include choices about which toys are made freely available and which may only be presented by practitioners – for example, an area with board books so that children can access

them freely, but also to keep the ordinary books to one side until better motor control means they are not ripped or eaten.

There should be as few tables and chairs as possible (if any) so children can move around freely and see across the room. Be aware of any changes in levels, not to necessarily remove them, but to consider how this cohort of children may (or may not) be able to negotiate them. Do remove any trip hazards, for both the children and practitioners who may be carrying babies to the nappy change area, for example.

Toddlers and walkers

Sometimes mobile babies start to use the bookshelves and cupboards as ways of helping them to balance and 'cruise' around the furniture. Do be aware of sharp edges and hazards at babies' head or eye level and the stability of the furniture when pulled.

By the time children are walking confidently, encourage them to walk on different levels, such as gentle slopes and shallow steps. It is good practice for them to walk with no shoes on, so they can feel the ground and the different textures, as well as the slope and unevenness of the ground.

Review your equipment

Reduce the number of chairs and tables to an absolute minimum. Under-threes are best on the floor, where they don't have to balance on chairs or reach across tables. Are the chairs that you are providing the correct size - so children's feet can reach the floor comfortably? If not, consider smaller chairs or benches, because the act of using core strength to balance and stay on a chair is very distracting and could potentially undermine learning. Think about how you feel perched on a high chair or barstool.

The effect of the physical environment on the emotional environment

The physical environment often reflects the emotional environment (see Chapter 2), as well as reflecting practitioners' strengths and interests. For example, if you have a practitioner who is interested in horticulture, you are likely to have a well-cared for and planted-up garden outdoors. One way to ease transitions through a larger nursery setting is to have the rooms designed to accommodate all the children moving up together, as a social cohort.

Childminders have a different set of challenges and opportunities. Often babies will continue to be cared for by the same childminder in the same rooms or house, until they leave – potentially four years later. Therefore, the children are already familiar with their surroundings. However, the challenge here is now for the childminder to ensure that the physical environment evolves and adapts as the children grow up.

In any type of setting, there are the physical restrictions of the building – for example, access to outdoors, as well as adhering to the statutory limitations on space, and adult:child ratios and facilities required, such as toilets and nappy change areas. Even in Forest Schools, which are learning environments without walls, there are still statutory welfare requirements and limitations that have to be taken into consideration.

'Flow' of the room or environment

The flow of the environment is vitally important. This will be affected by the manner in which the equipment, both permanent and temporary, is arranged within the space in the room. Plan the room by considering *how* the children will use the space. For example:

- Sit quietly and enjoy the books, then provide a space out of the main thoroughfare, with inviting looking cushions and chairs.
- Explore the sensory baskets; place them in an easily accessible place, such as on the middle of a rug near the centre of the room.
- Free flow to outdoors from indoors, making sure the pathway to the doorway is clear and visible from children's height.

Activities

Consider the emotional needs of the age range in the room. For example, are there babies who would benefit from having a rocking chair where you can have a cuddle? Would a sofa be useful for the toddlers to sit on together during story time?

Include photographs of the children displayed at the baby and young children's eye height, so they can see they are valued. Make sure these are updated regularly.

Have pegs, drawers, boxes or special cubbies for each child, so everyone knows they have a special space of their own to keep their precious belongings.

Encourage older children to help in the planning and layout of the room, so they gain a sense of belonging and ownership.

Review Your Practice

Plan the physical environment with the emotional environment in mind. (Think how the children might react to large, open spaces or small, hideaway spaces.)

Reflect on the physical layout and make up of the setting and how this meets the requirements of statutory ratios.

How is the balance of your babies/toddlers/preschool determined?

Could you incorporate family groups/mixed age grouping?

If your baby room is your flagship (and it should be), do you have the capacity to take all the babies throughout the setting?

Are the children's words captured, displayed or is the wall full of 'notices' for practitioners to remember to do things or information for parents? Which of these environments look like the practitioners value children the most?

Quick Summary

Share with parents

The activities and environment at home – for example, positive parenting, the home learning environment and parents' level of education – are among the most important factors in driving children's outcomes (Field, 2010: 38) in the early years.

Therefore, consider how practitioners can share this with parents to continue the learning and development at home.

Environments for talking and listening

Elizabeth Jarman is well known for her Communication Friendly Spaces ©, which are ideas for ways to have small, calm spaces suitable for sharing conversations and to engage in sustained shared thinking. Jarman (2013) suggests that becoming attuned to babies' preferences and interests helps to identify the environments in which they are confident, communicative and engaged. This may be different from baby to baby, so consideration must be given to the unique child and how environments can be differentiated for each child's communication preferences – for example, some babies like to be outdoors and will babble, point and watch other children playing when outdoors. Other babies may prefer to be with their key person (or another practitioner who is close to them) in a quiet corner together. Lansbury (2014: 48) describes this type of area as a 'safe and cozy yes place' where baby and adult can spend extended periods of time. As the baby grows into a toddler, this area could be a safe gated area as children become mobile.

Lighting

The way a room is lit can make a tremendous difference to the feel and look. Babies are still developing their vision from birth, and can initially only see contrasts (for example, black and white shapes) so the room needs to be lit in such as way that there is little glare, and preferably not all from the ceiling (Clare, 2012: 77) as this can then throw the adult's face into shadow for the baby.

In her Communication Friendly Spaces ©, Elizabeth Jarman's research suggested taking out strip lighting and replacing it with pendants and lamps, wall-mounted lighting and to generally have softer lighting conditions. Clare (2012) suggests that the use of colours with babies is thoroughly considered, or else there is a risk of over-stimulation. More and more settings are using neutral and natural materials in their baby rooms, such as hessian as backing to reduce noise and to give a calming background. In addition, easier-to-change displays and at toddler level are less likely to rip or be pulled off.

Review Your Practice

Lie down on the floor in each room and look at the environment from the children's perspective. What can you see? What does it sound like? Are there obvious places for children to go to and talk (either with practitioners or with other children)? How could this be improved? (Think of pop-up tents, net curtain or shower curtains to create spaces within the room.)

Case Study

Example of Elizabeth Jarman's Communication Friendly Spaces ©

Watch this Vimeo on Elizabeth Jarman's website (scroll to the bottom of the page to find the Vimeo link): www.elizabethjarmantraining.co.uk/index.php?option=com_content&view=article&id=2&Itemid=6

Although it features children up to and including primary school age, a lot of the key messages are the same – for example, decluttering and not over-stimulating with too many displays and hanging items, and including the children in choices in the environment wherever possible. See how many examples of different 'cosy corners' you can see in the Vimeo.

Consider the environment in your setting. How many cosy corners do you have? How could you differentiate this for different babies and children? (Think of outdoor dens, inside cushions and curtains, use of cardboard boxes.)

Environments for learning and growing – cognition

An enabling environment is linked closely to observation, assessment and planning (Hutchin, 2012: 32), especially with the rapidly changing needs of babies and very young children. It is very easy to underestimate children's abilities, if care is not taken to constantly review their progress. It is useful to reflect back on older photos and videos to remind yourself of the progress that children have made and to keep stretching and challenging them.

It is important to remember the familiar as well as the new and exciting, especially for younger children as this gives them a stable base to work from. It can be disconcerting for young children to find that 'your' room has all been changed over the weekend – think how you feel when your regular supermarket has moved everything around since you last visited.

Tidy-up time can be a time for fun, especially as toddlers become more independent and can help. Many children will often enjoy this 'grown-up' job, as well as encouraging a feeling of confidence and achievement. Giving children a five-minute warning, accompanied by a regular signal such as a tidy-up song or turning the lights on and off, will give them time to finish their play and emotionally prepare for the end of the session. Obviously the less you have to disturb children's play the better.

Activities

Small changes can sometimes really enhance the environment, such as putting crinkly paper on the floor of the crawling tunnel so the babies and young children have a different tactile and auditory experience.

Consider all the senses when planning activities.

Quick Summary

The seven senses

The first five senses are well known:

- sense of smell
- sense of sight
- sense of hearing
- sense of touch
- sense of taste.

However, there are two other senses that we also rely on.

Proprioception is knowing where your body is in space, so that you can sit on a chair without looking behind you or pick up a plastic cup without squashing it or dropping it.

Vestibular is having a sense of balance and motion, so you can walk on a moving ship, balance on a log and spin round in a circle without falling over.

Is the environment still suitable for this cohort of children?

Review your environment for the age and stage of the children that you have right now.

- Is it still suitable for this cohort of children? Is there enough challenge and sensory stimulation?
- Have you made the environment so 'safe' that there are no challenges any more, such as steps or changes in level?
- Do you have open, empty areas where children can run freely and also areas where children have to negotiate around obstacles?
- How do you imagine the flow of the room when full?
- How might the flow be rearranged for another cohort of children (say, those who attend on another day)?

Environments for inclusion and differentiation

It is almost always true that improving the environment for children with additional needs will improve the environment for all children. As an example, having a clear, visual timeline is beneficial for many children on the autistic spectrum, and is also very useful for every child (and adult) in the setting to be aware of what will be happening next in the daily routine. The environment not only gives babies and young children opportunities to move and explore new sensation, but their 'metacognitive and self-regulatory abilities are significantly affected by environment' (Moylett 2013: 26).

Longitudinal studies show that effective early educational environments have two important aspects:

1   'Real intellectual challenge'
2   Children are 'very much in control of their own learning'.

All practitioners need to be aware that parents or at-home young children may not be allowed to explore or touch things as they are in your setting. This could mean that they don't know that if you pull the bottom jigsaw from the shelf, all the other boxes may come down too.

Inclusion and the environment should reflect the culture of the setting and the cultures of the families attending the setting. This is so the children and families feel welcomed and valued.

Activities

For their cognitive, physical (sensory) and emotional development children need a learning-rich environment. All children need natural materials for their feel, smell and visual attraction.

For babies this is crucially important so all of their senses are stimulated right from the start. This includes very simple adjustments to the environment - for example, having a wide range of different surface types to lie on, and crawl on as they develop.

For young children the texture and the nature of the surfaces need to be varied - for example, a range of slopes, steps, grass and sand to practise walking on. This gives the dual outcome of sensory input as well as practicing different types of walking.

Is the environment suitable for everyone?

Review the environment from a multiprofessional's viewpoint. For example, how suitable is it for children who have:

- Visual impairment? Are doorways, edges of furniture and trip hazards clear to see against their background? If you have pale wooden furniture and a laminate floor, being able to see the edge of the table may be very hard.
- Hearing impairment? Are there a lot of hard, flat surfaces (blank walls, large window) that cause reverberation? Can you add curtains or hessian-backed displays to 'deaden' this confusing noise?

In the age group birth to three there are likely to be some children who don't have a formal diagnosis yet, so it is worth reviewing your environment just in case there are children who would struggle otherwise.

Always be watchful for additional needs or SEN even with your youngest children, and there may be intermittent additional needs such as when 'glue ear' (otitis media with effusion, OME) causes temporary hearing loss.

Quick Summary

Top three thoughts on good practice

1 Consider all the senses during sensory play. Do you always include a sense of smell? Do you present prickly or scratchy items?
2 Visual timelines support all children. How do children know what will be happening next? How can they judge how long until home time?
3 Regularly review your environment from the children's perspective. Is it cluttered? How would a child with a hearing or visual impairment experience the environment?

Case Study

The 'home corner'

Blackpool Local Authority has a significant travelling and fairground worker population, whose children, on occasion, attend local pre-schools and settings. They are usually physically very capable children and love to play in the 'home corner'.

One setting I was working with were very conscious that their home corner was a reflection of a kitchen and living room of a traditional house, with a layout and accessories unfamiliar to the traveller children who were attending the setting.

Therefore, they rearranged the area so it was more of a caravan shape, hung net curtains at the window and hung pictures of horses and ponies as decoration (a big part of this travelling community was their horses).

The practitioners reported back that the children had been thrilled to see their new home corner. One little boy, who had spoken very little the previous week, started telling his key person about his pony and learning to ride. The other children were also fascinated and were asking about the travellers' caravans and the horses.

How else could your home corner reflect other cultures? (Think of traditional cooking equipment, using empty boxes printed in Polish or other languages.)

The outdoor environment for babies and young children

There are many good reasons for being outdoors. Jan White (2008: 3) lists over a dozen unique benefits, from fresh air to an environment that 'feeds information into all the senses' to social interactions – and many of these are happening simultaneously, so children are getting a good holistic environment for learning, by simply being outside. However, it seems to become more problematic when considering babies going outdoors, with many fewer baby rooms having free flow access to the outdoors. With careful consideration of how to organise this environment physically – for example, if a separate, fenced-off area is needed or if another surface for the babies to sit on would be preferable, this is achievable (Clare, 2012). Practitioners still need to be attuned to children's interests and fascinations, and to appreciate going outdoors with babies is just as important as going outdoors with pre-schoolers.

Activities

There are some outdoors challenges, such as:

- Babies still mouthing items
- Babies and toddlers having an awareness of dangers
- Babies are not able to say whether they are hot/cold/comfortable
- Practical cover – for example, if one practitioner has to go in to change a nappy, what happens to the ratios?

Sometimes bringing outdoors into the indoor environment still provides some of the experiences for the babies – for example, putting snow onto a tray and bringing it into the baby room for them to play with, or having plant cuttings indoors. However, the physical environment outdoors is unique – the feel of the weather, the sounds and smells are a vital part of being outdoors. Sanitising this experience for babies reduces the benefits considerably.

Although childminders may not necessarily have access to a large, resourced garden, they do have the advantage of being able to access outdoors more easily on trips and outings into the local community (or even further afield), which also give ever-changing experiences in new places. This also offers opportunities for quality practice by offering access to different parks, which have 'physical challenge appropriate to their age and stage of development' (Clare, 2012: 77). Outdoor environments in a setting are much more diverse than indoor but are sometimes are less thoughtfully designed for babies – for example, not having overhead items for babies to watch from the prams or buggies; quieter areas away from the sudden noises of the older children and separate seating so practitioners can give bottles outdoors.

White (2008: 3) lists six 'ingredients' for a 'full menu of rich and satisfying outdoor provision' for young children each offering a 'highly holistic learning experience':

1   Natural materials outdoors
2   Experiences of the living world outdoors
3   Play with water
4   Physical play and movement
5   Imaginative and creative
6   Construction and dens.

Outdoors can be a calming space as well as an active one (White, 2008: 7), and new research is showing that children diagnosed with autism are much calmer while outdoors (Natural England, 2013).

Children can also feel less 'controlled' by adults outdoors (White, 2008: 8), which can be a significant aspect, especially as two-year-olds and older start to challenge boundaries and gain their independence. Being outdoors may be a more suitable environment for children to explore their independence, as they can choose to be quiet or be boisterous.

Review Your Practice

Consider Jan White's six ingredients. Does your outdoor environment offer all of these? How could you enhance them so all ages, from babies to older children, could have equal access?

Case Study

What nature teaches children, by Nilda Cosco (A TEDxRaleigh talk)

Some children spend most of their waking hours in childcare every weekday, where they can play outdoors and learn from nature. Interacting with plants and insects outside is found to be fundamental for children's health and well-being. In her talk, Nilda Cosco explains the importance of being outdoors as it releases the power of experiential learning and creates lifelong memories of nature: www.youtube.com/watch?v=Dhas9OEc1Lk

Look at the images of her setting's outdoor area. What is most noticeable?

Would you have stopped the boy picking the beans, standing on the wheeled truck?

What are your experiences of growing vegetables with children?

Do you have an 'enticing' environment outdoors?

Quick Summary

Key person

A key person in a setting is a named person who has special responsibility for their key children, their family and any other agencies involved with the family. This good practice is the practical application of Attachment Theory, which says that a baby's emotional well-being is greatly improved if he or she has at least one adult to whom they can 'attach' or bond with.

The key person role includes emotional support, keeping the child in mind, observing (and acting on, where necessary) any changes in mood, health or behaviour, liaising with parents and being a special person for their children.

This includes all areas of development, and often the key person is the first one to notice progress or problems with their key children, in all areas of learning and development.

Challenges for setting up environments

Practitioners have to be aware of children's ever-changing needs, as well as arranging the environment according to their own ethos and philosophy. For example, should a day nursery look like a home with comfortable armchairs or should it be more 'schooly' with chairs and tables to work at? Conversely, how much should a childminder's home look like an educational establishment, with displays on the walls and designated play areas?

There are some practical considerations within different environments. For example, keeping pets may be very natural for childminders or settings in rural areas, but present challenges in an urban day nursery (which may be closed over the weekend and holidays etc.).

Every setting will have restrictions and unique challenges, from being near a main road to having to pack away before the yoga class starts. These should be reviewed, discussed and monitored regularly to ensure that the environment is not having a negative impact on children's learning and development.

Opportunities

Practitioners have opportunities to make the environment suitably stimulating, accessible and challenging for babies and young children.

The environment at a setting may be able to provide opportunities that the home learning environment is unable to – for example, a climbing frame outdoors, messy play or pets. These environments will complement babies and children's learning experiences.

Conclusions

The physical environment can help or hinder good practice and babies' and young children's learning and development. Practitioners can ensure the physical environment is suitable by being aware of the components of a quality environment and understanding the impact this has on babies and young children. The outdoor environment in particular, with its natural challenges, can support independence, physical development as well as quiet areas for speech and language.

Every setting's physical environment is unique and should change and evolve with the babies and children who attend the setting. A childminder's home will look very different to a large day nursery, but both can provide opportunities for holistic development for babies and young children.

Further Reading and Research

Clare (2012: 73) discusses the suitability of high chairs for feeding babies and toddlers in a day nursery setting.

- How do you feed the babies and toddlers in a day nursery? Is this comfortable for you as well as pleasant for the babies?
- As a childminder, are you able to use a dining table effectively with suitably sized high chairs or similar?

'Sleeping outdoors is preferable for babies and toddlers' (Clare, 2012: 74): How often do the children sleep outdoors? What are the benefits and challenges of this?

References

Blum-Ross, A. and Livingstone S. (2016) *Families and Screen Time: Current Advice and Emerging Research.* Media Policy Brief 17. London: Media Policy Project, London School of Economics and Political Science.

Braithwaite, J. (2014) GRT. In *Inclusion for Early Years.* Abingdon: David Fulton.

Burton, A. (2015) *Supporting the Best Start in Life.* London: PHE.

Callanan, M., Anderson, M., Haywood, S., Hudson, R. and Speight, S. (2017) *Study of Early Education and Development: Good Practice in Early Education Research Report.* London: NatCen Social Research for the

DfE. Available from: www.gov.uk/government/collections/study-of-early-education-and-development-seed. Accessed 10 June 2017.

Clare, A. (2012) *Learning Environments for Babies and Toddlers*. London: SAGE.

Dowling, M. (2014) (4th edn) *Young Children's Personal, Social and Emotional Development*. London: SAGE.

Early Education (2012) *Development Matters*. London: DfE.

Evangelou, M., Sylva, K., Kyriacou, M., Wild, M. and Glenny, G. (2009) *Early Years Learning and Development. Literature Review*. Oxford: DCSF.

Field, F. (2010) *The Foundation Years: Preventing Poor Children Becoming Poor Adults. The Report of the Independent Review on Poverty and Life Chances*. London: Cabinet Office.

Goouch, K. and Powell, S. (2013) *The Baby Room. Research Summary 2*. Canterbury: Canterbury Christ Church University.

Gopnik, A. (2010) How Babies Think. *Scientific American* Vol. 303, pp. 76–81.

Harms, T., Cryer, D., Clifford, R. and Yazejian, N. (2017) (3rd edn) *Infant/Toddler Environment Rating Scale (ITERS-3)*. New York: Teachers' College Press.

Hutchin, V. (2012) *The EYFS: A Practical Guide for Students and Professionals*. Abingdon: Hodder Education.

ISSA (2014) *Measuring and Improving Quality in Early Childhood Environments*. The Netherlands: ISSA.

Jarman, E. (2013) *A Place to Talk for Babies*. London: Featherstone.

Laevers, F. (ed.) (1994) *Well-being and Involvement in Care Settings. A Process-oriented Self-evaluation Instrument*. Leuven: Leuven University.

Lansbury, J. (2014) *Elevating Child Care: A Guide to Respectful Parenting*. Createspace Amazon.

Lindon, J. and Brodie, K. (2016) *Understanding Child Development 0–8 Years* (4th edn). London: Hodder Education.

Mathers, S., Eisenstadt, N., Sylva, K., Soukakou, E. and Ereky-Stevens, K. (2014) *Sound Foundations: A Review of the Research Evidence on Quality of Early Childhood Education and Care for Children under Three. Implications for Policy and Practice Research*. London: The Sutton Trust.

Moylett, H. (2013) *Characteristics of Effective Early Learning*. Maidenhead: Open University.

National Strategies (2008a) *Early Years Quality Improvement Support Programme (EYQISP)*. Nottingham: DCSF.

National Strategies (2008b) *Social and Emotional Aspects of Development (SEAD)*. Nottingham: DCSF.

Natural England (2013) *Engaging Children on the Autistic Spectrum with the Natural Environment: Teacher Insight Study and Evidence Review*. Commissioned Report NECR116. Available from: www.naturalengland.org.uk

Siraj, I., Kingston, D. and Melhuish, E. (2015) *Sustained Shared Thinking and Emotional Well-being (SSTEW) Scale for 2–5 Year Olds Provision*. London: IOE.

White, J. (2008) *Playing and Learning Outdoors*. Abingdon: Routledge.

10 Effective partnerships

Early childhood teachers need to understand the influence of sociocultural contexts and family circumstances on learning, recognize children's developing competencies, and be familiar with the variety of ways that children may demonstrate their developmental achievements.

National Association for the Education of Young Children, 2009: 13

Introduction

Practitioners rely on information from parents about their babies, from care routines to food choices and soothing techniques. Parents are the most knowledgeable about their own children, so practitioners need to have two complementary skill sets – being able to communicate effectively and sensitively with parents and being able to meet the care and educational needs of their children. This will look different depending on the type of setting and the type of care provided (day care, sessional care, drop in, crèche etc.). For example, many childminders have a close relationship with a handful of parents over a long period of time, whereas practitioners in a busy baby room in a large setting may know many families, but for less than a year, because the children move into the toddler room.

Irrespective of the length of time you have known parents, it is an essential part of the practitioner and key person role to have an effective, meaningful and genuine relationship with parents and those with parental responsibility. This is vital for the successful sharing of information, which may sometimes include personal information about the baby in your care or possibly any concerns that you may have. In order to be able to do this, you will need to consider the parents' expectations of care and education for their baby or young child, their culture and home learning environment.

Parent partnership

Settings must (i.e. they have a statutory duty) provide parents with information on the Early Years Foundation Stage (EYFS), the types of activities the children do, how Special Educational Needs are supported, the food and drink supplied, the setting's policy and procedures, and staffing, such as key person (DfE, 2017: 33). In addition, there are a number of recommendations for good practice, such as parents should be kept up to date with their child's progress and development, and should encourage parents to share the two-year-old progress check with relevant professionals. These are the very basics of a good parent partnership. However, genuine, trusting and respectful joint partnership with parents and carers means that parents are actively involved with their children's learning and care in the setting – for example, parents taking observations and reflections into the setting to add to their child's folder. The growing use of electronic systems of recording has made sharing a video clip or photos easier than ever, and this should be encouraged. It is even more important when working with babies and young children, because parents will be the only source of information about the home learning environment and children's well-being.

Margy Whalley and her team at Pen Green research centre in Corby have researched with, worked with, employed and/or trained over 6,000 parents. The centre's ethos has always revolved around developing a 'comprehensive parent partnership programme that recognised the critical role parents have to play as their child's primary educators' (Pen Green, 2017: 1). When the research base was established in 1996, 'parents were involved with the advisory group for the Research Base'. This level of partnership is possibly unique, but it demonstrates what can be achieved if parent partnership is a core consideration of the setting. While working with parents in the setting, the parental group focused on the birth to three age range (Whalley and the Pen Green Team, 2008: 143) and used the four psychoanalytic theories of holding, containment, companionship and attachment.

Holding: Holding in mind, even when you are not there – for example, letting children know that you'll come back from leaving the room.
Containment: The adult (parent or practitioner) 'contains' the baby or young child's emotions, recognising and acknowledging them.
Companionship: 'An effective parent–infant exchange can have the quality of a conversation between equals'

Whalley and the Pen Green Team, 2008: 144

⚡ Quick Summary

Secure attachment

Secure Attachment is typical for the majority of children and is described as emotionally healthy. It is characterised by a child who is in distress after a brief separation, but can be comforted and settled by the caregiver reasonably quickly.

Page, Clare and Nutbrown (2013: 36) theorise that:

1 High-quality caregiver relationships are central to emotional development and learning in infants and toddlers.
2 Relationships take time to develop, so the key person must be given that time and opportunity to become attached to their key baby or key toddler.

In addition, the team videoed the parent–baby interactions and reviewed them with the parents. This allowed them to discuss the session, and also starts the dialogue around child development, expectations and making observations of their play. This has been termed 'reflective parenting' (Whalley and the Pen Green Team, 2008: 155) and demonstrates highly advanced parent partnerships. Many settings would have neither the time nor the environment to do this on a regular basis, but it does highlight some areas of good practice:

- Sharing information with parents about their own child is more meaningful than generic advice or information packs.
- Parents will have different levels of existing knowledge about children, child development and early education. Time spent finding out the parent's individual comprehension, their concerns and their experiences is time well spent.
- Involving parents must be a two-way exchange, so you can find out about them, their families and their children, as well as giving information from a practitioner's point of view of childcare and education.
- Not every parent may be as enthusiastic or passionate about child development (and some may feel they don't need to know, because *you* are the expert), so be mindful of this and adjust the amount of information sharing accordingly.
- Alternatively, there may be a group of parents who are very keen to find out more, so practitioners need to consider how to meet this need – for example, doing a parent's training session, having key group parents come in together or having an information-sharing open day with small workshops for parents.

 Quick Summary

Key person

A key person in a setting is a named person who has special responsibility for their key children, their family and any other agencies involved with the family. This good practice is the practical application of Attachment Theory, which says that a baby's emotional well-being is greatly improved if he or she has at least one adult to whom they can 'attach' or bond with.

The key person role includes emotional support, keeping the child in mind, observing (and acting on, where necessary) any changes in mood, health or behaviour, liaising with parents and being a special person for their children.

This includes all areas of development, and often the key person is the first to notice progress or problems with their key children, in all areas of learning and development.

Home learning environment

The home learning environment (HLE) is the type of play, learning and interactions that happen at home, including reading books, playing games together, counting together and talking together. It is 'strongly associated with children's intellectual and social development ... what parents do with their children is more important than who parents are' (Sylva *et al.*, 2004: 25). Similarly, in the Field Review, it states that:

> There is now a significant consensus amongst academics and professionals that factors in the home environment – positive parenting, the home learning environment and parents' level of education – are the most important.
>
> Field, 2010: 38

This has been demonstrated again recently as part of Professors Pascal and Bertram's research, High Achieving White Working Class (HAWWC) boys research project (Pascal *et al.*, 2016). This research analysed why a small number of boys from white, working-class backgrounds were performing in the top 5 per cent of children in England (as measured by the EYFS profile). One of the 'inner circles of success' (Pascal *et al.*, 2016: 13) was the home learning environment. The outcomes were very good for the boys where there was evidence:

> of warm, nurturing, attentive, relaxed but 'boundaried', parenting, with regular routines, provides the basic nutrients for optimal development; parents who enjoy spending time with their son, and support and encourage the young boy's interests and passions encourage self-motivation and self-directed learning.
>
> Pascal *et al.*, 2016: 17

Therefore, it makes good sense to work in partnership with parents to ensure the home learning environment is as good as can possibly be. This is stated in the EYFS (DfE, 2017: 13) as, 'practitioners must discuss with parents and/or carers how the [two-year-old progress check] summary of development can be used to support learning at home'. Note that this is a 'must', so there is a statutory duty to ensure this happens. The All-Party Parliamentary Group on a Fit and Healthy Childhood (2015: 38) also suggests that advice and support is given to parents about play, and that it is 'as essential as offering information about their feeding'.

For some parents, leaving their baby with someone else can be very stressful and even guilt inducing. The way in which parents reach their decision is 'complicated and unique to their individual circumstances' (Page, Clare and Nutbrown, 2013: 194). There may be genuine concerns from the parents about the baby 'transferring' their love to the practitioner, which need to be addressed and allayed.

Quick Summary

Professional love

This is a concept formulated by Dr Jools Page to explain the love that practitioners feel for the babies and children in their care. It is the affectionate and caring behaviours that happen when you care for babies and children, even though it is part of your professional role. Dr Page's research started with a focus on babies, but the concept is equally applicable to older children.

Reflective Questions

Partnerships with parents

Think about how you partner with parents in your setting. For many settings the partnership consists of information about the babies' and children's well-being coming from you, and essential information (such as bottles, comforter, pick-up times) coming from parents.

How much further do you extend the partnership? For example:

- Sending out and receiving photos and video clips
- Open days or evenings for existing parents to attend and ask questions
- Parents' evenings or meetings regularly throughout the year
- Joint planning of activities and the environment with parents
- Working with parents to develop their own skills in observation or schema
- Joint research project with parents.

Cultural care

Cultural identity can be defined as people who identify with particular groups based on their birthplace, country of origin, ethnicity, language, values, beliefs or worldviews (KidsMatter, 2012). It must be noted that not everyone in each group will be identical or all hold the same views, but it is an overview of the group. This cultural diversity is the difference between groups. Culture is one of the strands that weaves children's identity and sense of belonging. Children will have several areas of identity – for example, as an individual, in the family (oldest of two children), setting (youngest in the toddler room) and community (head teacher's son) or in the individual, microsystem and mesosystem respectively (Bronfenbrenner, 1979). They may have a stronger sense of belonging in one area over the others, and it is likely that this is the cultural group that they will most identify with. For example, they may recognise the setting as being a large part of their life, but may not yet be aware of the larger community links.

Differences in parenting across cultures

There may be significant differences in the ways that parents from different cultures expect children to behave, disciplining of children, gender expectations and possibly concerns about children losing their cultural identity when they become part of the setting's community. There may also be confusion from young children as they adapt to two different cultures.

Where parents have moved to a new culture, parenting practices may change to match the destination culture, but this seems to vary from culture to culture. For example, Japanese mothers' practice tends to match those of American mothers once in the US (Bornstein and Bohr, 2011). In addition, there are limitations because many of the tools and standards used for child development are 'still largely Eurocentric' (Bornstein and Bohr, 2011: 4).

Research has shown that well-educated and dual-income parents from Eastern Europe moving to the US 'report maintaining elements of their culture and parenting strategies, while actively participating in the larger society and adopting new values and childrearing practices' (Nesteruk and Marks, 2011: 821), thereby taking the best from each culture for their children. One of the challenges, however, was the perceived lack of respect from the children towards their elders in the destination culture. Interestingly, this has also been found in the Latin American, Asian, Middle-Eastern and African cultures who reside in the US. In Australia, it was found that in cultures where individualism and independence is seen as being important, the 'expression of emotion is encouraged and children are taught to communicate their personal feelings. Collectivist societies, however, tend to emphasise emotional control' (Wise and da Silva, 2007) to maintain group dynamics. For example, encouraging a child to discuss and be honest about feelings was important for 40 per cent of Anglo-American mothers, but by none of the Chinese-American mothers. There were also different expectations for child development, including language, obedience and self-regulation.

Within the UK culture

Practitioners must acknowledge and value children's 'experiences due largely to contextual and cultural differences. From a very early age babies and young children search for the meaning of the behaviours and speech of those around them' (David *et al.*, 2003: 32). It is accepted that between one year and three years old, children will begin to understand what is 'culturally acceptable behaviour and speech and this is the result of being involved in interactions during the first year of life' (David *et al.*, 2003: 9).

Reflective Questions

How cultures around the world think about parenting

In an article in the online *TED magazine* (2014), Amy Choi compares and contrasts how child-rearing ideas from Japan, Norway, Spain – and beyond – differ – for example, time spent outdoors, bedtimes and walking by yourself to the local shops. You can find the article here: http://ideas.ted.com/how-cultures-around-the-world-think-about-parenting/

Do some of these practices match your own practice?

What would you feel uncomfortable about letting young children do?

Reflective Questions

Where in the world?

www.youtube.com/watch?v=gIZ8PkLMMUo

In this TedxUCLA talk, 'What is the most important influence on child development?' by Tom Weisner, he discusses the well-being of the child – in particular, as being contextualised and dependent on where in the world the child lives and is growing up: 'By learning about the rest of the world, we will understand better how to take care of kids here and everywhere' (3 min 22 s).

How might living in a Westernised, educated society influence our thinking on children's well-being? (Think about where most of the research is conducted and with what type of children.)

How can understanding childhood elsewhere in the world help our understanding of childhood in our settings? (Think about the things we take for granted – for example, 'community of care' where there are multiple caregivers or the different ways in which boys and girls live after early childhood.)

How would *you* define well-being in this context? (Think of your own values and context.)

Weisner (2016: 113) cites Konner as describing cultural acquisition devices (CAD), which have four categories of mechanisms by which culture is acquired. These are:

1   Reactive processes (Classical conditioning, social facilitation or intentional conditioning)
2   Social learning (scaffolding, ZPD, imitation, direct instruction)
3   Emotional learning processes (attachment, emotional management through cultural rituals)
4   Symbolic processes (schematic learning, cognitive modelling).

The opportunities for babies to develop their own understanding of their culture will be present constantly. For example, what do adults do when a baby cries? Is he or she picked up immediately? Do adults always 'solve' problems without letting children try first? What happens on birthdays or religious festivals? Do adults encourage and support schematic play?

It is evident from these four categories that the acquisition of culture starts from birth and is also dependent on many other areas of development, such as personal, social and emotional development, language development and types of play that are encouraged. Benham (2016: 1) notes that it can sometimes be easy to make assumptions and jump to conclusions about family life but that when she visited homes as a paediatric nurse, 'you could maybe see they were also looking after an elderly relative for instance, or both parents were in high pressure jobs, and have little time to do the care, or if they did the care, they would forfeit time playing and reading to their children'. This is a reminder that family situations vary and there may be circumstances beyond the control of parents that could have an impact on their children's learning and development.

'Quality' is cultural

Some aspects of cultural differences are obvious, such as language, some less so, such as eye contact (Ionescu and Tankersley, 2016: 40) care and feeding routines. There are cultural similarities that practitioners need to be aware of, such as maternal depression (or post-natal depression) (Cuthbert *et al.* 2011). 'Pedagogy of care' is considered a universal quality service by Ionescu and Tankersley (2016: 16) because it considers children as being vulnerable, but equally as competent learners and communicators. However, Goouch and Powell (2013: 5) note that quality care is 'highly individual and subjective' varying from family to family, and that the concerns about relationships between baby and practitioner may threaten the relationships between baby and parent.

 Quick Summary

Pedagogy

Pedagogy is the combination of the methods of teaching, the ethos, the interactions between baby or child and practitioner, the learning environment and the curriculum. It is the *way* teaching is conducted, considered as a whole with the content. It could be considered to be the holistic methods by which teaching and learning occur.

Your own culture and its impact

Every practitioner has his or her own culture, heritage and background. For some practitioners this could be a large part of their personal identity, but others may have never reflected on their own culture. However, practitioners should examine their own cultural experiences, because they shape 'their perspective and to realize that multiple perspectives, not just their own, must be considered in decisions about children's development and learning' (National Association for the Education of Young Children, 2009: 1). For example, a practitioner's assumptions and expectations may affect the way that they assess both social and educational outcomes of children in their care (Stirrup, Evans and Davies, 2016). Cultural background may also affect language skill and the 'development of musicality form an early age' (Evangelou, *et al*, 2009: 82).

The culture of your setting

Settings have a culture that is shaped by the ethos, interactions and attitudes of the practitioners working there. For example, a philosophy around supporting each individual child and ensuring their well-being is a priority that will probably result in a strong key person system.

If the quality and quantity of interactions are valued, this gives a good foundation for interactions with parents – for example:

- Having a variety of different ways of communicating (email, text, letter, electronic records)
- Checking communications for gender bias (Is it always 'mums' or mums and dads?) and being sensitive towards family make-up (blended family, same-sex parents, single parent)
- Being aware of and empathetic to some of the challenges parents themselves have (EAL, literacy issues, post-natal depression, sleeplessness, anxiety about leaving a baby for the first time, breastfeeding, post-op considerations, financial issues if one parent is currently on maternity/paternity leave)
- Encouraging parents and extended family into the setting (not simply 'we have an open-door policy')
- Being thoughtful about the times of day for parents (mornings or lunchtimes may be preferable times to meet or talk).

Although being thoughtful about these things may take time and extra effort, it could make the difference between a parent feeling comfortable and confident in leaving their child or not. In turn, the babies and young children will pick up on this, so influencing their mood and well-being. It should be noted that sharing and collecting information should be done in a culturally sensitive manner, especially sharing information with others. When interpreting the data that have been collected, 'cultural diversity in childrearing' should be reflected (Anderson Moore et al., 2017: 8).

Reflective Questions

The culture of your setting

Reflect for a minute on how you would describe the culture of *your* setting. If you have a mission statement or core values, what do these say about working with parents?

Holistic links in this chapter

- *How the home learning environment can support holistic development*
- *Cultural and cognition development*
- *Partnerships with other professionals*
- *Quality and expectations from different cultures and parenting backgrounds.*

How the home learning environment can support holistic development

It is well established that the home learning environment has a significant influence on babies' and young children's holistic development (Sylva *et al.*, 2004; Field, 2010; Finnegan, 2016). This is both physical environment, but more importantly, the emotional environment and encouragement that parents and extended family can give to children. Practitioners can support parents and their home learning environment by providing activity ideas and sharing good practice in a sensitive and caring way.

Easy activities to share with parents

Help build your child's brain by talking to them right from the start.

For babies

- Play 'baby' games together (peepo or sticking your tongue out). Watch for your baby's reaction, and if they enjoy it, do it again.
- Respond to the noises your baby makes. Echo their cooing noises. Comment on what you think they might be trying to say - e.g., 'You like that, don't you?'
- Sing songs and look at pictures or books together. Your baby doesn't have to know what the words mean, they will enjoy spending time with you and hearing you talk or sing.

Review Your Practice

How often do you share with parents and carers how well their children are progressing? (Think about detailed sharing as well as the 'He's had a great day' conversations at the door.)

How do you know parents understand and further support learning at home? (Think about some of the jargon that is used in the Early Years sector - EYFS, PSED, progress check, long observation, next steps - do parents always understand?)

How do parents know that you have listened and incorporated their feedback into your plans? (Think of sharing photos with parents.)

For toddlers

- Talk about what you see and hear around you.
- Keep your sentences short and simple.
- Use sentences that are one word longer than your toddler uses. So, if they say mainly one-word sentences, you use two. This helps their understanding and teaches them what to aim for next.
- Keep dummies for bedtime – children who have a dummy in their mouth for a lot of the day don't get as much practice at talking. That can mean the sounds they use aren't clear and they may use fewer words.

(Finnegan, 2016: 11)

 Case Study

HAWWC

The High Achieving, White Working Class (HAWWC) boys project (Pascal *et al.*, 2016) investigated 30 or so families, where a boy in the family was achieving well above average (in the top 10 per cent at least in the country, on the EYFS Profile) against the statistical odds (i.e. they were young boys, white AND working class). The aim of the project was to identify how these boys and their families had achieved so much, and ultimately how these methods could inform good practice for other families in the same situation.

In an interview (Brodie, 2017: 39), Professors Chris Pascal and Tony Bertram explain how 'they weren't extraordinary parents. They were excellent parents – in extraordinary circumstances. So they were doing all the beautiful things that you want a parent to do'.

They go on to explain:

- They had someone special 'fall in love' with them (sometimes mum, sometimes an older sibling or other family member).
- The key person at their setting had formed a strong bond with both the child and the family (in some cases, extended family).
- The child's abilities were affirmed by their special person and the setting.
- Being outdoors seemed to be a common trait.
- Noticing what the boys were interested in.
- Routines, although these were flexible and responsive.

Read the full findings here: www.crec.co.uk/hawwc-boys

How can you work with parents and carers (and other significant people) in children's lives to help support their holistic development?

What could you implement from this piece of research?

Culture and cognition development

'Babies seem to be tuned to learn from, with and about, first the people and the cultural environment around them, followed by the material environment – they come into the world primed to be curious, competent learners' (David *et al.*, 2003: 9).

The local culture and community culture will affect both what babies and children learn and how they learn it. There may be very significant differences. For example, gypsy, Roma and travelling (GRT) often have more freedom to play outdoors (Braithwaite, in Brodie and Savage, 2015) with little or no adult supervision and spend very little time indoors, so learning indoors with adults could feel very different. However, this offers an opportunity to celebrate gypsy and traveller cultures, especially as it is rarely recognised or valued (Levinson, 2005; Cemlyn *et al.*, 2009), as well as enjoying learning outdoors.

Activities to support culture and cognition

Ask parents, grandparents and extended family for any culturally specific songs or music and any dances that accompany them.

Research and find the history of the area that the setting is in: what is the area's cultural background? Discuss this with the children and encourage them to think about what it may have been like years ago.

Review Your Practice

How do you respect and incorporate culture (your own and others) into your setting? (Think of sharing and celebrate your own culture as well as others.)

What type of activities would be meaningful cultural activities for babies? (Think about information from parents on their own routines, such as singing before naptime.)

How can including culture improve children's cognition? (Think about feelings of belonging and well-being supporting cognition.)

How can you sensitively and respectfully ensure that parents are aware that you are including some cultural references? (Think about participation.)

How could you work with other settings to expand your knowledge and understanding about other cultures and heritages?

Partnerships with other professionals

Integrated health and educational care is currently being championed in England – for example, the two-year-old 'Progress Check' (DfE, 2017: 13). This is a three-way check on toddlers' development, with information from parents, the health visitor and the educational establishment

Case Study

Quarry Bank Mill

I am lucky enough to live near Quarry Bank Mill, Styal, which was the inspiration for the TV series *The Mill*. Every schoolchild in the area will almost certainly have been on a school trip to the mill to see the working and living conditions of children of their own age who were apprenticed there.

Styal village, St Bartholomew's church, the mill and the river Bollin running alongside it are reminders of our local cultural heritage, built by Samuel Greg in 1784. In addition, this local piece of history gives a window onto the later cotton boom in the mid-nineteenth century, when Manchester was dubbed 'Cottonopolis'. Even today in Australia and New Zealand you will occasionally still find the department where you buy cotton bed sheets referred to as 'Manchester'.

Although taken for granted by many local children, this piece of cultural history usually makes them think about how life has changed in the last 200 years and how it affected the local area.

Find out more about the Apprentice House at Quarry Bank Mill: www.nationaltrust.org.uk/quarry-bank/features/the-apprentice-house-at-quarry-bank

Find out more about the apprentices who inspired the Channel 4 drama *The Mill*, here: https://quarrybankmill.wordpress.com/2013/07/29/apprentice-life-at-quarry-bank/

What sort of local culture do you have near you? (Think about things you may 'take for granted' – for example, local industry or local landmarks.)

How can you make your culture relevant to young children? (Think of the impact on the rest of the community, such as jobs or amenities.)

What can children learn from this?

Quick Summary

Top three thoughts on good practice

1 Consider all the senses during sensory play. Do you always include a sense of smell? Do you present prickly or scratchy items?
2 Visual timelines support all children. How do children know what will be happening next? How can they judge how long until home time?
3 Regularly review your environment from the children's perspective. Is it cluttered? How would a child with a hearing or visual impairment experience the environment?

(i.e. the Early Years setting). It is self-evident that it is beneficial to have as many perspectives as possible drawn together to be able to assess the holistic development of a toddler accurately.

Ideally, there would be a holistic approach to all services, including midwives, paediatricians and children centres, and this would be from pregnancy (Best Beginnings, 2016).

Information that supports good working partnerships

Ensure that the setting has a record of the health visitor for every child (a requirement for England).

Keep in contact with your local authority to ensure you are up to date with any new legislation, training or guidance available.

Make strong links with the pre-school or nursery on to which the babies and young children will move. If this is within your own setting, make sure there are thoughtful handovers, with time taken for children to settle in and pertinent information shared.

 Reflective Questions

Working with outside agencies

Do you have a quiet, private area where you can exchange ideas about child development with outside agencies, without being interrupted by the phone or doorbell?

What do you think the priorities of the other professionals will be and how do you integrate this into your care and education of the children? (Think how a speech and language therapist may focus on communication, a physiotherapist on physical development, teacher for the deaf on room acoustics.)

Do you have procedures for liaising with other agencies? (Think about who is responsible for arranging meetings, who chairs meetings and takes notes, how do you approach out of setting meetings?)

Quality and expectations from different cultures and parenting backgrounds

As the UK becomes an increasingly multicultural country, it is important to be able to adapt appropriately to a range of different situations without losing the quality of the care and early education being provided in the setting. However, 'quality' can be problematic to define at any point, but, as David *et al.* note (2003: 74): 'quality is a value-laden concept, which makes comparisons, particularly those across national or cultural boundaries, difficult to interpret'. The Effective Provision of Pre-School Education (EPPE) project (Sylva *et al.*, 2004) found that one of the biggest indicators of quality in the most effective Early Years settings they studied was the adult-child relationship, especially around interactions. It is from these quality interactions that they coined the term 'Sustained Shared Thinking'. To be able to make these relationships effective, it is important for practitioners to understand the background and cultural expectations of the children and family.

The quality of the home learning environments (HLEs) 'vary with social class' (Evangelou *et al.*, 2009: 9), and research shows that a good-quality setting can compensate for the HLE.

 ## Quick Summary

Sustained shared thinking

Sustained shared thinking is defined as:

> an episode in which two or more individuals 'work together' in an intellectual way to solve a problem, clarify a concept, evaluate activities, extend a narrative etc. Both parties must contribute to the thinking and it must develop and extend.
>
> Sylva *et al.*, 2004: 36

These are the two-way interactions that occur from birth and support babies' and children's thinking processes and knowledge base.

Useful information for sharing

Find out from parents their expectations from their baby or child attending the setting and make sure that you share policy and procedures.

Think about having open days or evenings where you can explain how the setting works, any distinctive ethos or philosophy, such as Forest School or Montessori, and core statutory components such as the key person system and the two-year-old progress check.

Review Your Practice

How does your setting welcome all parents? (Think of parents who may not be used to leaving their children with paid professionals.)

If you ask for a parent's views on childcare, do you always incorporate it into your practice? (Think of corporal punishment or 'only' using English while in the setting.) If not, how do you broach that with parents? (Think of your setting's policies and procedures, research and best practice examples.)

How do different cultures define or view a 'quality' setting? What are the implications about our English views on quality? As a more multicultural country, how do we adapt to this?

Quick Summary

Share with parents

The activities and environment at home – for example, positive parenting, the home learning environment and parents' level of education – are among of the most important factors in driving children's outcomes (Field, 2010: 38) in the early years.

Therefore, consider how practitioners can share this with parents to continue the learning and development at home.

Challenges

It is likely that practitioners will work with babies and young children from increasingly diverse backgrounds, including cultural and linguistic. This may require more diverse pedagogy (Wall, Litjens and Taguma, 2015) and may create challenges for settings that are less flexible or are caught unawares. The types of challenges that may affect children and families from culturally diverse backgrounds include, but are not restricted to, migration and resettlement, the effects of trauma, discrimination, racism and sexism.

The political climate at any time can both be a challenge and an opportunity. In times of austerity and budget cuts, it is a challenge when there are fewer multi-professionals available and less local authority support. However, this also offers an opportunity for practitioners to become skilled to offer some support to parents themselves.

Opportunities

Working in partnership with parents opens a world of opportunities to explore different cultures and traditions, and also to celebrate and value the things we may take for granted. For example, ask parents about the sports that they play, whether they are involved in dance or other physical activities that they may be able to bring into the setting and share with the children. This is not only a good parent partnership, but also good role models as you demonstrate to children that physical activity is for life.

Conclusions

Effective partnership with parents is a meaningful, respectful, two-way relationship. It is partly a statutory duty in England under the EYFS, but it is also beneficial for the care and well-being of the babies and young children too. The home learning environment (HLE) is key to babies' and young children's good outcomes, and this can be supported and helped by practitioners via the parent partnership. However, cultural diversity also needs to be taken into account and practitioners must be aware of their own cultural biases and norms while caring for and educating babies and young children. This is not to say that anything different needs to be done, but that there is an awareness of their pedagogical background. Similarly, it is useful to have effective partnership with other professionals to help promote holistic learning and care.

 Further Reading and Research

The third edition of the excellent *Involving Parents in their Children's Learning* (2017), by Margy Whalley and the team at Pen Green, has some new chapters and updated material.

The Reggio Emilia Approach is recognised for its collaboration and co-construction of knowledge. Find out more here: www.reggioemiliaapproach.net/

For inspiration on practical ideas: Thornton, L. (2014) *Bringing the Reggio Approach to Your Early Years Practice*. Abingdon: Routledge.

For a more in-depth study of the approach: Wharton, P. and Linda Kinney, L. (2015) *Reggio Emilia Encounters: Children and Adults in Collaboration*. Abingdon: Routledge; Asmussen, K., Feinstein, L., Martin, J. and Chowdry, H. (2016) *Foundations for Life: What Works to Support Parent–Child Interaction in the Early Years*. London: Early Intervention Foundation.

This is a comprehensive review of 75 early intervention programmes that are available to parents in the UK, evaluated in terms of cost and impact on the children. These programmes are designed to give support, advice and confidence to parents, in order to improve the quality of young children's environment. The review is about 'how to help parents improve how they relate, engage, communicate, play and live with children so as to improve children's experience of childhood and hopefully enhance their capability to flourish and avoid harm' (Asmussen *et al.*, 2016: 6). The aim is not to simply treat 'symptoms' but to improve the quality of interaction to 'generate real opportunity and reduce risk'.

The focus of the review is on attachment, self-regulation and behaviour, and cognitive development programmes. Each area is analysed and the results from each programme discussed in detail. This makes this review very valuable for students who may need detailed analysis and practitioners who can confidently guide parents towards programmes that are suitable for their needs.

Ann Clare's book, *Creating a Learning Environment for Babies and Toddlers*, has a very useful chapter on 'Parents and the Environment' (p. 100 onwards) that discusses partnership from the parent's perspective.

Families

Are you sure about who has parental responsibility?

You can check for the latest updates and any changes in legislation here: www.gov.uk/parental-rights-responsibilities/what-is-parental-responsibility

In their booklet, *Including Different Families* (2017), the organisation Stonewall explains how to include families with gay parents and how to tackle bullying. Although written with schools in mind, the top 10 tips for including families, starting on p. 30, have some good ideas for parents of children in Early Years settings too. Find the booklet here: www.stonewall.org.uk/sites/default/files/including_different_families_lo.pdf

Megan Beren's (2013) research showed that, even though training on same-sex families was clearly needed, most teachers had neither training nor development. It was found that the majority of teachers wanted training so they could be more inclusive and more welcoming. Find the full research document here: www.learninglandscapes.ca/images/documents/ll-no13/beren.pdf

A site that offers advice to parents about all aspects of parenting is Family Lives: www.familylives.org.uk/advice/your-family/parenting/parenting-in-same-sex-relationships/

The National Strategies Early Years document *Quality Improvement Support Programme (EYQISP)* has some useful ideas for training sessions for staff or for self-reflection on working in partnership with parents and valuing the home learning environment. See p. 35 onwards for a set of four modules on each subject.

References

All-Party Parliamentary Group on a Fit and Healthy Childhood (2015) *Play*. Association of Play Industries. Available from: http://outdoorplayandlearning.org.uk/downloads/. Accessed 8 June 2017.

Anderson Moore, K., Bethell, C. Murphey, D., Carver Martin, M. and Beltz, M. (2017) *Flourishing From the Start: What Is It and How Can It Be Measured?* Child Trends. Available from: www.childtrends.org/publications/flourishing-start-can-measured/. Accessed 10 June 2017.

Asmussen, K., Feinstein, L., Martin, J. and Chowdry, H. (2016) *Foundations for Life: What Works to Support Parent-Child Interaction in the Early Years*. London: Early Intervention Foundation.

Benham, K. (2016) *Reflections on Family Diversity*. Available from: www.kathybrodie.com/guest-post/family-diversity/. Accessed 6 June 2017.

Beren, M. (2013) Gay and Lesbian Families in the Early Childhood Classroom. *LEARNing Landscapes* Vol. 7 Iss. 1, pp. 61-79.

Best Beginnings (2016) *The 1,001 Critical Days*. Available from: www.1001criticaldays.co.uk. Accessed 11 June 2016.

Bornstein, M. and Bohr, Y. (2011) Immigration, Acculturation and Parenting, in Tremblay, R.E. Boivin, M. and Peters, R. (eds) *Encyclopedia on Early Childhood Development* [online]. Montreal: Centre of Excellence for Early Childhood Development and Strategic Knowledge Cluster on Early Child Development.

Brodie, K. (2017) *Personal, Social and Emotional Well-being in Young Children*. Wilmslow: Rainmaker Academy.

Brodie, K. and Savage. K. (2015) *Inclusion and Early Years Practice*. Abingdon: Routledge.

Bronfenbrenner, U. (1979) *The Ecology of Human Development: Experiments by Nature and Design*. Cambridge, MA: Harvard University Press.

Cemlyn, S., Greenfields, M., Burnett, S., Matthews, Z. and Whitwell, C. (2009) *Inequalities Experienced by Gypsy and Traveller Communities: A Review*. Manchester: Equality and Human Rights Commission.

Choi, A. (2014) *How Cultures around the World Think about Parenting*. Available from: http://ideas.ted.com/how-cultures-around-the-world-think-about-parenting/. Accessed 10 June 2017.

Clare, A. (2012) *Creating a Learning Environment for Babies and Toddlers*. London: SAGE.

Cuthbert, C., Rayns, G. and Stanley, K. (2011) *All Babies Count: Prevention and Protection for Vulnerable Babies*. London: NSPCC.

David, T., Goouch, K., Powell, S. and Abbott, L. (2003) *Birth to Three Matters: A Review of the Literature. DfES Research Report Number 444*. Nottingham: Queen's Printer.

DfE (2017) *Statutory Framework for the Early Years Foundation Stage. Setting the Standards for Learning, Development and Care for Children from Birth to Five*. London: DfE.

Evangelou, M., Sylva, K., Kyriacou, M., Wild, M. and Glenny, G. (2009) *Early Years Learning and Development. Literature Review*. Oxford: DCSF.

Field, F. (2010) *The Foundation Years: Preventing Poor Children Becoming Poor Adults. The Report of the Independent Review on Poverty and Life Chances*. London: Cabinet Office.

Finnegan, J. (2016) *Lighting up Young Brains*. London: Save the Children.

Goouch, K. and Powell, S. (2013) *The Baby Room. Research Summary 2*. Canterbury: Canterbury Christ Church University.

Ionescu, M. and Tankersley, D. (2016) *A Quality Framework for Early Childhood Practice in Services for Children under Three Years of Age*. International Step by Step Association (ISSA).

KidsMatter (2012) *Why Culture Matters for Children's Development and Wellbeing: Early Childhood Initiative*. Available from: www.kidsmatter.edu.au. Accessed 4 June 2017.

Levinson, M. (2005) The role of play in the formation and maintenance of cultural identity: Gypsy children in home and school contexts. *Journal of Contemporary Ethnography* Vol. 34, pp. 499-532.

National Association for the Education of Young Children (2009) *Developmentally Appropriate Practice*. NAEYC. Available from: www.naeyc.org/DAP. Accessed 5 June 2017.

National Strategies (2008) *Early Years Quality Improvement Support Programme (EYQISP).* Nottingham: DCSF. Available from: www.foundationyears.org.uk/2011/10/early-years-quality-improvement-support-programme/. Accessed 10 June 2017.

Nesteruk, O. and Marks, L. (2011) Parenting in immigration: Experiences of mothers and fathers from Eastern Europe raising children in the United States. *Journal of Comparative Family Studies* Vol. 42 Iss. 6, pp. 809–25.

Page, J., Clare, A. and Nutbrown, C. (2013) (2nd edn) *Working with Babies & Children: From Birth to Three.* London: SAGE.

Pascal, C., Bertram, T., Delaney, S. and Nelson, C. (2016) *High Achieving White Working Class (HAWWC) Boys Project.* Birmingham: Centre for Research in Early Childhood.

Pen Green (2017) *A History.* Available from: http://research.pengreen.org/history/ Accessed 10 June 2017.

Stirrup, J., Evans, J. and Davies, B. (2016) Early years learning, play pedagogy and social class. *British Journal of Sociology of Education.* Available from: www.tandfonline.com/doi/full/10.1080/01425692.2016.1182010. Accessed 26 May 2017.

Stonewall (2017) *Including Different Families.* Available from: www.stonewall.org.uk/sites/default/files/including_different_families_lo.pdf. Accessed 10 June 2017.

Sylva, K., Melhuish, E., Sammons, P., Siraj-Blatchford, I. and Taggart, B. (2004) *The Effective Provision of Pre-School Education [EPPE] Project. Effective Pre-School Education: A Longitudinal Study funded by the DfES 1997–2004.* London: DfES.

Wall, S., Litjens, I. and Taguma, M. (2015) *Pedagogy in Early Childhood Education and Care (ECEC): An International Comparative Study of Approaches and Policies.* Department for Education Publications. Available from: www.gov.uk/government/publications

Weisner, T. (2016) Relationships and social trust in Early Childhood program, in K. Sanders and A. Guerra, *The Culture of Childcare.* Oxford: Oxford University Press.

Whalley, M. and the Pen Green Team (2008) (2nd edn) *Involving Parents in their Children's Learning.* London: SAGE.

Wise, S. and da Silva, L. (2007) *Differential Parenting of Children from Diverse Cultural Backgrounds Attending Childcare. Research paper No. 39.* Melbourne: Australian Institute of Family Studies. Available from: https://aifs.gov.au/publications/differential-parenting-children-diverse-cultural-bac/executive-summary. Accessed 4 June 2017.

11 What does the future hold?

In the light of the moon, a little egg lay on a leaf.

Carle, 1994

Introduction

It is incredibly difficult to prepare children for a future that we may find hard to predict – just as it would be difficult to predict, without prior experience, that the Very Hungry Caterpillar's egg will turn into a beautiful butterfly. Technology, in the form of phones, interactive screens and travel is pervasive and this is unlikely to change. In fact, more and more technology is appearing in less predictable places, such as being able to take a 'phone' call on your watch. However, this is not the only arena where there are an exponential number of changes being made. The strides being made in neuroscience mean that we can now 'see' inside even the youngest brains, so we can start to predict how babies 'think' by the areas of the brain that 'light up'. Staying with biology, more and more pre-term babies are now part of everyday settings. Sometimes these babies and children can have unknown health or cognitive challenges that scientists are only just beginning to uncover. As well as physical health, mental health and well-being are being discussed more openly, enabling debates about how this may affect babies and young children. Finally, the way that childcare is organised, where parents pay professionals to look after their children, encouraged by government subsidies, may have long-term effects on babies and young children. In all these areas – technology, neuroscience, health and childcare – there are opportunities and challenges for babies' and young children's holistic development. Some of these seem to be following a reasonably predictable trajectory, while others are completely unknown.

In this chapter, these areas are discussed using the current evidence and with a perspective of how we can support babies and children now, even though the future is unknown. Instead of activities for this chapter, there is a 'Read and reflect' section, with readings that practitioners are encouraged to access and reflect upon.

Screen use and babies' development

The increasing and inescapable presence of 'screens', whether that is iPads, iPhones or other tablets, in every environment is unlikely to change in the near future. In fact, as technology becomes more affordable, it is likely that children and even babies will be exposed to screens during every part of their life. Already there are attachments so young children can see a screen while in their buggy, in a bouncer or even on the potty. Currently, the research is in its infancy

on this omnipresence of screens, although there is a growing interest in the long-term impact that this may have on both the children and the wider family (Steiner-Adair and Barker, 2014; Hourcade *et al.*, 2015). There are concerns that 'addiction' to screens is damaging young children's developing brains in much the same way as cocaine addiction would (Kardaras, 2016).

It is already well established that language development and skills require more than just exposure to language (Evangelou *et al.*, 2009). They are dependent on the interactions, the dance reciprocity and complex social cues between people, without which there would be very little or no development of language. However, screen technology is merely exposure to language, bypassing the two-way exchange that is typical of a quality interaction and lacking any facial or body language cues.

Blum-Ross and Livingstone (2016) argue that focusing on the amount of time that children spend in front of screens is misleading. Although this is easily measurable, and easily adapted, it overlooks the vital aspects of social interaction and self-esteem. They suggest that parents should, instead, be considering the wider holistic development of their children and how the opportunities to spend time playing physically or interacting with others have been reduced while their children are in front of screens. In addition, there are growing concerns about Internet safety as videos and games that are intentionally made to look suitable for children are, in fact, decoys for much more sinister material (Subedar and Yates, 2017).

Challenges

Being able to give your baby or child a video to watch while out for a meal is very tempting. At least you get to eat your food in peace, but the 'interruptions' during mealtimes – for example, talking about waiting times, discussing the food likes and dislikes, encouraging the use of cutlery and use of manners – are golden opportunities for sustained shared thinking. It is becoming a common sight, however, to see a family with young children take a seat and simply pass a 'screen'

Quick Summary

Sustained shared thinking

Sustained shared thinking is defined as:

> an episode in which two or more individuals 'work together' in an intellectual way to solve a problem, clarify a concept, evaluate activities, extend a narrative etc. Both parties must contribute to the thinking and it must develop and extend.
>
> Sylva *et al.*, 2004: 36

to the children to amuse themselves. This becomes particularly challenging when combined with the increasing access to the Internet in public places and the safety of the material on the Internet.

Opportunities

Being able to use technology and understand the infinite possibilities for expansion will be commonplace, essential even, for the future of babies and young children. They will be casual consumers, full-time employers or innovators – or something that we don't yet know about. Feeling comfortable using technology will be paramount.

Supporting babies and young children to be questioning about their choice of games or videos and discussing them, just as you would do a choice of book or toy, will help them to think about choices and help you to understand their motivation. This can also start a sustained shared thinking conversation and support the critical thinking element of the Characteristics of Effective Learning.

Read and Reflect

The American Academy of Pediatrics (AAP), which you can find on this website: www.aap. org, regularly update their website with recommendations based on the latest research. You will be able to find research, articles and YouTube clips on here about specific areas (such as 'media use in the under-2s') as well as general guidance.

How does this compare with current UK guidance? For example: the advice given by Alicia Blum-Ross and Sonia Livingstone, from the London School of Economics and Political Science: http://eprints.lse.ac.uk/66927/1/Policy%20Brief%2017-%20Families%20%20 Screen%20Time.pdf

Or this 2016 research about the links between type 2 diabetes and screen time by Nightingale *et al.*, which can be accessed here: http://adc.bmj.com/content/early/2017/02/ 06/archdischild-2016-312016

Use of technology by practitioners

There is an increasing use of technology in settings (Rutter, 2016) by practitioners, who are using tablets or iPads or laptops to record observations, assessments and planning. These have many advantages, including keeping parents updated, providing folders of work, easy-to-track cohorts and individual children, less bulky than paper, quickly comparing across settings for large chains and giving prompts for material to include. However, as with all computer systems, the output will only be as good as the practitioner's input. Therefore, if the practitioner has little knowledge of child development and fails to understand the significance of the observations, then it is wasted effort to include them in any system, electronic or otherwise. Unfortunately, it may be harder to spot a practitioner who is struggling with child development concepts when using a computerised system because they generally allow tick boxes without proof of knowledge. Although electronic recording systems have many advantages, they are not a substitute for practitioners having good child development knowledge and knowing their children well.

Another use of technology for managers and leaders is that of electronic systems that both record and predict when the regulatory requirements need updating, such as First Aid training, fire drills, training requirements, food hygiene etc. This is a good time-saving tool for managers, because it reduces the amount of checking for (and potentially missing) due dates on training. One benefit of such systems is that they can form part of the evidence for meeting statutory requirements for Ofsted or Local Authority inspection. However, just as with the other electronic systems, these are only as good as the information that is entered, with the temptation to rely too heavily on the computer notifying staff, rather than checking personally every so often.

As global web summits and webinars become more popular and accessible (Brodie, 2017), practitioners are able to learn from other cultures, other countries and other pedagogies. This will broaden knowledge and help practitioners to reflect on their own practice. It may be that it gives an appreciation for how good their current practice is, compared to other parts of the world, or they may want to improve practice with their children, having learned of the way that others approach education and care. The ability to access information via the Internet reduces the need for practitioners to leave the setting, which is especially useful for childminders who have the additional problem of closing the whole setting when attending training.

Challenges for practitioners and managers

Although many practitioners may have smart phones or be able to use a satnav., there are still many practitioners who are not confident with using technology as sophisticated as observation recording systems or management systems. In addition, many local authorities are moving their own systems to online only – for example, booking onto courses, accessing local authority updates and filling out SEN referrals or requests. Many central government updates, such as EYFS revisions, are circulated online and settings are expected to print them off or read them online. For some settings this is no problem, but there are still many settings, such as childminders, packaway settings or those in very rural areas, where there is no Internet access (or limited access), which makes this challenging or impossible. There is also an assumption that everyone will be able to pay for or have access to a printer.

Data protection becomes more complex when information is stored electronically, especially if it is stored on a setting's laptop that the manager or owner takes home. In many settings, there

is still some confusion about access, security and retention of information. For up-to-date information, go to the website for the Information Commissioner's Office (ICO), which is the UK's independent authority set up to uphold information rights in the public interest, promoting openness by public bodies and data privacy for individuals: https://ico.org.uk/for-organisations/guide-to-data-protection/

Opportunities – technology makes it easier to share

Computing power now means we can share images, videos and information instantly with parents and carers. This can help to reduce parent's anxiety over leaving their children and is especially useful if their child is a baby or non-verbal, so can't explain about the day that they've had. Similarly, practitioners can record short messages for their key children, so that the children know that they are being kept in mind. It is also easy to share news, announcements and accomplishments on social media – for example, Facebook or Twitter – but this must be done using rigorous policies and procedures and with the express permission of parents or those with parental responsibility.

The ease with which technology can now be used (for example, swipe screens) means that even the youngest children can access sophisticated technology such as videos, interactive books and facetime with others (the 'videophones' that science fiction predicted a generation ago!). This opens up digital worlds that will undoubtedly expand into areas as yet unknown, which is incredibly exciting. It also comes with a caveat that young children will need support and guidance on using this technology to ensure they are safeguarded, and for their mental and physical well-being.

With imagination and innovation, the technology currently used to simply record observations could be more multi-functional – for example, incorporating child development information and training into the electronic systems or receiving updates from government sites, which would increase their utility and effectiveness.

On balance, the use of electronic systems for both practitioners and managers is more beneficial than not. When staff and mangers get used to using the systems, these become easier to keep up to date and refresh. Inevitably, more and more local authorities and other multi-agencies will use, and expect others to use, electronic systems to coordinate information between the Private, Voluntary and Independent (PVI) sector settings and all other agencies. For children, providing their safeguarding and well-being is prioritised (as with any other activity) there are some incredible opportunities to use technology to connect with others and support their learning.

Read and Reflect

Go to the European Early Childhood Education Research Association (EECERA) website, where you will find the Digital Childhoods - Special Interest Group: www.eecera.org/sigs/digital-childhoods/ Here they have the latest publications, books, journals and conferences – for example, Arnott, L. (ed.) (2017) *Digital Technologies and Learning in the Early Years.* London: SAGE.

Due to the fast-changing nature of technology in the Early Years, it is worth revisiting this at regular intervals to see what is new.

What might neuroscience be able to tell us in the future?

Being able to predict what fascinates and stimulates baby's brain has moved from watching baby's eye gaze to watching the biology of the brain and the blood flows. This means being able to spot typical and atypical brain patterns – for example, the differences in the brain displayed by babies with autism, which *could* mean that autism is not diagnosed through observation of behaviours, but from a brain scan at a very early age. This has many implications, including the negative connotations of labelling, but for practitioners it could determine how to interact more effectively with the babies identified from the very start (Hazlett *et al.*, 2017) supplying important, extra time when it matters the most. Note, however, that brain scans only give an image of the blood flow through the brain (this is what 'lights up' the charts). It is how these images are then translated or overlaid into babies' and children's learning that gives the insights into how learning may take place. It could be that some nuances of learning may get lost in the reading of the charts or that individual children simply learn in different ways, thus making generalisations problematic.

Brain imaging and non-invasive techniques for studying brain activities will become more sophisticated in the future. The flourishing discipline of neuroscience will start to uncover links between areas of learning, demonstrate the biological responses in the brain during experiences and also where there may be disconnects. For example, Jones *et al.* (2015) used an electro-encephalogram (EEG) (a test that detects electrical activity in the brain) on 6- and 12-month-old babies to investigate their socio-cognitive development. They found evidence that supports the Interactive Specialisation (IS) hypothesis (Johnson, 2000), which supposes that the brain develops through a holistic mixture of movement, genetics and body, rather than the theory that areas of the brain simply mature according to age. Interestingly, their results were most pronounced during live, naturalistic interactions, again suggesting that babies benefit the most from real social interactions.

Quick Summary

Why incorporate 'neuroscience' into Early Years practice?

Neuroscientists affirm that 'billions of synaptic connections are made within the first five years of life' (Conkbayir, 2017: 22) and that practitioners are part of this process, through planning environments, developmentally appropriate activities and sensory experiences.

The process of incorporating neuroscience into Early Years settings with practitioners may have challenges (including a proliferation of 'neuromyths'), but is worthwhile because it vindicates good practice based on science (causation not correlation) and adds another layer of knowledge to understanding about how young children think, learn and develop.

Aside from giving evidence to support the IS hypothesis, the conclusion that real social interaction is beneficial for a baby is hardly likely to be revolutionary for most baby room practitioners. However, the neuroscience can now show *how* this is beneficial, so this can start to be translated into the exact types of interactions that babies and young children need from practitioners to elicit the optimum social responses. The fact that generally received, good practice may have science to reinforce it should be seen as a positive advance.

Similarly, EEGs are now being used to analyse eye gaze in typically developing babies between one and eight months, to give new understanding of how a baby's brain develops (Kulke *et al.*, 2017). The results show how babies are able to shift attention more efficiently as the brain develops and their eye gaze patterns change. Again, it is not too surprising that babies become more able to control their attention and eye gaze as they get older. However, these results may give an indication of how the brain architecture (in particular, the intracorical connections) may affect attention, so activities that improve these areas of the brain are likely to improve attention as well.

The most recent advances in brain imaging and autism show that, in mice, when the cerebral cortex brain region begins to form, an 'overload of neural connections typically observed in autistic brains' (University of Maryland, 2017) has been detected. This gives some insight into the early development of autism-related neural networks, which may lead to interventions or further developments in the understanding of the autism continuum.

These are only three examples of recent research studies, but there are many more that are emerging. It is almost inevitable that there will be studies, or groups of studies, that will either reinforce good practice or change the way that practitioners work and think about child development.

Challenges of interpretation and use of neuroscience

Neuroscience is still developing and growing, and there will almost certainly be many more innovations to come. However, there must be some caution exercised because interpretation of the areas of the brain that 'light up' during scans is still open to some discussion and conjecture. The results still need to be deciphered with due regard to what is already known about child development.

The other big challenge is making practitioners aware of the current research and, most importantly, how this can improve their practice. Neuroscience can be considered to be a world away from playing with children day to day, but there are some very relevant discoveries being made through research. Sometimes the research may simply confirm what is already considered good practice, but there will be revelations that may make practitioners stop and consider how or why they do things they way they do.

Opportunities afforded by neuroscience

The opportunity to understand babies' thought processes is undeniably exciting and incredibly useful as a reflective tool on good practice. There are further possibilities for the future, such as investigating the effects of trauma or malnutrition or multi-lingualism or almost any other aspect of children's growth and development. The type and number of holistic links between different areas of development will be particularly interesting to see.

Read and Reflect

A good book to start with is Mine Conkbayir's *Early Childhood and Neuroscience: Theory, Research and Implications for Practice* (2017). This book explains about brain architecture, how hormones affect the brain and developing a 'healthy' brain. Most importantly, this book then goes on to describe the relevance to Early Years practice and *why* we need to know this information, including exploding some neuroscience myths.

The National Forum for Neuroscience in Special Education is dedicated to sharing insights into the latest research and increasing dialogue around special education. Find their latest research on the NAHT website here: www.naht.org.uk/welcome/news-and-media/key-topics/special-education-needs/national-forum-for-neuroscience-forum-in-special-education/

How biology is transforming perspectives and methodologies

Increased understanding of how babies grow, especially genetic and biological patterns, is already uncovering some interesting holistic links. For example, genetics and biological links have already been established between the molecular mechanisms of critical and sensitive periods (Boyce and Kobor, 2015). An expanding area of research is into the measurable, biological effects on children who are growing up in different environments. This can be considered to be the area where 'nature versus nurture' becomes the interplay between 'nature and nurture'.

There has been research into genetic markers that could be used to personalise interventions (in this example, for 2–5-year-olds and a literacy intervention and the dopamine D4 receptor gene). 'Irrespective of cognitive level, children who carry this variant may be more receptive to the same parental, educational, or environmental influences than those who do not' (Howard-Jones, 2014: 24). Put another way, there may be some children who are strongly dependent on the quality of the interactions or instruction and will only respond to some specific interventions (sometimes called 'orchids' – analogous to a delicate flower that needs specific circumstances to thrive) and children who will adapt and flourish in a range of learning environments, responding positively to many different types of interactions (sometimes called 'dandelions' – analogous to a flower that will grow in a wide range of environments, sometimes harsh). One conclusion from this is that children may be biologically programmed, from birth, to react differently to their environments and to interventions, so finding the correct one for the 'orchids' will be essential, although to have just two categories (orchid or dandelion) seems to be simplistic and lacks nuance.

Existing research has already shown that different alleles of the same gene make children (and therefore people) more susceptible or less susceptible to environmental factors and their own emotional regulation (Goldsmith, Pollak and Davidson, 2008). Children may have a genetic predisposition (i.e. determined from conception by their DNA) to the influence that their environment will have on them. This could be more positive or more negative, across a continuum of responses. For example, an adult may have all the genes to predispose towards certain disorders (schizophrenia, PTSD, alcoholism) but they may never be triggered because there was never a set of environmental conditions to trigger them. The diathesis–stress model states that you need an environmental stressor and trigger to set off the behaviour. In practice, this means that two people could have exactly the same experiences, but will have different responses and therefore outcomes. 'The discovery of the molecular, epigenetic processes by which environmental conditions can regulate the activation or deactivation of genes' is described by Allen and Kelly (2015: 66) as 'among the most compelling, emergent stories in developmental biology'.

In addition, there is more and more evidence that 'maternal exposure to adversity during pregnancy leads to life-long effects in offspring' (Matthews and Phillips, 2012: 95). These have important consequences for society as a whole, because it could provide a biological explanation for repeated 'behaviours in populations exposed to adversity' (Matthews and Phillips, 2012: 95). Even from the point of conception, a baby may be predisposed to certain stress responses, via the maternal, epigenetic programming. This is at a biological level, so even though the baby may never directly experience those stressors or triggers, the mother has already passed on a predisposition. For example, babies of mothers who witnessed the World Trade Center attacks in New York while pregnant (particularly 3rd trimester) had different cortisol levels present than those who did not, which could only be explained by this experience (Yehuda *et al.*, 2005). This may partially explain how cycles of behaviour are repeated and may also present a solution to overcoming adversity that happened a generation beforehand.

It has already been identified that young children have individual responses to early adversity (Allen and Kelly, 2015). Some children are particularly vulnerable but others seem to have exceptional resilience, explaining why some children seem to grow and thrive, even though their environment has many difficulties or they may have experienced great adversity. It is important to understand this, because the level and type of intervention need to be appropriate to the individual child and their circumstances. This may be explained by genetics, for example, but more importantly we need to recognise first that there are differences in susceptibility that will affect intervention efficacy (Belsky and van Ijzendoorn, 2015), and the nature of resilience in different children.

Links between health and poverty

Living in poverty adversely affects children's well-being and development in all areas, including health, socio-emotional, cognitive and language development, and educational achievement. Children from poorer backgrounds lag behind at all stages of education. By the age of three, poorer children are estimated to be, on average, nine months behind children from wealthier backgrounds, and this intellectual gap increases throughout their school years. By the age of 16, children eligible for free school meals achieve 1.7 grades lower at GCSE than those not eligible for free school meals (Mathers *et al.*, 2014).

In his book *The Health Gap*, Sir Michael Marmot explores how people at relative social disadvantage also suffer from health disadvantage. He explains that 'what happens to children in the early years has a profound effect on their life chance and hence their health as adult' (Marmot, 2016: 112). This is becoming an increasingly evident problem, with things like food banks becoming a part of life: the Trussell Trust gave out 1,182,954 three-day emergency food supplies in 2016/17. Marmot suggests that good early child development is shaped by the children's environment, but it requires equity from the start, from social mobility to levels of poverty to the quality of care that children receive from parents and state, to ensure the best start in life to lay the foundations for the rest of their lives. By their very nature, predicting global financial markets, government priorities and local reactions to these are extremely difficult, but it can be predicted that neglecting children's best interests will, inevitably, affect the next generation.

Understanding how mental health affects young children

It is already well documented that both prenatal depression (e.g. Pearson *et al.*, 2012; Parfitt *et al.*, 2013) and postnatal depression (e.g. Kawai *et al.*, 2017; Vieites and Reeb-Sutherland, 2017) affect babies' development, particularly social development. In these situations, the adults tend to stop responding to their babies' interactions because they may feel tired, sad, depressed, have difficulties concentrating or feel apathetic. For a stark example of this, watch the brief YouTube clip (search 'Dr Tronick still face experiment') where a mother is interacting with her baby, giving positive facial expressions, smiling and responding. When asked to have a 'still face', i.e. no responses to her baby at all, the baby very quickly becomes distressed and tries a variety of strategies to get the mum's attention again. Current studies into these types of conditions may help to improve support given to parents (both mothers and fathers) before, during and after pregnancy, to prevent or reduce the effects of poor mental health.

Better health for babies and pregnant mums

Improvements in health care have resulted in many more premature babies, and even very premature babies, surviving. However, the reduced white matter in the immature brains of premature babies can trigger a range of complications, from general developmental delay to sensory impairment, linguistic processing and inattention-type attention deficit disorders (Carpenter, 2015). Currently there is research being done into various intervention programmes that may improve this situation. The research of Spittle *et al.* (2015: 2) into a range of intervention programmes has shown that 'early intervention programmes for preterm infants have a positive influence on cognitive and motor outcomes during infancy, with cognitive benefits persisting into preschool age'. They also found that there was great variance in the type and delivery of the programmes, so a direct comparison was difficult. They have not identified the *most* effective programme. More recently, Hadfield *et al.* (2017: 27) have identified that 'children born preterm have poorer outcomes than children born full-term', but that it is not all bad news, as the quality of the caregiving environment can improve outcomes.

Similarly, research into describing and treating development disorders is constantly shedding light on new conditions. For example, foetal alcohol spectrum disorder (FASD) is considered more often when discussing children's health and behaviour since Professor Barry Carpenter disseminated information about this condition (Carpenter, 2013).

Challenges

Babies and young children are captive to their biology – even pre-birth babies are affected by their mother's health and circumstances. Knowing where to start can be a challenge. Is it with pregnancy or pre-birth (as with the Scottish pre-birth to three curriculum) or is it with the wider society to value children's health and care as a matter of course? It may fall to settings to meet these challenges and campaign for better understanding about pregnancy, baby and child development in the wider society to offset some of the negative side effects.

Opportunities

The diverse and wide-ranging research into health, from genetics to mental well-being to preterm births, indicates the many ways that the biological and developmental sciences are taking an interest in the birth to three age range. It is becoming increasingly obvious that the results from this research will affect practice and pedagogy as the sector begins to review practice and environments through these lenses. Although a definitive intervention programme or support approach has not been found, there are opportunities to incorporate methodologies that seem to work in a number of areas. For example, quality interactions seem to be important, from the perspective of PND and health and poverty.

 Read and Reflect

Research in the areas of health and biology is fast-moving and warrants further investigation. Good journals to start with include *Infant Behavior and Development* (available from: www.journals.elsevier.com/infant-behavior-and-development/) and *Developmental Psychobiology* (available from: http://onlinelibrary.wiley.com/journal/10.1002/(ISSN)1098-2302)

For a UK perspective, *Early Child Development and Care* (www.tandfonline.com/toc/gecd20/current), and for a European perspective, *European Early Childhood Education Research Journal* (EECERJ) (available from: www.eecera.org/journal/).

Changes in childcare

Childcare choices and children's development

If more babies are going to be in settings, and that seems to be the current trend in England, then policy and practice need to be suitable to meet this new demand. Consideration must be given to the quality, as well at the quantity, of professional childcare that babies and children are getting. It has been established for some time (since the EPPE research by Sylva *et al.* (2004)) that 'good-quality childcare has . . . long-standing benefits for children's language development and educational outcomes' (Finnegan, 2016: 3). However, simply increasing the number of government-funded childcare hours available to parents does not mean it will all be good quality or that it will meet the needs of the babies and young children. Elfer and Page (2015: 1782) believe that the type of childcare offered needs to evolve through 'the "voices" of the babies themselves', via communities of practice and innovative processes and practices.

The current UK government have pledged to offer more 'free' childcare (i.e. funded by central government, so free to parents at point of use) to parents in England, with the aim of encouraging parents back to work even sooner. There are two complications with this system. First, although the care is 'free' for the parents, it is effectively being subsidised by the companies that comprise the large private, voluntary and independent (PVI) sector in England. This system will therefore rely on the PVI sector being buoyant enough to support it. Realistically, it is likely that larger, national chains will provide the extra places because they can sustain this financially (Rutter, 2016: 25), possibly resulting in a consolidation of the many small private, voluntary and independent settings into just a few large chains or groups. This may also mean that existing schools and academies will need to start offering care and education for babies and children, which will necessitate a review of their staff qualifications, staff deployment and the physical environment (milk kitchens and nappy-changing areas, for example).

Second, this means that a growing number of children will be starting their lives partly in the care of people who are not their parents, so that the quality of care and early education should be improved in line with the increased effect it will have on the next generation. However, research from Hadfield *et al.* (2012) has already shown that the most highly qualified staff are rarely put in the baby room. Finnegan (2016: 3) has since proposed that 'an early years teacher in every nursery in England by 2020' would raise quality in settings and improve the outcomes for many children, but particularly those children in poverty.

Childminders occupy an interesting niche in the childcare sector in the UK. Traditionally they work alone, or with one assistant, from their own homes. This means that the children get a home-like environment, usually with different aged peers to play with, sometimes siblings and often enjoy excursions out of the setting environment as well. This is in sharp contrast to the daily practice of many day nurseries, pre-schools and two-year-old provisions. However, these can often be disproportionately affected by underfunding because they are often operating with much smaller budgets and have less flexibility with regard to staff. The combination of factors may mean that there will be fewer registered childminders, with childcare becoming a choice of informal care (with relatives, for example) or day care nurseries. Brind *et al.* (2014) state that there were 55,900 registered childminders in England in March 2013, a decrease of three per cent from the 57,500 recorded in June 2011. By 2016, this figure had further decreased to 46,600

Quick Summary

Secure attachment

Secure attachment is typical for the majority of children and is described as emotionally healthy. It is characterised by a child who is in distress after a brief separation, but can be comforted and settled by the caregiver reasonably quickly.

Page, Clare and Nutbrown (2013: 36) theorise that:

1 High-quality caregiver relationships are central to emotional development and learning in infants and toddlers.
2 Relationships take time to develop, so the key person must be given that time and opportunity to become attached to their key baby or key toddler.

(DfE, 2017: 1), a decrease of 19 per cent in five years. The current funding issues are unlikely to stop this fall in numbers, which will reduce the choice for parents of the type of childcare they would like their children to enjoy.

Challenges

In the PVI sector, keeping the quality of the setting while still being financially viable is a constant struggle. The recent political rhetoric has been to offer 'free' childcare, while not acknowledging that some settings are, effectively, subsidising this offer to parents. One method of doing this is to keep the adult to child ratio to the statutory minimum, meaning there are fewer adults per child. This will almost inevitably mean fewer quality adult interactions and less sustained shared thinking, with fewer benefits for the babies and children attending the setting.

There are concerns that smaller, unique childcare providers, such as childminders, will not be an option for many parents as they become financially untenable.

Read and Reflect

The Family and Childcare Trust website is excellent for up-to-the-minute information on policy, research, business information, training and parent information: www.familyandchild caretrust.org/

They also offer a number of free toolkits that can give practical support, such as extending the school day to cover the early education hours.

Opportunities

If it becomes apparent that the government's aspirations for 'free' childcare are still a target for them, there may be opportunities for an overhaul to the PVI sector, with providers represented as a group to government to ensure fair funding, training and improvement of quality.

There is an opportunity for parents to state the type and quality of settings they would like their children to attend, which may influence the sector as well.

 Case Study

24-hour care

The natural culmination of extended hours of day care, combined with extended work hours (such as 24-hour shops) is that nurseries will routinely offer care at any time of the night or day, any day of the week.

How might 24-hour care with a practitioner affect very young children? (Think of attachment and professional love.)

How might 24-hour care change the skill set that practitioners need? (Think of safeguarding, shift patterns, their own families.)

How may 24-hour care affect the physical environment of the setting? (Think of sleeping areas for staff and children, food preparation, relaxation space.)

 Quick Summary

Professional love

This is a concept formulated by Dr Jools Page to explain the love that practitioners feel for the babies and children in their care. It is the affectionate and caring behaviours that happen when you care for babies and children, even though it is part of your professional role. Dr Page's research started with a focus on babies, but the concept is equally applicable to older children.

Practitioners working in the childcare sector

Pedagogy

Mathers *et al.* (2014: 8) suggest that quality pedagogy relies on interactions and relationships; play-based approaches (where children can take the lead); communication and language; and opportunities to move and be physically active. This mirrors the three prime areas of the EYFS: communication and language; physical development; and personal, social and emotional development (PSED). Play-based pedagogy seems to be ubiquitous in the current climate, certainly in the UK and also elsewhere. However, it is important to understand how this translates into good practice in the setting and into a developmental appropriate curriculum. For example, free flow play indoors and outdoors has many benefits, but thought must be given to how this would work for toddlers who are just walking, especially if there are non-mobile babies in the same space. In the future it may be that there is more emphasis on a movement-based curriculum or an outdoor/forest school aspect to every setting, favouring the prime area of physical development.

 Quick Summary

Pedagogy

Pedagogy is the combination of the methods of teaching, the ethos, the interactions between baby or child and practitioner, the learning environment and the curriculum. It is the *way* teaching is conducted, considered as a whole with the content. It could be considered to be the holistic methods by which teaching and learning occur.

Quality practitioners

Taggart (2014: 173) suggests that training for practitioners in early childhood education and care (ECEC) should be '*ethical* as opposed to one which is purely instrumental or rooted in a patriarchal notion of women's supposed unique suitability' and in particular, the notion of compassion would overcome the 'false dichotomies between discourses of "children's rights" and "care". The research of Mathers *et al.* (2014) analyses the international evidence to show how vital it is to have good-quality Early Years provision, including what 'quality' means from a practitioner's perspective. They found that 'in short, good quality staffing underpins good quality practice' with general educational level of practitioners, specialised Early Years training, both formal and informal training, continuing professional development after initial training and on-the-job supervision all having a 'positive impact' on quality (Mathers *et al.*, 2014: 24). Interestingly they also note that the 'research is both less rich and less consistent when it comes to children under the age of three'. One of the constant problems is the number and variation of qualifications available, which are difficult to compare like for like, and no clear follow-up when practitioners do join settings. This means that defining a 'quality' route of training, education and practice for practitioners in the baby room is much more difficult than for those practitioners working in the pre-school room. Mathers *et al.* (2014) note that mentoring, coaching and peer support may be more effective than one-day's training out of the setting.

It has already been identified that there are differences from practitioner to practitioner in the 'quality and quantity of adult interventions that are relevant for the promotion of language in young children' (Laevers, 2015: abstract), but identifying relevant and beneficial training for baby room staff is more difficult. Kalliala (2011) analysed a form of training or intervention called Kangaroo care (a skin-to-skin method of caring for babies). The aim was to see whether this type of intervention would improve practitioners' sensitivity and enhance their activation skills towards the well-being of the under-threes in Finnish day-care centres. The results were positive, with 'significant differences in quality' between the intervention group and the control group, demonstrating that targeted and specific training for practitioners who care for babies is worthwhile and necessary. Training and qualifications are not the only motivating factors for quality practitioners. Elfer (2015: 508) states that when staff 'feel cared about and understood, including their emotional responses to the work, both positive and negative, they are more likely to be more attentive and responsive to individual children and families'. However, there are many practitioners who still feel that they have little or no say in the set-up of their environments, control of their rooms or ability to provide for their individual children. This can result in low-cost or shabby environments (Goouch and Powell, 2013: 6). Most concerning in this piece of research was that baby room practitioners rarely had 'dedicated spaces for participants to enjoy breaks and time away from the babies'. It is to be hoped that, in the future, the hard physical work, sometimes emotionally draining and multifaceted role of a baby room practitioner will be appreciated.

It is remarkable that there are still only three per cent of practitioners who are men. Statistically it must be assumed that there are more men who would be outstanding childcare professionals (just think how many dads, granddads, uncles, brothers and cousins who are 'good with children'). Hopefully the future will bring more good-quality male practitioners into the profession, which could improve outcomes for children and give them male role models.

Challenges for practitioners

Early Years teaching is not currently seen as a profession by many outside of the sector. This may be partly due to the lack of nationally recognised pay, conditions and qualification requirements that are characteristic of teachers in the state sector. Baby room practitioners in particular may feel undervalued (Hadfield, 2012). A challenge that the whole sector faces is moving away from the discourse of the 'cost' of childcare towards the quality and benefits of professional childcare. Funding of the sector will, of course, have a big impact on professional recognition, quality and morale. It is to be hoped that the future brings some cross-party political solutions.

Definitions and descriptions of a 'quality' setting and 'quality' practice are notoriously difficult in such a diverse sector. However, the future could bring a closer focus on this as more and more parents take advantage of government schemes for their children, and the proportion of babies and young children affected increases.

Opportunities for practitioners

In quality settings there are more and more opportunities for babies and children to be involved with different experiences, which may not be possible (or desirable) in the home – for example, playing in the forest, experiencing fire pits and using real tools. As physical development moves more into the spotlight, especially as the Chief Medical Officer's recommendations are included in the revised EYFS, there are likely to be more opportunities for practitioners to be creative with their physical play for children.

The traditional 'training day' out of the setting may be replaced by more innovative and blended methods of mentoring, coaching, training and teaching, possibly using technology such as webinars, summits and online courses. There are two big advantages to these. First there is no travel required, saving time and money and they may be more practical for many. Second, they allow easy and affordable access to the knowledge and expertise of specialists from around the globe.

There are many opportunities for men to enter the childcare profession, and this is to be welcomed. There are some chains (such as LEYF: www.leyf.org.uk) that are very successful at recruiting and retaining male practitioners. There are opportunities to learn from these settings for the whole sector.

Read and Reflect

The next step for the Early Years workforce, I would argue, is that they need to partici-pate in determining their own expertise and knowledge base, rather than accepting the modelling of it on educational roles which may only in part fulfil what they consider their purpose to be.

Dyer, 2016: 1

Mary Dyer makes a strong argument for the professionalism of the workforce. Read her full blog here: www.bera.ac.uk/blog/professionalism-and-the-early-years-practitioner and discuss with a colleague how much these experiences reflect your own.

How does this compare with Early Childhood Educator in the US? Go to their website and review some of their membership organisations: www.cdacouncil.org/resources/find-ece-organizations

Have a conversation with a colleague about why you feel there are so few men in Early Years.

What can be done to change the situation (if you think it needs changing)?

Conclusions

A big challenge is that we do not know where the next technological or biological breakthrough will come from or how significant it will be for the lives of the babies and young children. Undoubtedly there are areas of science and technology that are being researched today that will have impacts on Early Years good practice for years to come, whether that is understanding how areas of the brain are structured to reinforce learning or how the body grows and matures. However, an even greater challenge is being able to access the scientific knowledge and then translating that into 'on the ground' good practice in settings. This obstacle may be best overcome by closer interdisciplinary working, across education, science and psychology, and a greater focus on the critical early years in a child's life.

As practitioners understand more about emerging sciences, such as neuroscience and how this affects a baby's learning and development, experiences can be more developmentally appropriate, more challenging, more exciting or more emotionally balancing, setting the scene for the rest of the baby's life.

There can be some educated deductions made about the future in which the babies and children of today will grow up – for example, that technology such as smart phones is likely to become more sophisticated and ever-present. Biology, medicine and neuroscience are likely to find more answers to questions, and probably find more questions along the way. However, there is a lot of unpredictability about the type of world that the babies today will find themselves in as adults.

It would be tempting to simply ignore the thoughts of the future, because our predictions and suppositions may be a long way from the truth. However, the babies and children of today rely on their practitioners to prepare them for the unknown future. The most reliable way of doing this is to give children good resilience, self-esteem and well-being, both physical and mental. It is to be hoped these children will flourish in the future, as the beautiful butterfly, from all the nurturing experiences that they will have in their settings.

References

Allen L.R. and Kelly B.B. (2015) Committee on the Science of Children Birth to Age 8: Deepening and Broadening the Foundation for Success; Board on Children, Youth, and Families. Washington, DC: Institute of Medicine National Research Council.

Belsky, J. and van Ijzendoorn M.H. (2015) What works for whom? Genetic moderation of intervention efficacy. *Development and Psychopathology* Vol. 27 Iss. 1, pp. 1-6.

Blum-Ross, A. and Livingstone, S. (2016) *Families and Screen Time: Current Advice and Emerging Research.* Media Policy Brief 17. London: Media Policy Project, London School of Economics and Political Science.

Boyce, W.T. and Kobor, M.S. (2015) Development and the epigenome: The 'synapse' of gene-environment interplay. *Developmental Science* Vol. 18, pp. 1-23.

Brind, R., McGinigal, S., Lewis, J. and Ghezelayagh, S. with Ransom, H., Robson, J., Street, C. and Renton, Z. (2014) *Childcare and Early Years Providers Survey 2013.* London: Department for Education.

Brodie, K. (2017) *Personal, Social and Emotional Well-being in Young Children.* Wilmslow: Rainmaker.

Carle, E. (1994) *The Very Hungry Caterpillar* [Board Book]. New York: Puffin.

Carpenter, B. (2013) *Fetal Alcohol Spectrum Disorders.* Abingdon: Routledge.

Carpenter, B. (2015) Prematurity and the challenge for educators. *SEND Magazine* March/April 2015.

Conkbayir, M. (2017) *Early Childhood and Neuroscience: Theory, Research and Implications for Practice.* London: Bloomsbury.

DfE (2017) *Childcare and Early Years Providers Survey 2016.* London: DfE. Available from: www.gov.uk/government/statistics/childcare-and-early-years-providers-survey-2016. Accessed 10 June 2017.

Dyer, M. (2016) *Professionalism and the Early Years Practitioner.* Available from: www.bera.ac.uk/blog/professionalism-and-the-early-years-practitioner. Accessed 10 June 2017.

Elfer, P. (2015) Emotional aspects of nursery policy and practice – progress and prospect. *European Early Childhood Education Research Journal* Vol. 23 Iss. 4, pp. 497-511.

Elfer, P. and Page, J. (2015) Pedagogy with babies: Perspectives of eight nursery managers. *Early Child Development and Care* Vol. 185 Iss. 11-12, pp. 1762-82.

Evangelou, M., Sylva, K., Kyriacou, M., Wild, M. and Glenny, G. (2009) *Early Years Learning and Development. Literature Review*. Oxford: DCSF.

Finnegan, J. (2016) *Lighting up Young Brains*. London: Save the Children.

Goldsmith, H., Pollak, S. and Davidson, R. (2008) Developmental neuroscience perspectives on emotion regulation. *Child Development Perspectives* Vol. 2 Iss. 3, pp. 132-40.

Goouch, K. and Powell, S. (2013) *The Baby Room. Research Summary 2*. Canterbury: Canterbury Christ Church University.

Hadfield, K., O'Brien, F. and Gerow, A. (2017) Is level of prematurity a risk/plasticity factor at three years of age? *Infant Behavior and Development* Vol. 47, pp. 27-39.

Hadfield, M., Jopling, M., Needham, M., Waller, T., Coleyshaw, L., Emira, M. and Royle, K. (2012) *Longitudinal Study of Early Years Professional Status: An Exploration of Progress, Leadership and Impact. Final report*. London: DfE.

Hazlett, H. *et al.* (2017) Early brain development in infants at high risk for autism spectrum disorder. *Nature* Vol. 542, pp. 348-64.

Hourcade, J., Mascher, S., Wu, D. and Pantoja, L. (2015) Look, my baby is using an iPad! An analysis of YouTube videos of infants and toddlers using tablets. *Proceedings of the 33rd Annual ACM Conference on Human Factors in Computing Systems,* pp. 1915-24.

Howard-Jones, P. (2014) *Neuroscience and Education: A Review of Educational Interventions and Approaches Informed by Neuroscience*. London: Education Endowment Foundation.

Johnson, M. (2000) Functional brain development in infants: Elements of an interactive specialization framework. *Child Development* Vol. 71 Iss. 1, pp. 75-81.

Jones, E.J.H., Venema, K., Lowy, R., Earl, R.K. and Webb, S.J. (2015) Developmental changes in infant brain activity during naturalistic social experiences. *Developmental Psychobiology* Vol. 57, pp. 842-53.

Kalliala, M. (2011) Look at me! Does the adult truly see and respond to the child in Finnish day-care centres? *European Early Childhood Education Research Journal* Vol. 19 Iss. 2.

Kardaras, N. (2016) *Glow Kids: How Screen Addiction Is Hijacking Our Kids - and How to Break the Trance*. New York: St. Martin's Press.

Kawai, E., Takagai, S.,Takei, N., Itoh, H. Kanayama, N. and Tsuchiya, K. (2017) Maternal postpartum depressive symptoms predict delay in non-verbal communication in 14-month-old infants. *Infant Behavior and Development* Vol. 46, pp. 33-45.

Kulke, L., Atkinson, J. and Braddick, O. (2017) Neural mechanisms of attention become more specialised during infancy: Insights from combined eye tracking and EEG. *Developmental Psychobiology* Vol. 59, pp. 250-60.

Laevers, F. (2015) *Making Care and Education More Effective through Wellbeing and Involvement. An Introduction to Experiential Education*. Leuven: Centre for Experiential Education.

Marmot, M. (2016) *The Health Gap: The Challenge of an Unequal World*. London: Bloomsbury.

Mathers, S., Eisenstadt, N., Sylva, K., Soukakou, E. and Ereky-Stevens, K. (2014) *Sound Foundations: A Review of the Research Evidence on Quality of Early Childhood Education and Care for Children under Three. Implications for Policy and Practice Research*. London: The Sutton Trust.

Matthews, S.G. and Phillips, D.I. (2012) Transgenerational inheritance of stress pathology. *Experimental Neurology* Vol. 233 Iss. 1, pp. 95-101.

Nightingale, C.M., Rudnicka A.R., Donin A.S., Sattar, N., Cook, D., Whincup, P. and Owen, C. (2016) Screen time is associated with adiposity and insulin resistance in children. *Archives of Disease in Childhood*. doi: 10.1136/archdischild-2016-312016

Page, J., Clare, A. and Nutbrown, C. (2013) (2nd edn) *Working with Babies & Children from Birth to Three*. London: SAGE.

Parfitt, Y., Alison Pike, A. and Ayers, S. (2013) The impact of parents' mental health on parent–baby interaction: A prospective study. *Infant Behavior and Development* Vol. 36 Iss. 4, pp. 599-608.

Pearson, R., Melotti, R., Heron, J., Joinson, C., Stein, A., Ramchandani, P.G., and Evans, J. (2012) Disruption to the development of maternal responsiveness? The impact of prenatal depression on mother–infant interactions. *Infant Behavior and Development* Vol. 35 Iss. 4, pp. 613–26.

Rutter, J. (2016) *Understanding the Childcare Provider Market*. London: Family and Childcare Trust.

Spittle A., Orton J., Anderson P.J., Boyd R. and Doyle, L.W. (2015) Early Developmental intervention programmes provided post hospital discharge to prevent motor and cognitive impairment in preterm infants. *Cochrane Database of Systematic Reviews* Iss. 11, Art. no. CD005495.

Steiner-Adair, C. and Barker, T. (2014) *The Big Disconnect: Protecting Childhood and Family Relationships in the Digital Age*. New York: HarperCollins.

Stirrup, J., Evans, J. and Davies, B. (2016) Early years learning, play pedagogy and social class. *British Journal of Sociology of Education.* Available from: www.tandfonline.com/doi/full/10.1080/01425692.2016.1182010. Accessed 26 May 2017.

Subedar, A. and Yates, W. (2017) The disturbing YouTube videos that are tricking children. Available from: www.bbc.co.uk/news/blogs-trending-39381889. Accessed 9 June 2017.

Sylva, K., Melhuish, E., Sammons, P., Siraj-Blatchford, I. and Taggart, B. (2004) *The Effective Provision of Pre-School Education [EPPE]. Project Effective Pre-School Education: A Longitudinal Study Funded by the DfES 1997–2004*. London: DfES.

Taggart, G. (2014) Compassionate pedagogy: The ethics of care in early childhood professionalism. *European Early Childhood Education Research Journal* Vol. 24 Iss. 2, pp. 173–85.

University of Maryland (2017) Autism may begin early in brain development: Brains of mice with autism-like symptoms develop neural defects when first circuits take shape. *ScienceDaily*. Available from: www.sciencedaily.com/releases/2017/01/170131124146.htm. Accessed 16 May 2017.

Vieites, V. and Reeb-Sutherland, B. (2017) Individual differences in non-clinical maternal depression impact infant affect and behavior during the still-face paradigm across the first year. *Infant Behavior and Development* Vol. 47, pp. 13–21.

Yehuda, R., Mulherin Engel, S., Brand, S., Seckl, J., Marcus, S. and Berkowitz, G. (2005) Transgenerational effects of posttraumatic stress disorder in babies of mothers exposed to the World Trade Center attacks during pregnancy. *Journal of Clinical Endocrinology & Metabolism* Vol. 90 Iss.7, pp. 4115–18.

Index